The Fighting Irish

by

William Gildea
and
Christopher Jennison

Prentice-Hall, Inc.
Englewood Cliffs, New Jersey

The Fighting Irish by William Gildea and Christopher Jennison
Copyright © 1976 by William Gildea and Christopher Jennison

Book Design by Joel Weltman
Art Direction by Hal Siegel

Printed in the United States of America

Prentice-Hall International, Inc., London
Prentice-Hall of Australia, Pty. Ltd., Sydney
Prentice-Hall of Canada, Ltd., Toronto
Prentice-Hall of India Private Ltd., New Delhi
Prentice-Hall of Japan, Inc., Tokyo
Prentice-Hall of Southeast Asia Pte. Ltd., Singapore
Whitehall Books Limited, Wellington, New Zealand

10 9 8 7 6 5 4 3 2 1

Library of Congress Cataloging in Publication Data
Gildea, William.
  The fighting Irish.

  1. Notre Dame, Ind. University—Football.
I. Jennison, Christopher, joint author. II. Title.
GV958.N6G54   796.33′263′0977289   76-20566
ISBN 0-13-314641-3

To Our All-Star Eleven:

**Mary Fran, William Sr., Mary, Billy, David, Maria;
and
Annice, Keith, Emily, Nicky, and Ned**

Acknowledgments

Valuable assistance in acquiring the pictures was provided by Fred Cantey at Wide World, Art Lee at UPI, Gene Ferrara at the New York *Daily News,* Tom Logan at Culver Pictures, Malcolm Emmons, Bruce Harlan, and Roger Valdeserri's staff at the Notre Dame Sports Information Office, particularly Norma Villanucci, who responded cheerfully to a barrage of eleventh-hour requests.

Much research was done at the International Sports and Games Research Collection at Notre Dame with the thoughtful cooperation of its director, Herb Juliano.

Thanks also go to Frank Coffey, Jacques deSpoelberch, Chet Grant, Mark Hannan, Mrs. Robert J. Monahan, Ara Parseghian, Robert G. Smith, and Venlo Wolfsohn.

Contents

1
The Notre Dame Mystique

The campus, even from a distance, suggests hallowed ground, an imposing place of history and legend, heroism and achievement. The golden dome of Notre Dame shines brilliantly even on days the sun doesn't. The Sacred Heart Church steeple juts majestically above the great hardwood trees. The huge mural of Jesus, arms upraised, stands tall and protective against the fourteen-story library wall.

Up closer, tradition is everywhere. The first college dormitory in the country to offer private rooms still stands and bears the name of Notre Dame's founder, Rev. Edward Sorin. The yellow-bricked stadium invokes memories of Knute Rockne. The science building is named for Rev. Julius Nieuwland, discoverer of the base for synthetic rubber; as a brilliant chemistry student, Rockne worked with Nieuwland.

Football is intertwined with much of the place—because of Rockne. If school leaders from Sorin to the present built a university to be proud of, it was Rockne who called much of the known world's attention to it. "Knute Rockne died in 1931," says a Notre Dame man, "but he's as much alive today as he was in 1930."

The ghost of George Gipp, Notre Dame's most famous football player, resides in Washington Hall, a school official relates only half-jokingly. Walking past that old stone building, he remarks, "They say ghosts are born when a restless person dies young. Gipp was restless and he died young."

Even the campus firehouse offers its own unique history. It contains a room preserved the way it was when another legendary football coach, Frank Leahy, lived there. It was a convenient place to sleep for a coach who would only rarely take the time from his work during football season to spend an evening with his family at home.

The grotto, where there are candles to light and kneelers to pray on, is the place where former great football players had their pictures taken before big games. Johnny Lujack knelt there. So did Bob Williams. And scores of others. And when their pictures were printed in newspapers and magazines, much of the nation prayed along with them on Saturdays.

A reverence prevails—sometimes a blithe reverence. The library mural, which faces the stadium, is called "Touchdown Jesus" because of the upraised arms. The statue of Moses, pointing skyward, is said to be declaring Notre Dame "No. 1." Rev. William Corby, one of seven chaplains sent by Notre Dame to the Union forces during the Civil War, is depicted in a statue giving general absolution to the Irish brigade at Gettysburg. Because of the raised arm he is called Fair Catch Corby.

There are living links to the Notre Dome tradition. Some who might be easily encountered are Ed "Moose" Krause, cigar-smoking athletic director with a frame to match his nickname; 84-year-old Chet Grant, sprightly athletic historian who played quarterback in 1916 and later under Rockne; Rev. Robert Rioux, whose special project is shaping into a formal organization that loose legion of Notre Dame admirers known as the subway alumni.

Assorted relics certify the tradition. In the library basement is a small pulley system from the plane that carried Rockne to his death in a cornfield near Bazaar, Kansas. There is a copy of the March 7,

1927, *Time* magazine with Rockne on its cover and an accompanying article relating that the coach tells his men to "eat no chocolate, cocoa, greasy fried potatoes, pork, or bananas." A yellowing newspaper, the October 7, 1950, *South Bend Tribune*, displays a remarkable headline. "Irish Upset!" screams the front page headline set in huge type. The headline is purposely upside down. In another building is a football that Gipp carried. In another place is an authentic Texas longhorn, memento of Notre Dame's victory over Texas in the 1971 Cotton Bowl.

The longhorn got there through the persistent efforts of Ara Parseghian, Notre Dame's twenty-second coach, who won 95 games in 11 seasons, second only to Rockne. Parseghian gave to Notre Dame of the sixties and seventies what Leahy did in the forties and early fifties and Rockne did just before and during the twenties: football teams to shout about. Parseghian woke up the echoes, bringing students tumbling outside into the cold and snow to take

The finest center in Notre Dame history, Adam Walsh, with Rockne. Walsh played against Army in 1924 with two broken hands. At one point Walsh got so tired of hearing about the Four Horsemen, he invited the 11 regulars to vote on which part of the team was more important, the backfield or the line. The linemen won the vote 7-4.

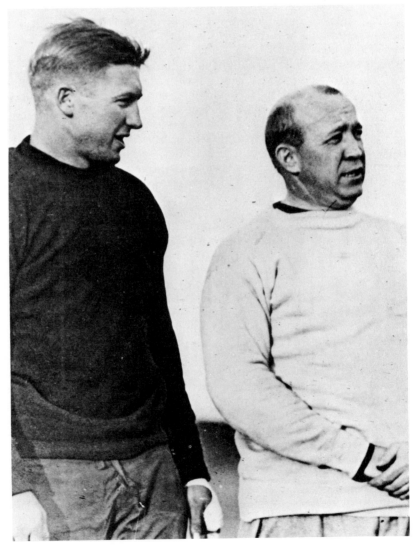

part in some of the wildest pep rallies known to mankind and giving to all those 178 Notre Dame alumni clubs around the world a new spirit and focus. It was cheer, cheer for old Notre Dame, once again.

Here is a scene from the so-called Era of Ara:

"Win one for the Gipper," the graying, baldish man is shouting into a microphone as a mob of students sends up a deafening roar. It is a Friday night rally before an important game and Pat O'Brien, who played Rockne three decades before in the film *Knute Rockne, All-American,* is back on campus, stirring the memories.

Outside the old field house, firecrackers are exploding. Inside, the students scream and throw rolls of toilet paper, and just occasionally, listen to the voice from the past. High over Pat O'Brien's perspiring head are two students, hanging precariously from a girder and dangling a sign that reads "Welcome Back Knute."

"This isn't a rally, it's a great war," the actor says, and there's another roar of approval. Then comes the Rockne speech: "Go out there and crack 'em, crack 'em, crack 'em, crack 'em. Fight to live. Fight to win. Win, win, win, win . . ." Occasionally, Pat O'Brien flinches as a roll of toilet paper comes flying perilously close. But he keeps on talking and the words are effective.

"Win, win, win, win . . ." The roar extends across the campus this cold, otherwise quiet night in Indiana.

The excitement was even more sustained a few years later, before Notre Dame's 23-13 victory over Southern California in 1973, the pivotal game in a perfect season.

"I never saw anything like that week," says athletic director Krause, who arrived on campus as a student in 1930. "There wasn't just one pep rally before that game. There was one every night of the week, starting the previous Sunday. I spoke at two of them. Even when the players would be walking to class, the students would cheer them on.

"It was so much that Ara was worried the team might peak too soon. But he did a terrific job. You could see at practice that he was keeping them under control, working them up gradually. In the tunnel before the game, they were ready. They were jumping up and down. And when they charged out on the field, it was like they were running into the Colosseum in Rome. The cheer that went up—well, it was the greatest cheer I've ever heard before a game."

Such a tradition was years—many successful years—in the making. Rockne, in 13 seasons, won an incredible 105 games, lost only 12, and gained three national championships. Warm and colorful, he was loved by almost everyone who met him and countless others who only heard about him. One writer declared the two most dynamic personalities he ever met were President Kennedy and Knute Rockne. A decade after Rockne came Leahy, who brought success of similar proportion. In 11 seasons, he won 87 games, lost just 11, and produced six undefeated seasons and four national championships.

Parseghian knew of these records and something about the Notre Dame tradition when he arrived—but not everything.

"When you first come to the campus, coming up Notre Dame Avenue, you see the golden dome and you can feel the history and tradition that goes with it," he says, looking back on the experience after a year of retirement.

What surprised him, though, was "the magnitude of Notre Dame on a national scale" and its effect on him as Notre Dame coach. "I don't want to put down the other schools like Ohio State or Alabama," he adds, "but we're national. The demands on your time being with a national institution are much more. I was always talking coast to coast with writers, meeting with alumni from all over, recruiting all over the country."

Seldom did he go anywhere—New York, Los Angeles, Miami, New Orleans, Dallas—when he was not recognized. Once, while

Ara Parseghian, who was celebrated for his ability to pump up the emotions of his players as well as the thousands of howling students at football pep rallies, such as this one just prior to the 1966 Michigan State game.

driving with a coaching colleague to an all-star game, Parseghian was describing the fishbowl existence of a Notre Dame coach when the car stopped for a light and a man operating a jackhammer came running up, signaling for Parseghian to roll down his window.

"Aren't you Ara Parseghian?" he asked.

"Yes, as a matter of fact I am."

"Well, I'm from Sioux Falls and I want to know why you don't have any South Dakota boys on your football team."

As coach, Parseghian worked almost endless hours, beginning each day at 5 A.M. He would drink coffee at Milt's Grill in downtown South Bend, then, while most people still slept, would begin coaches' meetings and film sessions. There would be no spare moments in his day—and he rarely got home before 10 P.M. Mail would arrive daily by the pound. Invitations to speak and requests for interviews would pour in. As spring arrived following his first season, Parseghian could count only 17 nights he had spent at home since the previous September; a seemingly endless round of communion breakfasts, football lunches, and awards dinners had followed the season.

The demands never slackened, but Parseghian met them all. "I was always an energetic person," he says, looking back at his Notre Dame years and those before. "As a youth I always wanted to be involved not only in football but in as many activities as I could get involved in. I played most of the sports in high school, college, and the navy. I was even on the golf team in high school. I was always drawn to athletics and I'd throw myself completely into them."

His dynamism rivaled Rockne's and Leahy's. He worked as hard as Leahy. He commanded the respect, and affection, of his players like Rockne. They looked to him for leadership when he first got there—and he responded. What he did was discover a quarterback, John Huarte, who had toiled in obscurity for two years. Parseghian built his first Notre Dame team around Huarte and resurrected the school's winning tradition.

"No one had expressed confidence in him," recalls Parseghian. "He was a quiet individual. By way of background, he's a Basque. By nature, Basques are reserved, quiet people. He didn't have the confidence. I think that's what I was able to give him. I believed in his abilitites. When he saw that I believed, he believed."

"Finding Huarte was quite an accomplishment," says Krause. "Here was a kid who hadn't even won a monogram and he's coming up to his senior year. Well, Ara sat him down and told him he was the No. 1 quarterback and by the time he went into the season he was like a veteran."

Notre Dame went on to a 9-1 season, Huarte was awarded the Heisman Trophy as the nation's outstanding player, Parseghian was hailed as a miracle worker, and Notre Dame was back in the business of cranking out legends after some lean years.

"Parseghian and Leahy were both emotional coaches," says Krause. "So was Rockne. Ara had that talent for getting a team physically, mentally, and emotionally ready for a game. Most coaches can get a team physically ready. It's harder to get them mentally and emotionally ready.

"Ara's teams always were. You could watch the players and see it. They'd be jumping up and down throughout a game. Every play was a victory. And they'd keep it up the whole game. I think the key was

The still beauty of the campus in autumn, a perfect setting for the unique excitement of Notre Dame football.

The team takes the field and Notre Dame stadium explodes.

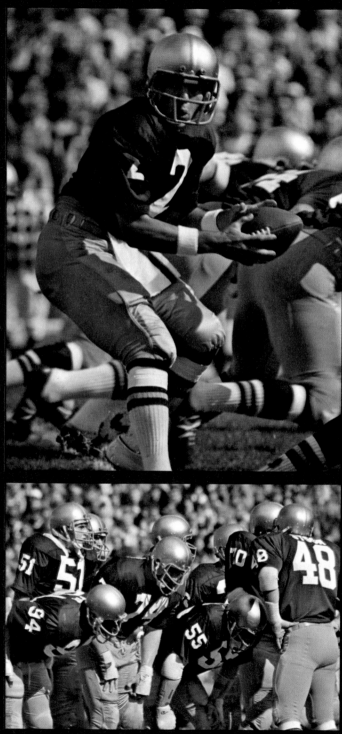

(Top) Alone in a crowd, Tom Clements directs the attack.

Jim Stock calling defensive signals.

Against U.S.C. in the 1975 contest, Jerome Heavens dives for a crucial first down.

The archetypal gladiator, in this case Greg Marx.

Opposite Page:
(Top right) Al Hunter starting his 52-yard touchdown sprint against U.S.C. in 1975.

(Bottom) The latest in the proud dynasty of Notre Dame quarterbacks, Joe Montana.

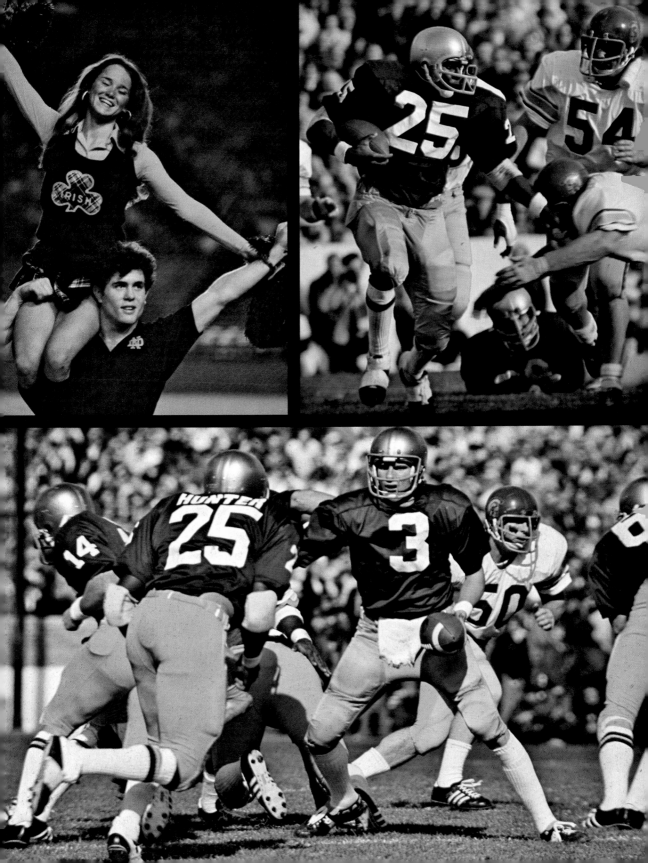

The legend was not betrayed: Ara went out a winner.

bringing them to this peak just as the game started. That's the sign of a great coach.

"Then, too, Ara would use some of Rockne's psychology. Winning, winning, winning is all Ara would talk about until pretty soon the players were convinced they could win. He was a coach with leadership qualities that brought out the spirit on campus."

The result was Notre Dame's first national championship in 17 years in 1966, a 9-0-1 season; the first undefeated, untied season since 1949 in 1973; and, largely through Parseghian's persuasion, a change in the school's policy of not accepting bowl bids and five subsequent post-season appearances.

But the pressures on Parseghian were relentless—and they had their effect.

"They existed for him his very first year," says longtime Notre Dame observer Chet Grant. "The Pitt game that first year was supposed to be an easy one and Notre Dame barely won. The U.S.C. game was a terrific blow, having it won only to lose out. In fact, many games over the Parseghian years were decided one way or the other in the fourth quarter. Notre Dame would go into the last quarter just ahead or just behind. These games were good for everybody else; they were a great spectacle. But they were killing him."

Opponents would point toward Notre Dame, as Parseghian himself did as Northwestern coach, adding that much more pressure. "Every Saturday," says Parseghian, "was an absolute must."

"Every game is a bowl game for us," adds Krause. "Everybody wants to beat Notre Dame. Heck, if I was on the other side I'd want to, too. Duffy Daugherty says it was easy getting Michigan State ready to play Notre Dame. Purdue ended our long streak during the Leahy era in 1953 but few remember Purdue lost all its other games that season, except one."

In an unusual portrait of Parseghian in the Notre Dame library—it is made of 104 pieces of variously colored inlaid wood —one can see something of the toll the job took; his expression seems to be a pained smile. When Parseghian took command in 1964, he was a dark-haired, youthful looking 40 years old. When he retired at 51, he looked his age. His hair was graying fast. So was his complexion.

"My first year we were 9-1 and came within a couple of minutes of the national championship," he recalled shortly after resigning. "The next year we were 7-2-1 and you'd have thought it was a disaster.

"I didn't think that type of pressure could happen. When I was at Northwestern, there was pressure because the Big Ten was well recognized as the premier conference, but there was no way I could even imagine the responsibility of being the Notre Dame coach until I arrived on campus and came to learn it.

"The only way to experience the pressure is to sit in the coach's chair and wear the coach's shoes. Then you'll totally understand all the ramifications, the responsibilities, the demands on your time."

Frank Leahy said similar things as long ago as 1949: "When you are a coach at Notre Dame, you don't control your personal life. You belong to the people. I notice now that I become fatigued a little earlier each day. My family would be happy if I decided to discontinue coaching. In 1947, during the winter months, there was one

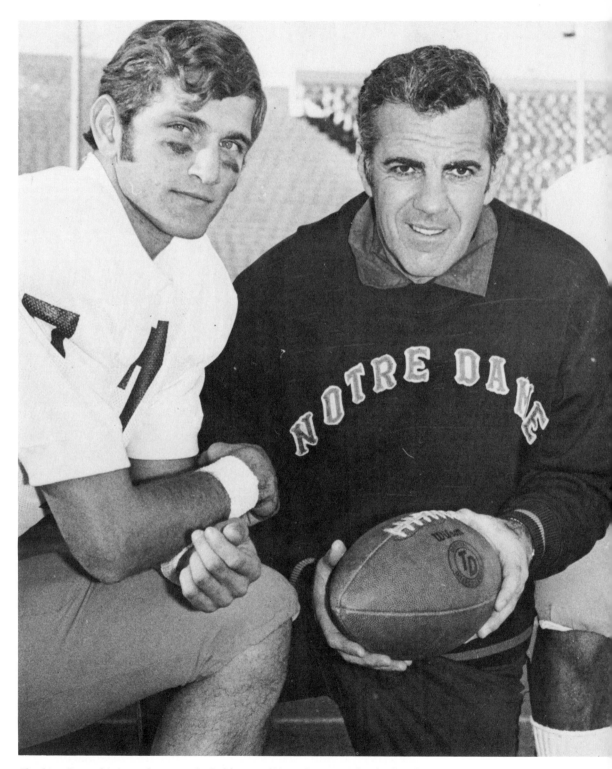

Flanking Parseghian are the men who hold most of Notre Dame's individual and career passing and receiving records. Joe Theismann is on the left, and on the right is Tom Gatewood, Theismann's favorite receiver.

stretch when I was home only six nights in ninety. The rest of the time I was out speaking."

The job ruined Leahy's health. It almost ruined Parseghian's. Suffering from high blood pressure and jangled nerves, he had sense enough to get out in time. He almost changed his mind—after his last regular-season game as coach, a disastrous 55-24 defeat by Southern California.

"It was the most agonizing, most disappointing game for me," he says. "When I got home, my wife thought I might change my mind. I vacillated on it. I thought possibly I could not go out after all those years with a loss like that.

"Then I realized I had made an intelligent decision before, an unemotional decision. I decided if it was a good decision in the middle of the season it should still be a good decision. If I had based decisions on emotion, I'd have changed my mind an awful lot in 25 years of coaching.

"So I stuck with the decision."

That producing legends is no easy matter was likewise known by Rockne. Even he, who set the standard of Notre Dame excellence, had trouble living up to his own goals. At halftime of a game in 1925 he collapsed in the locker room, an emotional, sobbing wreck. After the season he escaped to Europe to get away from it all.

Further, Rockne even suffered much criticism from alumni after skipping the Carnegie Tech game of 1926, which Notre Dame lost in a shocking upset, to scout the Army-Navy game in Chicago. Telegrams piled high in his hotel room that night. Yet that was the only game Notre Dame lost that year—and only the sixth Irish defeat dating all the way back to 1918. Still, the question was raised, What have you done for us lately?

Part of the Notre Dame legend has it—and this is certainly understandable—that one evening on the way back to his office after a particularly trying day Parseghian came upon a bust of Rockne in the Athletic and Convocation Center, paused in front of it, and pointing a finger, said to the statue, "You, you started all this."

This is true to a certain extent, but not precisely. Rockne was neither the founder of the game at Notre Dame nor the inspiration of the school's spirit. What he did was make the most of both, propelling Notre Dame into a national institution. "Rockne," says Chet Grant in his book, *Before Rockne at Notre Dame,* was "a finder, not a founder."

The source of the Notre Dame spirit, Grant believes, is "a fighting Frenchman," Notre Dame's founder, Father Sorin. Starting from the motherhouse of the Congregation of Holy Cross in Le-Mans, France, Sorin crossed the Atlantic, then the eastern part of the United States, making the last part of his journey to South Bend by oxcart with seven Holy Cross brothers in November 1842.

Upon arriving at the site of the university, he dedicated the "delightful solitude" to the Mother of Jesus. Hence, the school's colors, Gold and Blue, the patron Lady's colors. The notion that the school's colors included green grew from "The Fighting Irish" nickname first used in the 1920s.

Demonstrating a fighting spirit that later was to be dramatized by football, Sorin and the other priests and brothers braved harsh winters and virtual poverty while building their university. In April

1879, they received their sternest test. The main building and several others burned down.

"If it were all gone," Sorin said, "I should not give up." Which is to say, "We may be down, but we're not out." This, to historian Grant, represents the essence of the Notre Dame spirit.

By the time of the fire, a new game already was being played on campus, the American game of football. One day in 1887 came a notice in the weekly Notre Dame *Scholastic:* "The University of Michigan football team is expected here next Wednesday to play a match game of football with the Notre Dame Association. W. Harless and G. De Haven, former students of this place, are leading members of the varsity organization. The Michigan University team holds the college championship of the West."

Thus began intercollegiate football at Notre Dame. Michigan won, 8-0, by scoring two touchdowns, each worth four points. The *Scholastic* reported: "After spending an hour taking in the sights of the campus, the Wolverines donned their uniforms of spotless white and repaired to the Seniors' campus.

"Because of the recent thaw, the field was damp and muddy, but the players of both sides plunged into the play with no regard for their cleanliness or comfort. To make our players feel more familiar with the game, the scrimmages at first were between sides chosen irrespective of college. After several minutes of this practice, play was halted, players returned to their respective sides and the real game was begun.

"Since the game had to be finished by noon, it was limited to one period of 30 minutes' duration. This resulted in a score of 8-0 in favor of Michigan on two touchdowns. The game was interesting, and has started an enthusiastic football boom. It is hoped that coming years will witness a series of these contests.

"After a hearty [noon] dinner had been enjoyed by the two teams, the Rev. President Walsh thanked the Ann Arbor boys for their visit and assured them that a cordial reception would always await them at Notre Dame. At one o'clock, the carriages to catch the train at Niles were ready, and amid the rousing cheers of Notre Dame students, the Michigan players departed, leaving behind them a most favorable impression."

Informal campus games became more common and the school's weekly noted of one such affair: "It proved more fully than before the capability of our boys to become famous, even champions, in handling the Rugby Egg."

In April 1888, Michigan returned for two games on consecutive days. The first was held in downtown South Bend. "The first inning was interrupted by a number of wranglings over the rules, but the second went through smoothly," it was reported. Michigan won, 24-6. The next day the Michigan team came out to the campus. The *Scholastic* related: "After partaking of dinner in the senior refectory and a short ride on the lake, they got ready and appeared on the grounds at two o'clock." The visitors won again, 10-4.

Harvard School of Chicago became Notre Dame's first victim in 1888, and Northwestern was shut out in the only game of 1889. After two years when no games were played, Notre Dame football returned in 1892 and has been played continuously since then. A notice was posted: "This is the college cheer—'Rah! 'Rah!! 'Rah!!!

This jaunty group, posed with what appears to be a watermelon, represents Notre Dame's first intercollegiate football squad, pictured here in the Fall of 1887. Sitting from left to right are Harry Jewett, Joe Cusack, Henry Luhn, Ed Prudhomme; standing from left to right are Joe Hepburn, George Houck, Ed Sawkins, Frank Fehr, Pat Nelson, Gene Melady, and Frank Springer.

Gold and Blue!!! 'Rah! 'Rah!! 'Rah!!! N.D.U.!!!!"

A writer for the *Scholastic* observed: "The players are strong and willing, but they need a coacher [*sic*] to teach the individuals how to unite mind, body and spirit in the common cause; how to play with and for each other to the best interest of the team."

In 1894 and 1895, two part-time coaches directed the team, and in 1896 Frank E. Hering, who stayed for three years, became the first full-time coach after serving at Bucknell University. His top player and the young man generally regarded as the best all-round Notre Dame athlete of the nineteenth century was John F. Farley, later a priest at the school. He was fast and known for his end runs. Big John Eggeman, 1897-99, was a rugged center who sometimes had to be triple-teamed by opponents.

The most famous pre-Rockne player was Louis J. "Red" Salmon, driving fullback of the 1900-1903 teams who stood about 5-feet-10 and weighed 170. He was known for his punting, dropkicking, breakaway running, and blocking. At a time when most players accorded star status came from the East, Salmon made Walter Camp's third team All-America. In Salmon's senior year, 1903, Notre Dame outscored its opponents, 292-0, for eight victories and a scoreless tie with Northwestern. The students loved it and prizes were given for the best organized yells from the stands at Cartier Field.

With an increasingly involved student body cheering them on, the Notre Dame players scored their most lopsided victory ever in 1905, 142-0, over American Medical of Chicago. After a 25-minute half during which Notre Dame took a 121-0 lead, the second half was shortened to eight minutes to give the medical students time to eat before catching a train home. The Irish scored 27 touchdowns but missed 20 extra points.

Harry "Red" Miller, who enrolled in 1904, would be the eldest of Notre Dame's most famous football family. He was "invited" to Notre Dame by coach Henry J. McGlew, known as Fuzzy for his curly hair. Such an invitation would come to be known as recruiting. Miller was followed to Notre Dame by his brothers Ray, Walter, Gerry, and Don, one of the Four Horsemen; and by sons Tom and Creighton.

The most significant pre-Rockne year was 1909. The Irish football program had gained steadily the three previous years, the combined record being 20-2-1. Scores such as 64-0 and 88-0 suggested that Notre Dame was outgrowing its opposition.

One team it had never beaten, however, was powerful Michigan, coached by Fielding "Hurry Up" Yost, a legend himself. Michigan and Notre Dame played eight times before 1909 and Michigan won every time. But that 1909 season opened with three one-sided victories for the Irish. Then came the most important two weeks in the pre-Rockne era. They were to travel as far east as Pittsburgh, then to Ann Arbor for a date with Michigan. The feeling at Notre Dame was that the Irish were on the verge of national recognition.

Walter Camp, who was in the process of picking an All-America team, journeyed to the Pittsburgh game. Notre Dame's coach, Frank C. "Shorty" Longman, Irish fullback in 1904-05, was quoted as saying, "My men are in good condition and we are able to present

Louis J. (Red) Salmon was Notre Dame's first All-America, making Walter Camp's third team in 1903. He was a skilled punter, dropkicker, runner, and blocker. His career and single season scoring records still stand in the Notre Dame record book, and no one has bettered his points-per-game average (11.7 in 9 games in 1903), or his career touchdown total (36).

our best front. Pittsburg [sic] has one of the best aggregations in the East, but I have no fears for my men."

More than 5,000 Notre Dame rooters showed up, only about 2,000 fewer than the Pittsburgh rooters. The Irish won, 6-0, on an early touchdown by Lee Mathews worth five points, plus an extra point. Another back, Pete Vaughan, received much credit. "His line plunges were irresistible and he was largely instrumental in overpowering Warren, the giant Pitt tackle," said one account. It also was reported: "The game itself was a revelation to the Pittsburgh fans, who were surprised to find the Westerners adept at the modern game."

On to Michigan. The Irish knew what was at stake: acclaim as western champion. And it is equally clear that Michigan knew it would be in for a rough game. Its freshman coach watched Notre Dame play Pittsburgh—scouting, it's called these days—and reported back: "The Hoosiers play football all the time and they go as far as any team can go without calling forth penalties for roughing from the officials."

The scouting report apparently lacked some specifics. By all accounts, the Irish thoroughly surprised Michigan with numerous short passes, just over the line of scrimmage. It took Michigan quite a while to adjust. When it finally did, a crucial play inspired the Irish. Leading 5-3, they blocked what seemed a certain field goal and went on to win 11-3.

"What makes me so doggoned mad is that we might have won the game," Michigan Coach Yost was quoted as saying. "These are the worst kinds of games to lose. They leave a worm in a man's heart to gnaw and gnaw. Oh, I don't know, I'm sick and tired of the whole business; it is certainly discouraging."

Yost went on to contend it was just a practice game, but Walter Eckersall, the famous quarterback and referee, writing in the Chicago *Tribune*, helped shape public opinion to the contrary. "Notre Dame, by defeating Michigan so decisively, earned the right to be ranked with Minnesota and Wisconsin, the leading aspirants for the title in this section," Eckersall wrote.

Almost the entire Notre Dame student body reacted to the victory with a huge celebration that included a bonfire and a number of speeches by school officials praising the team. This was one of the first times that interest in football seemed to grip practically everyone on campus. And this was just the beginning.

The next year Rockne enrolled. Contrary to an impression that has grown over the years that he had only vaguely heard about the Indiana school, Notre Dame had established a football stature in the Midwest that would have been hard for Rockne to have overlooked.

By 1912, the Irish were positively terrorizing opponents. In a game they won, 74-7, the Adrian coach asked his counterpart, John L. Marks, if he could send players back into the game who had been substituted for, which was then against the rules, because he had used them all. Marks agreed, but then later noticed an unfamiliar player on his bench. The player was from the other team.

"You're on the wrong bench," Marks said.

"I know it," said the player. "I've been in that scrap four times already, and they're not going to send me back in if I can help it. I've

Knute Rockne as a 25-year-old senior. This picture was taken shortly before the 1913 Army game, a contest that inaugurated one of the sports' most famous rivalries.

had enough." Marks let him stay.

Against Wabash that season, fullback Ray Eichenlaub ran for 400 yards in a 41-6 Notre Dame victory. Aboard a streetcar after the game, as they headed for the train depot, the Wabash players were crowded in the aisle as an older woman carrying several packages got on and shouldered her way toward the back of the car. "One side," a player shouted, "here comes Eichenlaub's mother."

Few games in the history of football left a deeper impact than the Army-Notre Dame game of 1913. It marked the birth of one of the most colorful series in sports, one filled with drama and crowd appeal. Played on the plains at West Point, the 1913 game introduced Notre Dame football to the East. By the next decade, Notre Dame followers annually came pouring forth from the subway exits of New York City to see their adopted team.

It was in the 1913 game, won 35-13 by Notre Dame, that Charles "Gus" Dorais and Rockne made the forward pass fashionable. On one play, Rockne slipped, then got up and came back a few steps to take a pass. That was the birth of the buttonhook. "Gus," Rockne supposedly said in the huddle, "I just discovered something. If I stop and come back, I can get away from my defender."

The Army series was highlighted by Gipp's greatest game in

1920, the naming of the Four Horsemen by Grantland Rice in 1924, Rockne's win-one-for-the-Gipper speech of 1928, Jack Elder's 96-yard run with an intercepted pass for the 1929 game's only touchdown, Army's two colossal wartime victories, and the monumental 0-0 tie of 1946.

Officials from both schools viewed with increasing distaste the extraordinary amount of gambling that took place when the teams met. About $5 million was bet on the 1946 game. At Army's request, the series was discontinued after 1947, though it was resumed in 1957 and played intermittently after that. Notre Dame, which leads the series 30-8-4, has always been grateful to Army for its part in spreading the Irish fame.

As coach, Rockne did more to spread that fame than any single person. Before him, it was largely Irish Catholic immigrants who either sent their sons to Notre Dame or rooted for the school from afar. At that time, Notre Dame had the image of a "poor boys' school" that immigrants could identify with. And many Catholics who felt out of the American mainstream also found a certain security in Notre Dame.

Rockne, himself a Norwegian immigrant, attracted a more diverse following that eventually included a cross section of all Americans as he built a national schedule and took his teams to the people. The Irish would travel so much players would sing "Home Sweet Home" as they climbed aboard Pullman cars and the team came to be called the Ramblers. This was particularly true in 1929, when a

Grantland Rice, whose story of The Four Horsemen immortalized both himself and Notre Dame.

new stadium was being built and all games had to be played on the road. Enormous crowds became the order of the age; four times between 1927 and 1930 crowds at Chicago's Soldier Field surpassed 100,000, twice reaching 120,000.

By his personality and achievements, Rockne attracted young men to Notre Dame who otherwise surely would have gone elsewhere, and this remained true even after his sudden, dramatic death in 1931. The legend endured nicely, as an incident from the Leahy era suggests. For an important game with Purdue, Leahy assistant Joe McArdle occupied a place in the scoreboard with a phone to the Irish bench. When Steve Oracko kicked a game-winning field goal, a voice, McArdle's, cried out, "God bless you Oracko." Word spread that Rockne's voice had been heard from the sky.

Before the 1973 Sugar Bowl between Alabama and Notre Dame, Alabama coach Bear Bryant cited Notre Dame's unique heritage. He said he wept as a youth when he heard that Rockne had died.

So great was Rockne's impact that the years immediately following his death brought an inevitable letdown. His successor was Heartley "Hunk" Anderson, so loyal a Rockne aide, the story goes, that he once was about to take on a truck driver even burlier than himself, who had been crowding the car Rockne was in—but Rockne held him back.

Anderson's nickname of Hunk fit perfectly with all those heroes over the years whose very names added luster to their deeds: Red Salmon, Shag Shaughnessy, The Gipper, Buck Shaw, Slip Madigan, Curly Lambeau, John "Clipper" Smith, Johnny "One Play" O'Brien, Moon Mullins, Moose Krause, Dippy Evans, and, of course, Rock. For still more color, add a few creations of an ever-industrious publicity department: Bill Shakespeare, "The Bard of Staten Island"; Angelo Bertelli, "The Springfield Rifle," and Terry Hanratty and Jim Seymour, "Fling" and "Cling."

Hunk Anderson, however, enjoyed less success as Notre Dame coach than he had as Notre Dame player, when he made All-America as a guard in 1921. The Irish of 1933 sank to a 3-5-1 record, were shut out six times (one game was a scoreless tie), and managed only 32 points all season. It was time to bring back another legend—one of the Four Horsemen, Elmer Layden.

Well before he became known as one of the Horsemen, Layden contributed to another dimension of the Notre Dame mystique. Like so many future greats in their early days at the school, Layden wanted badly to get away. His problem, not a unique one, was homesickness. He went back to Davenport, Iowa, several times before finally settling down at South Bend.

Rockne, himself, almost left. One of his first jobs as a student had been cleaning up the chemistry lab after hours. When some property was stolen, he was blamed for not locking up. Discouraged, he packed his bags and was heading out when a few classmates overtook him and persuaded him to return.

Gipp left at least twice. A native of Michigan, he was constantly being lured by Michigan coach Fielding Yost and it is said that Rockne twice showed up on the Michigan campus to fetch Gipp and escort him back to Notre Dame.

As coach, Layden quietly put together a remarkable record over seven years—47-13-2—that at most schools would have been hailed as an unqualified success. He took a scholarly approach to the game, caring genuinely about his players' academic welfare. One of his discoveries was that Bill Shakespeare had trouble with English. Or so legend has it.

"Despite the good record under Elmer, this was the only true

In later years the team would be greeted by throngs of admirers at the South Bend railroad station, but this homecoming, despite the stirring win over Army, was unheralded. Standing in the middle is the hero, George Gipp, his raincoat slung over his arm, and apparently watching out for his valise.

period of football de-emphasis at Notre Dame," says Chet Grant, who served as an assistant under Layden. "People talked about de-emphasis in the fifties under Terry Brennan, but they never mentioned the word until the record started to go bad.

"Layden got rid of red-shirting and controversial, high blocking. Everybody who came out for the team got a uniform. There were many more walk-ons then. He didn't believe in high-powered recruiting. He had a chance to get Tom Harmon, for example. Harmon came to the campus, but Elmer simply said he'd like to have him come. That was all. He also didn't believe in running up scores." In 1939, Layden's team compiled a 7-2 record while outscoring the opposition only by 100-73. Such close scores made Notre Dame followers nervous.

"The Army game of 1940 was particularly disturbing to some university officials because we should have won by two or three touchdowns," Grant says. "We were fortunate to win, 7-0, when Steve Juzwik intercepted and ran 81 yards for the only touchdown. Only 7-0! It was shocking." So when Layden announced he was taking the position of National Football League commissioner after the 1940 season, he left Notre Dame with numerous blessings and a few sighs of relief.

Then came Leahy, who vowed to win not just most of the games but all of them. And he almost did. Notre Dame's 39-game unbeaten streak stretched over five seasons. A dogged recruiter, Leahy promised one prospect, who wanted to be an agriculture major, one thing Notre Dame did not offer, that he would supply a tutor and the chap would become Notre Dame's first agriculture graduate. That was a promise even Leahy could not deliver. But he could not have been more serious when he promised the worried mother of another prospect that his own mother would look after the boy.

In 1953, before the Notre Dame-Oklahoma game, Leahy's wife, Florence, tripped over one of their children's toys at home and broke her hip. Rather than bother her husband at practice, she went to the hospital and had a cast put on. When Leahy arrived home late that night and saw her he was upset.

"Why didn't you tell me?" he asked.

"I didn't want to take you off the field before the big game." Then she added, "It could have been worse. It could have been Johnny Lattner with his leg in a cast."

Leahy reflected a moment and replied, "You're right, Florence, that would have been worse."

Those were the days when Catholics all over, some even with rosaries in hand, would listen to the Irish games on the 115-station Notre Dame network and root for "their" team. To many, Notre Dame football represented a religious mission. But when *Life* magazine, in a 1949 article, suggested that the players themselves seemed to consider their games a religious mission, the Notre Dame *Scholastic* declared irately that "*Life* left a distasteful cast on what otherwise might have been a pretty good story," adding, "Larry Coutre might just as well have scampered for three touchdowns had he been absent from Mass that morning."

Still, it has always been hard to overlook Notre Dame's religious connections. Late in the Irish-Oklahoma game of 1952, a policeman was seen kneeling and praying near the Notre Dame dressing room. A spectator remarked, "Uh, oh, he's calling up Notre Dame's reserves."

Another story is told of a reporter seeking out the team chaplain before a Southern Methodist game. "Would you introduce me to him?" the reporter asked a Notre Dame official, who replied: "Which one, the offensive chaplain or the defensive one?"

Leahy himself, in moments of frustration, often would begin a lecture to a player by telling him, "You're not worthy to represent Our Lady." Shortly, he would find forgiveness.

Even in more recent times, religion remains a part of Notre Dame lore. Jim Lynch, one of Parseghian's eleven All-Americas of 1966, was debating whether to attend Navy, where his older brother went, or Notre Dame. A priest is said to have suggested: "Your

family has done its part for country, now you should do something for God."

Before his last game, the 1974 Orange Bowl against Alabama, Parseghian, noting a student campaign to win one for him, asked reporters, "Can you imagine Catholics winning one for a French Armenian Presbyterian?" The outcome, a victory, proved another gain for ecumenism.

The Notre Dame mystique, with all its ramifications, was so well suited to Hollywood that three feature-length films resulted, as well as dozens of small dramas in other films. In all these productions, the hero must recover from an injury, pass a brain-cracking exam, or sever ties with gamblers to play in the big game, the Notre Dame game.

In the fall of 1931, Universal International released *The Spirit of Notre Dame* and dedicated it to Knute Rockne. Several Notre Dame players made appearances, including the Four Horsemen, Frank Carideo, and Adam Walsh. The uncomplicated plot involved a cocky and talented running back named Bucky O'Brien, graduate of

Every year at the beginning of spring practice, the team bursts through a huge paper shamrock for the benefit of several dozen press photographers. Repeating the process in this picture is Emil Sitko, taking a handoff from Coach Leahy, while Leon Hart and Jim Martin, co-captains in 1949, hold on to the sign.

Hookerville High, who comes to Notre Dame and announces himself as Hookerville's Flash. Obviously patterned after Gipp, O'Brien gets himself into trouble with the coach as a result of much ball-hogging and loud-mouthing. At the same time, a lineman named Truck McCall is seriously injured and hospitalized. O'Brien's return to grace and McCall's recovery coincide with—what else?—the Army game, won by Notre Dame in the very last seconds. Lew Ayres played O'Brien; Truck McCall was played by Andy Devine.

The production was successful enough to encourage Warner Brothers to undertake a film biography of Rockne several years later. The first director, William K. Howard, was fired after a confrontation with the studio over how the material would be handled.

Who could resist this kind of entertainment?

The day after Notre Dame whipped Stanford in the 1925 Rose Bowl game, Rockne and several of his players toured some Hollywood studios. From left to right are Elmer Layden, Harry Stuhldreher, Don Miller, Douglas MacLean (then starring in *Introduce Me*), Rockne, Anne Cornwall (one of the Wampas Baby Stars in 1925), and tackle John Weibel.

Howard reportedly preferred a serious portrait of Rockne, while the studio was said to prefer a more "rah-rah" approach. Lloyd Bacon succeeded Howard and ended up using most of Howard's original material.

Knute Rockne, All American provided Pat O'Brien with an identity that very nearly type-cast him for the rest of his career. He literally threw himself into the part, acting in several of the action sequences with such abandon that his false nose would pop off. He studied films of Rockne for hours, mimicked the gestures and postures, and memorized the ringing speeches. O'Brien even claimed to have played against a Rockne-coached team, as a member of the Marquette squad in 1921, and added that he had made a 67-yard run against the Irish that afternoon.

The film also included a lengthy portrait of Gipp, played by a slim youngster named Ronald Reagan, who successfully conveyed some of Gipp's blithe spirit, partly by chewing gum. It was an unpretentious and happy movie; it's made clear that Rockne's spirit and memory will warm the hearts of Notre Dame men forever.

The movie's world premiere was celebrated on October 4, 1940,

In *Knute Rockne All-American*, Pat O'Brien played Rock, and Ronald Reagan appeared as the Gipper. This shot records a conversation in which Rockne is persuading Gipp to forget about baseball and join the football squad.

at four theaters in South Bend. More than 10,000 persons attended, including O'Brien, Reagan, and Mrs. Rockne. After the film opened in New York, Bosley Crowther wrote in *The New York Times* that the picture was filled with exciting action, but ended his review with thudding faint praise, saying it was "one of the best pictures for boys in years."

Another New York critic declared: "The strongest reaction I had after seeing a preview was that it will serve as a powerful influence on those who have had their doubts and fears about the game itself. Parents who have wondered if football was worth the risk their sons were taking in playing it, parents who have wished their sons would give it up, will, I think, find the answer to their fears in the story of Knute Rockne."

There was yet another movie that has something to do with Notre Dame, though Notre Dame wishes it never happened. It was called *John Goldfarb, Please Come Home* and had less to do with Notre Dame than Arabs, oil wells, and harems. The manner in which the Notre Dame administration and football team were portrayed sparked a major controversy that was finally settled by the New York State Court of Appeals.

The idea for the movie began with the Francis Gary Powers spy plane incident. William Peter Blatty, who would later score big with *The Exorcist,* got together with producer Steve Parker and director J. Lee Thompson and all thought that something funny might result from a movie based on Powers' misfortune. Parker's wife, Shirley MacLaine, was enlisted as the leading lady, and 20th Century Fox contracted to release the film.

The plot, such as it is, involves the King of Fawzia, played by Peter Ustinov, and his attempt to schedule a football game with Notre Dame. When an American U-2 plane crash occurs in his country, the King offers to trade the pilot for a chance to take on the Fighting Irish. The State Department insists that Notre Dame agree; what else could it do? So the game is on. Meanwhile, Shirley Mac-Laine has joined the King's harem and ends up scoring the touchdown that wins the bizarre game for Fawzia.

It wasn't the loss but rather the manner in which the Notre Dame coaches and players were portrayed, with dissolute ugliness, that prompted the university to bring suit against Fox for invasion of property rights. The film was supposed to be released on Christmas Day, 1964, but on December 17 New York Supreme Court Justice Henry Clay Greenberg granted a preliminary injunction against distribution of the film and the book based on the film. Subsequent arguments and appeals attracted much attention, but Greenberg's decision was finally reversed by the Appellate Division, and the reversal was upheld by the New York State Court of Appeals.

Like most books banned in Boston, *Goldfarb* received publicity greatly out of proportion to its worth. Almost 25 years after reviewing the film biography of Knute Rockne, Bosley Crowther wrote that *Goldfarb* not only defamed Notre Dame but did irreparable harm to humor and the human race.

So Notre Dame survived that crisis nicely as it did another controversy involving *Life* magazine in the fall of 1953. As was its custom, *Life* did a picture spread, Notre Dame players being the subject. The trouble was all the players had their teeth knocked out.

The school's fathers were deeply troubled by this and hastily dispatched to *Life,* along with a protest that the magazine had misrepresented the roughness of the sport, the rare statistic that 94 percent of the players had all their teeth. Three weeks later *Life* apologized and published more appropriate, clean-cut pictures that might have passed for toothpaste ads.

Around this time, there were other sorts of pictures demonstrating the virtues of Notre Dame. A favorite was Leahy and family kneeling in prayer or posed in front of a Christmas tree. The public also was reminded quite often of what Leahy was telling the youth of America: He would close his speeches at pep rallies, for example, with poems that stressed fair play, brotherly love, family life, and patriotism. He would often tell his players, "Always stay close to Our Lady."

Even after he had left the scene at Notre Dame, Leahy attracted attention to the school, often in his heroic struggle against leukemia, arthritis, and other illnesses. In December 1970, he was inducted into college football's Hall of Fame, but his health was such that he had to be helped down the aisle. Always a man of determination, he shrugged off the assistance of one of his former stars, big George Connor, when they reached the steps to the stage. "I'll take it from here," said Leahy, and he did.

When Parseghian came along to stir up the players, students, alumni, and subway alumni, Leahy was among the happiest onlookers. Ten seasons had gone by between the two coaches, the same number that had elapsed between Rockne and Leahy. "He's rekindled the Notre Dame spirit," observed Leahy, upon returning to campus.

That spirit still lives.

2 Knute Rockne

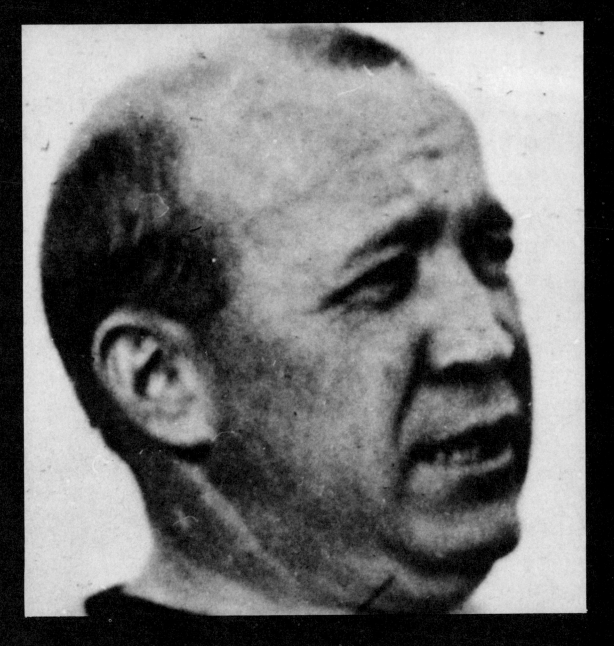

We are becoming so hardened by misfortune and bad luck that it takes a mighty big calamity to shock this country. But, Knute, you did it. We thought it would take a president's death to make a whole nation shake their heads in real sorrow and say, "Ain't it a shame he's gone?" Well, that's what this country did today, Knute, for you. You died one of our national heroes. Notre Dame was your address but every gridiron in America was your home.

—Will Rogers
March 31, 1931

Mighty things from small beginnings grow, wrote the poet Dryden long before just that happened near the south bend of the St. Joseph's River in Indiana. Rev. Edward Sorin, whose journey began in France, arrived there in 1842 and built a school. Knute Kenneth Rockne, who came from Norway, spread its fame like no other man. He did it with the purely American game of football, beginning in the humblest of ways. When he was finished, the names Notre Dame and Rockne were known throughout the land, and were practically synonymous.

Beyond the Midwest in 1913, not much was known of the picturesque little school when a small group of Notre Dame football players, traveling 900 miles from what many effete Easterners of the day considered almost uncivilized territory, showed up at West Point for a November 1 game. There were 18 of them, and just 14 pairs of cleats. This motley collection was about to make football history, lay the foundations of the Fighting Irish as a national tradition, and offer up a name that would grow increasingly large in the national consciousness—Rockne.

Only 12 Notre Dame players managed to get onto the field that day, the contest being one of the first recorded instances of a football coach not willing to risk using his substitutes. And that coach, Jesse Harper, under whom Rockne emerged from obscurity with a flourish that was to mark most of his deeds, would have employed just the minimum 11 had it not been for one player's refusal to obey orders. This was a shocking display for the time, acts of defiance among athletes not having become commonplace until more than a half century later.

The right halfback snapped his shoelace in the course of the game and a benchwarmer named Bunny Larkin brazenly refused Harper's edict to remove his shoes and hand them over immediately to the man in need. Instead, Larkin ran into the game himself.

Lasting fame that afternoon, however, was reserved for two others—Gus Dorais, who passed the ball like most of the known world had never seen before, and Knute Rockne, who made the catches. *The New York Times* man proclaimed the news: "The Westerners flashed the most sensational football ever seen in the East." Thus, it must have been so. *The Times* account continued: "The yellow leather egg was in the air half the time, with the Notre Dame team spread out in all directions on the field waiting for it."

The coach with the Notre Dame mascot, an Irish Terrier named Clashmore Mike. In a decade of heroes—Lindbergh, Dempsey, Ruth—Rockne became one of the most revered, and to this day his greatness warms the memories of all who knew him.

How did it happen? In part, because Army sent a scout to South Bend who watched the Irish literally run over little Alma, 62-0. Girded for a ground game, the Cadets proved surprised and baffled by an attack so arcane that it featured 17 forward passes, 15 of them completed. And the passes covered 35 and 40 yards, no less.

One that started the rout went soaring out to the baldish and bandy-legged, 145-pound end, Rockne. He had been limping badly and therefore not taken seriously by the Army defense. Then, miraculously it seemed, Rockne was not limping at all but running at full speed under Dorais's long throw for the inevitable touchdown.

Was this Rockne limp a first example of what would become a staple of Notre Dame football, an ailing hero somehow overcoming pain to accomplish the improbable? No, it was just a little Rockne trick, a feigned injury to lull the defenders. One of the oldest tricks in the book, it might be said today. Rockne was one of the earliest practitioners.

Dorais and Rockne came together again for another bit of history, a coin flip for a coaching job in Iowa. Dorais won and went. Rockne stayed around Notre Dame, became Harper's assistant, then head coach in 1918, discovered George Gipp, assembled the Four Horsemen, recorded five perfect seasons, and amassed a 13-year record of 105-12-5.

Notre Dame became the football club the cab driver, the barber, the mechanic, the file clerk, the man without an alma mater could identify with—not only because it won most of the time but because of the way it did, orchestrated by the flamboyant Rockne.

"Alumni" sprouted in every section of the nation because of Rockne's personality. He was a brilliant chemistry and Latin student, a summa cum laude Notre Dame graduate; a gifted speaker and salesman, the only person, in the opinion of Grantland Rice, who could follow New York Mayor Jimmy Walker as an after-dinner speaker; a maestro of color and drama.

"Rockne was a man of many parts but the most important was his vitality," said Chet Grant, who played for Rockne. "Every man who came in contact with him felt his magnetic presence. He was effervescent, a harlequin, a practical joker, a quipper."

Rockne, twirling his ever-present cigar, loved to tell of an imaginary Swedish cousin of his who had so herculean a physique that he received a football scholarship to a top midwestern school. He was given a summer job at a campus building as a carpenter. The first day at work he crashed through the scaffolding three stories to the ground.

Passersby rushed to their fallen hero. The first words, according to Rockne, that he said were: "Iz der boss mad?" Assured that he wasn't, he said: "Goot. Ay vas coming down for nails anyvay." And Rockne would roar with delight at his own joke.

Stories of how he brought his players to a fighting pitch became legend. He told a group of linemen, "The only qualifications for lineman are to be big and dumb." Then, turning to the backs, lest they feel suddenly inflated, he declared, "To be a back, you only have to be dumb." And when one player told him, "I'll never play for you again," he shrugged and said, "You never have."

Once he entered the dressing room before a game and observed his players joking around. He called for attention. Then, when all was quiet, he pulled a sheet of paper from his pocket. It was a telegram. His boy, Jackie, had pneumonia and he might not live, Rockne said. "He asks that you win for him," Rockne told his players. The coach looked like he was going to cry. The players responded and won—but Rockne's son did not have pneumonia. He was perfectly healthy at the time.

At halftime of the 1925 Northwestern game, with Notre Dame trailing 10-0, he roared to his team, "I'm finished with you. I'm going to sit in the stands for the second half." If that locker room door wasn't knocked down by a team panting to get out for the second half, no door ever was. Notre Dame won, of course, 13-10.

For sheer fury among players, there wasn't anything to match that day—until 1928 and the Army game. In reply to Rockne's impassioned plea to win one for the greatest of all Notre Dame heroes, the dead Gipp, a crazed Jack Chevigny is said to have crossed the goal line screaming "One for the Gipper" and a sophomore end, Johnny O'Brien, who did little before or after and thus earned the nickname "One Play," ran under a desperation pass and scored the deciding touchdown in a 12-6 Notre Dame victory. The New York *Daily News* ran a back-page banner: "Gipp's Ghost Beats Army."

If that wasn't heady enough, the stuff of 1929 should suffice. Rockne had suffered an attack of phlebitis; there was a clot in his leg.

Rockne's communication with his athletes was extraordinary. He knew which of his men needed gentle coaxing, and which required sterner direction. In this picture he appears to be practicing the former. The player to his right is Bert Metzger, a small but ferocious guard who played for Rockne from 1928-30.

Doctors told him to give up coaching; he told the doctors what he thought of their advice. And so it was that he was carried from his sick bed to the Carnegie Tech game in Pittsburgh.

"I don't care what happens after today," he told his players, who immediately grasped the idea that he wanted to win more than live. After exhorting them to fight and win, which they did, Rockne collapsed. But the clot luckily never left his leg. That happened another day.

It was later in the season, a big game at Soldier Field, a crowd of 112,912, Southern California the opponent. Rockne felt he must leave his sickbed again. He did, and the Irish won, 13-12, in the kind of game not recommended for a coach with a blood clot. That night the clot dislodged, passed through Rockne's heart, missed his brain, and settled in his other leg. Could it have happened any other way?

Rockne saved some of his most successful psychology until the final game of his final season, 1930. Notre Dame arrived in Tucson, Arizona, for final workouts en route to another Southern California game.

For much of the season, a former Rockne assistant then working on the West Coast, in a plan craftily engineered by Rockne himself, went to great lengths to belittle the Notre Dame team, all in an effort to lull Southern California. Rockne also used the sly campaign to incite his own players; not only did he not tell his men what he was about but tacked up on his bulletin boards every reference from the West Coast that besmirched the Irish team's good name.

If that wasn't enough, when West Coast writers showed up in Tucson to watch a Notre Dame practice, Rockne downplayed his team's chances in grave tones. This was a team wracked by injuries, he stressed. And a star, Jumping Joe Savoldi, All-America fullback from Milan, Italy, of all places, was out too. He had admitted to being divorced; players then weren't even allowed to be married.

To be certain the Western writers got the message, Rockne arranged a practice for them to watch. Before it, he had his players switch jerseys and positions, putting linemen in the backfield, and vice versa, and leaving them to bumble through the workout. The writers thought them clods, decided that the backfield was too big and slow and the line too small, wondered what sort of teams this outfit had been playing back East that it could win all its games, and uniformly predicted a rousing U.S.C. victory.

For the final touch, Rockne, suffering still another phlebitis attack, called together the squad; then, with everyone looking on, ordered his trainer, Scrapiron Young, to change the bandages on his heavily veined legs. Rockne said his doctors had warned him not to make the trip and he asked the trainer, in a voice all could hear, "Do you think I should continue on?" Before Young could answer, he recalls in his book, *With Rockne at Notre Dame,* the players cried out, "Rock, you can't leave us now."

Having gotten both teams in the proper mood, Rockne watched with assurance while most of the 73,967 in the Los Angeles Coliseum and all of the U.S.C. team viewed with amazement what took place on the field. Notre Dame won easily, 27-0. It was the last game Rockne coached for Notre Dame.

By then, Rockne's predecessor, Jesse Harper, had been proven eminently correct in his recommendation of Rockne as coach and

Jesse Harper coached Notre
Dame for five years and
helped the Indiana college
gain national prominence.

athletic director. "You won't regret it," he told the school's leaders. In Rockne, Harper saw an immigrant who would work tirelessly to succeed. But not even Harper could envision the hundreds of thousands of people who would come to identify Notre Dame as their school and embrace Rockne as their kind of man.

Rockne's father, a carriage maker, had come to America from Norway in 1893 to exhibit some of his work at the Chicago World's Fair. Shortly, he sent for his wife, three daughters, and only son. The family was raised not far from the White Sox baseball park. Rockne played a little sandlot baseball. In one particularly heated game between neighborhood rivals he had his nose smashed with a bat during an argument, which did nothing for his fairly homely countenance and caused his mother to decide that football might not be as dangerous a pastime for her son as she had previously thought.

He played football in high school, but not particularly well. He was better in track, specializing in the half mile and was fairly adept at the pole vault. Football fascinated him, though, no more so than the day when he watched the famed Walter Eckersall, later a University of Chicago star and noted referee, lead the Chicago high-school champions over the Eastern champion team. Rockne liked the way Eckersall orchestrated the game as quarterback.

Still, football did not seem to be in Rockne's future. He never finished high school; he was dismissed from one for skipping classes to practice track with teammates, then sent to another that did not have a track team. Finally, he quit to take a series of odd jobs, settling on the post office, where he stayed for three years. Meanwhile, he continued to run track for the Illinois Athletic Club. Two friends from the club suggested he accompany them to Notre Dame and enroll. After extended questioning by the priests because of his lack of a high school diploma, he was admitted. It was 1910.

Rockne wasted no time in trying out for football, but did not like his first coach, one Frank "Shorty" Longman. Nor did Longman think much of Rockne's talents. Rockne got nowhere under Longman but became a regular on the 1911 and 1912 teams of John L. Marks. Then came Harper, who had the idea that it might be easier to pass over opponents than perpetually run at them. He told Dorais and Rockne to try throwing the ball around rather than just kicking it during the summer of 1913.

These were by no means sophisticated pass patterns those two worked. Rather, they were simply learning how to pitch and catch. Rockne discovered that if he caught the ball fully against his chest it would often bounce away. He tried gathering the ball in with his hands, and it worked. What chance did Army have that year against such enlightened tactics?

By the time Rockne graduated in June 1914, he knew what it was like to win. As a player he never lost, in two season under Marks and one under Harper. One score was 116-7, St. Viator the victim. In his senior year, he was team captain. He thought of going on to medical school but after leaving the campus briefly returned to Notre Dame as head track coach, assistant football coach, and chemistry instructor.

Even as an assistant, Rockne earned respect as a shrewd coach. It was 1915, Notre Dame was playing a powerful Army team led by Elmer "The Great" Oliphant. One of the good Irish players that year, Edward "Slip" Madigan, recalled: "Rockne was still a boy. Hadn't lost his hair yet. He was not even the head coach, only Jess Harper's assistant. I don't think Harper realized it before the day, and neither did us boys, but after Rock's brilliant thinking in the big clinch in that game, it dawned upon us all that he was the brains of the Notre Dame team."

And just what did Rockne do? It was late in the game, 0-0, and Oliphant attempted a 50-yard drop kick field goal that could win for Army. The ball hit the crossbar and bounced back. When Oliphant lined up on defense, as a deep back, Rockne noticed the Army star's dejection over the missed field goal. "Look at that Oliphant," Madigan remember Rockne saying. "He's down in the mouth. Look at him. Got his head down. Don't know he's in the game. Asleep at the switch."

Harper was busy tending to an injured Notre Dame player, so Rockne looked down the bench and called on little Arthur "Dutch" Bergman, a speedster who once held the world record for 40, 50, and 60 yards. Rockne rushed Bergman into the game and sent another substitute in with the play.

"Tell Cofall to do the passing and tell him to make the throw to Bergman in back of Oliphant. You'll be lucky if you can get in two plays before the gun—so make the first one good."

As ordered, quarterback Stanley Cofall fired that pass to Bergman, who had run around behind Oliphant. The gun sounded even as Bergman was racing down the field for the winning touchdown in what Madigan judged was the most spectacular finish to any game he had seen.

In 1916, Rockne, still an assistant, made the discovery that would insure everlasting fame for himself, the subject, and Notre Dame football. He noticed this fellow dropkicking a football with consummate ease. The name was George Gipp. Rockne invited him out for the freshman team. A few weeks later, in a freshman game, Gipp drop-kicked a 62-yard field goal. That was the start of something grand.

Rockne and Gipp had much in common. Both arrived at Notre Dame by accident. Rockne, when he thought at all about college, thought of Illinois. Gipp, from Laurium, Michigan, was driving a taxi in his home town when he received a baseball scholarship to Notre Dame on the recommendation of a former Irish star who had come from the same area in the upper peninsula of Michigan. Both Rockne and Gipp were older than most freshmen, Rockne being 22, Gipp 21. Both enrolled as Protestants; both became Catholics. Both died after glorious undefeated seasons, 1920 in Gipp's case, 1930 in Rockne's.

Gipp was the quintessentially disarming athlete, always cocksure no matter the situation, unflappable at all times while those around him dissolved in the very emotions he created. Or so Notre Dame historians have related. He is said to have walked around with a faint smile, bemused by student pep rallies, just then coming into vogue, and cheers for him in particular, while he was more anxious to repair to the solitude and pleasure of a downtown South Bend pool hall.

There he became known for mixing shots of whiskey with his games on the green felt. "My main job was to haul Gipp out of the pool room," his roommate and fellow halfback, the late Dutch Bergman, once reminisced. "Now George was a big man and I never weighed over 145. Sometimes he would threaten to punch me in the nose."

That was because of the insults Bergman would hurl at Gipp. Once Bergman had Gipp momentarily incensed, the little guy would take off in a sprint, with Gipp hot after him. "I always could run faster and I never had any trouble letting him chase me right back to the campus," Bergman said.

A prima donna not begrudged that status because of the heroics he produced, Gipp was decades ahead of his time in his style of play, the first player to step out of bounds rather than take a senseless hit when he was hemmed in. He also would leave the tackling to others whenever possible to save wear on his body.

Gipp did just about everything a single player could do to Army in his last season, 1920. This was considered his greatest game. He rushed for 124 yards, passed for another 96, and added 112 more on kick returns while leading the Irish to a 27-17 victory.

Halftime of that game produced one of the Gipp legends. Army was leading, 17-14, and Rockne delivered a stormy pep talk. Gipp, the story goes, relaxed all the while, sitting in a corner smoking a cigarette. Finally, Rockne is supposed to have turned all his wrath at the star halfback. "And you, Mr. Gipp, I don't suppose you care if we win or lose!" To which Gipp is supposed to have replied, "That's where you're wrong, Rock. I've got $500 on this game." He then stood up, flipped aside his cigarette, and the rest is history.

Or is it? It didn't happen that way, according to Chet Grant, who played with Gipp under Rockne and was there. "If Gipp had said that, he would have been showing up Rockne, and he never would have done that," Grant says.

George Gipp. He smoked, drank, stayed out late, gambled, shot pool, and otherwise conducted himself in a fashion the stern Rockne disapproved. But he also played football; running, passing, and kicking better than anyone in his, or most other times.

But Gipp did smoke—and there was money, plenty of it, bet on that game. "We all had money on it," Grant continues. "The players did. Students and downtown fans had sent money along with us to bet with the Army players and students. It was done purely in a sporting manner. It was the thing to do at the time.

"Chet Wynne, our fullback, didn't have any money, so Gipp went around before the game and collected money from us. He'd say, 'Give me $10,' and you did. I didn't like it. But he overpowered me in a very casual way. I didn't like him at the time, but I didn't want him to think me a cheapskate. So I must have valued his opinion of me."

Grant says Gipp "paced himself" in that Army game because he had no choice. "He hadn't had enough sleep. He never had enough. So if he ran off tackle for, say, five yards, that was it. He could have added two or three more by pumping, but he conserved his energy until he could really go. And once he got that step, he was gone."

One might have predicted a stellar performance by Gipp in the 1920 Army game had one seen Gipp in the 1919 Army game. This was no ordinary player. Displaying unusually quick thinking—he is said to have noticed an official about to signal an end to the first half—Gipp, from his halfback position, said something like, "Hurry, gimme the ball," as his team lined up near the Army goal line. The startled center responded with a direct snap and Gipp ran to daylight and a touchdown while others stood agape, everyone being so surprised there was little if any contact between opposing lines.

Sports writers began noticing Gipp and filing accounts similar to one before the 1919 Indiana game that Arch Ward did, writing under the by-line he used in his younger days, Archie Ward: "George Gipp is expected to be a prime factor in bringing the championship of Indiana to the Gold and Blue archives. Gipp weighs 175 pounds. He is a hard man to stop when skirting the ends and as a hurler of the forward pass he has few superiors in the West. His educated toe, however, is his greatest asset. In recent rehearsals Gipp registered several drop kicks from the 53-yard mark. He has not been forced to display his booting ability in previous contests, but his accuracy in hoisting the oval across the bars from all angles of the field may play a prominent part in stiff battles, such as the encounter with Coach Stiehm's men."

Indiana proved not very stiff a battle as Notre Dame, behind Gipp, rolled to a perfect season, 9-0, which it repeated the following year, 1920. As each game unfolded, press reports on Gipp grew even more glowing until Ring Lardner suggested simply, "Have the team line up, pass the ball to Gipp, and let him use his own judgment."

Gipp also did some off-field running, especially around Chicago in 1920, after the Northwestern game. He went to town to visit his friend Grover Malone, a Chicago high-school coach who had been Gipp's blocking back the previous year. "There were stories that Gipp had to be 'poured' on the train back to South Bend," Grant says. "But I doubt that. No matter how much he drank, I'm certain he wouldn't participate in any vulgar scene. It would be more dramatic for him to show that his drinking had no effect on him."

If Gipp did not accomplish more than most on the field—his running, kicking, and passing feats inscribed the term triple-threat into football jargon and his 2,341 yards remains to this day the Notre Dame career rushing record—he outdid just about all mortals in death.

If it is difficult to separate fact from fiction in Gipp's lifetime, it is almost impossible to do so at his deathbed, but one thing seems certain—he remained as self-assured as ever. Having contracted a strep throat that would prove fatal, there being no penicillin to work a cure, Gipp lay near death only a month after playing so brilliantly as to become the gauge by which all great Notre Dame football players are measured.

Rockne, wanting to cheer him up, brought him news that he had been named All-America by Walter Camp. "Isn't that great news, Gipp?" Rockne marvelled. "To be selected on Camp's team is a wonderful honor. Aren't you proud of it?"

"Well, that's jake, Rock," Gipp replied.

Moreover, Rockne passed on this further dialogue: "George," he said, "it's tough to go." And Gipp, reportedly in a whisper but with a thin smile, replied, "What's so tough about it?"

Gipp's cockiness has raised doubts for some that he could ever have been so maudlin as to request that the boys win a game for him. That and the fact that Rockne, known for his guile as well as his coaching, is the sole source of the story. But could anyone other than a heretic dare to believe it could have been any other way?

Says Grant: "My reaction for a long time was that it was a ploy, that Gipp wouldn't say it. But I've changed my mind. I wouldn't for a moment reject the possibility the whole thing is legit."

When Gipp died, 1,500 Notre Dame students marched in a snowstorm ahead of the casket, escorting the body to the train station. Francis Wallace, chronicler of Notre Dame football, put it this way: "The snows of Christmas powdered the grave of Thanksgiving's hero."

What could Rockne do for an encore? A lot, it turned out. After Gipp came a stream of talented players who had become conscious of Notre Dame, the football power. Though 1921 was a rebuilding year, Rockne still produced a 10-1 record. It was a season that produced some touchy moments: a 10-7 defeat at Iowa that left Rockne infuriated because he deemed his men overconfident before the game; controversy over the Rockne "shift," including Army's threat to cancel its game just before kickoff because it claimed the Irish backs were not coming to a complete stop before the snap of the ball, and finally, a scandal involving several Notre Dame players, who were kicked off the team for playing in two professional games.

It was also the year the Four Horsemen arrived—Harry Stuhldreher, Jim Crowley, Don Miller, and Elmer Layden. They would not be known as Horsemen until their senior year; in fact, they weren't known much at all their freshman season except to be noted along with several others playing the same positions. And in 1922, as Rockne produced still another successful season, 8-1-1, the eventual Four Horsemen were in and out of the lineup in different combinations. Layden wasn't in much at all and complained to Rockne about it before the Army game. "All right, Layden, I'll let you start," said Rockne, and he was never sorry. The four famous backs were united for the first time in the next-to-last game of 1922.

The Irish promptly lost the last game of 1922 to Nebraska, a Notre Dame irritant that was the only blot on a 9-1 record the next season, 1923. But nobody else could beat Notre Dame, that year or the next, the fitting climax to a 10-0 season coming in the Rose Bowl—Notre Dame's only bowl appearance until 1970—against a Stanford team coached by Pop Warner and led by Ernie Nevers.

Stunning as it may seem when contrasted with the giants of the modern game, the Horsemen were mere scatbacks. Stuhldreher weighed 158, Layden 162, and Crowley and Miller the heavyweights at 164. In later years, people sometimes remarked to one or another that they must have lost weight over the years. Actually, they were heavier as they got older.

Good as these four were, they would have been no better known than many other Notre Dame backs were it not for the 1924 Army game when Grantland Rice got off his famous account beginning, "Outlined against a blue-gray October sky, the Four Horsemen

When this picture was taken at New York's Polo Grounds shortly before Notre Dame's 1924 game with Army, these four were just another good Notre Dame backfield. Three hours later, *Herald Tribune* reporter Grantland Rice was ranking their might second only to destruction, famine, pestilence, and death. These were the Four Horsemen: Don Miller, Elmer Layden, Harry Stuhldreher, and Jim Crowley.

rode again today. . ." Some have accused Rice of getting carried away; the Irish won only by 13-7.

But there was an explanation for the deathless prose. The idea was planted by a Notre Dame publicist, historically a breed whose ingenuity at spreading the news, and sometimes creating it, perfectly complemented football teams that often managed the improbable.

Notre Dame's minister of information in 1924 happened to be a movie freak who saw *The Four Horsemen of the Apocalypse* something like six times, including the night before Notre Dame left for the Army game in New York. At halftime, he pointedly told a group of writers that he thought the Notre Dame backfield was running over Army like the *Four Horsemen of the Apocalypse*. Only Rice got it.

Like no other passage written, Rice's words made a household name of Notre Dame—even if it sometimes sorely inconvenienced the new Four Horsemen. Layden later recalled, "Next to flying, about which I remain a devout coward, I like riding a horse least. Yet it always seemed that whenever Stuhldreher, Crowley, Miller, and Layden got together, someone wanted to put us on horses."

Rockne loved it. His fame spread along with Notre Dame's. He became a speaker in demand; his word was taken as gospel. There wasn't anything he couldn't overcome, it seemed, except his baldness. He was a symbol of virility; almost everyone called him Rock. One of the few who didn't was his wife, Bonnie, who stayed contentedly in the background. She called him Kan-ute.

Fame brought pressures, and annoyances, to Rockne, it seemed almost everyone he knew was trying to get a Rose Bowl ticket from him at the end of the 1924 season. He received 700 pounds of mail between the last game and the Rose Bowl. But, ever shrewd, Rockne used even such matters as ticket troubles to win his players over. He told a few about his tribulations, stirring in them some anxiety for him that they would lose against Stanford.

Eddie Anderson played varsity football for four years, 1918-21. He led the team in pass receiving in 1920 and 1921, was selected as an All-America in 1921.

For three seasons Anderson's partner at end was Roger Kiley, who made All-America teams two years in succession, 1920-21. Kiley and Anderson were selected to our pre-Leahy all-time Notre Dame team.

Of greater concern to Rockne was acclimating his players to warmer temperatures for the big game. Did he leave early for California? Not exactly. The resourceful Rockne decided he could acclimate his players to hot weather while at the same time spreading the name of Notre Dame across the country. So he arranged a Southern train tour, starting in New Orleans, hardly the most direct route to the West Coast, then journeying across Texas and the Southwest. At Tucson, Rockne was met by former Irish player Slip Madigan, then coaching St. Mary's in California. Madigan informed Rockne of one of Stanford's favorite plays, a Pop Warner creation that had Nevers throwing the equivalent of a screen pass. Madigan's report solidified Rockne's faith in scouting. Layden scored three touchdowns, including two on interception returns of 80 and 70 yards as Notre Dame won, 27-10.

The years 1925 through 1928 were a mix of satisfaction and setback for Rockne. He produced four more winners with records of 7-2-1, 9-1, 7-1-1, and 5-4, the 1928 record being as close as he came to a losing one. Attendance at Notre Dame games increased steadily until it surpassed an average of 50,000 a game.

Yet the records, which would be regarded in most places as a huge success, did not measure up to the standard Rockne already had set for himself and his successors. Recruiting competition increased. So did Rockne's outside commitments: coaching clinics, writing and radio, motion picture shorts, public relations for the Studebaker Corporation of South Bend that sharply increased his travel schedule. His health deserted him for the first time. Worn down by the pressures of his schedule, he needed a trip to Europe after the 1925 season to refresh himself. He was wooed by other schools and actually signed in 1927 to coach Columbia, a commitment he failed to keep.

Rockne won some historic games in the years between the Four Horsemen and the perfect seasons of 1929 and 1930: when he plucked from the bench in the final minutes of the Southern California game of 1926 a little left-handed passer, Art Parisien, who threw to Johnny Niemiec for a 13-12 victory; when he delivered his Gipper speech in 1928 and Army fell, 12-6.

But Rockne lost some that almost broke his spirit: 27-0, his worst loss, to Army in 1925, when he might have used that Gipper speech; 19-0 to Carnegie Tech in 1926, when he confidently skipped the game to scout Army-Navy in Chicago only to become inconsolable when he got the bad news from Pittsburgh; one-sided losses to Carnegie and Southern California, the only time he ever suffered consecutive defeats, to close out the 1928 season and usher in his most glorious years yet.

There were precious few hints of the good times to come. The 1928 team hardly looked capable of spawning an undefeated successor. Rockne, in fact, to make his 1928 players fighting mad and extract every last bit of their potential, referred to them as the "Minute Men," as in, "They'll be in the game one minute and the other team will score," a comment he repeated frequently to reporters.

But while most observers thought the Irish of 1928 would surely fall to Army, Rockne, surprisingly, seemed confident. According to Ed Healey, now 81 and living in Niles, Michigan, a former Dartmouth and pro star who was then assisting Rockne with his linemen, Rockne displayed particular optimism at a luncheon with Eastern writers the day before the game at the Westchester Country Club, where Notre Dame stayed regularly before playing in New York.

The next day Healey found out why. "I was holding the door to the dressing room," Healey said, "and I was told by Rockne not to let anybody in. He had something special to say." It was his famous win-one-for-the-Gipper speech. "And when I tell you it was a terrific accomplishment beating Army that year," Healey added, "you can mark it down."

The 1929 team faced a treacherous schedule arranged by Rockne and compounded in its difficulty because the new Notre Dame stadium was being built and the team had to play all its games on the road.

After the first game of the season, Rockne was forced to bed. He had been stricken with phlebitis, a blood clot in his leg. His doctor advised him to give up coaching. Rockne's concession was to hand over the coaching duties to an assistant, Tom Lieb, for six of the nine games.

From home, Rockne would call long distance to talk to his starters and Lieb in the locker rooms before kickoffs. Then came the fourth game of the season, one he decided he would not miss under any circumstances—Carnegie Tech.

Francis Wallace, in his book *Knute Rockne*, recalled watching with a few others from behind a row of lockers as Rockne gave one of his most impassioned halftime speeches. Another man behind the lockers was a Dr. Maurice Keady, who whispered: "If he lets go, and that clot dislodges, hits his heart or his brain, he's got an even chance of never leaving this dressing room alive."

John Niemiec threw the pass to Johnny O'Brien that won the 1928 Army game, supposedly the "one for the Gipper." But unlike O'Brien's one play fame, Butch Niemiec carved a solid reputation for himself. He was the team leader in scoring and passing in 1927, and in 1928 completed 37 passes, a mark that wasn't bettered until Angelo Bertelli came along in 1941.

"I don't know when I've ever wanted to win a game as badly as this one," Rockne told his players. Then, beginning to shout: "I don't care what happens after today. Why do you think I'm taking a chance like this? To see you lose? Go out there and crack 'em, crack 'em, crack 'em. Fight to live. Fight to win. Fight to live. Fight to win, win, win, win." He collapsed as they poured out of the dressing room, but it was only a momentary setback.

Not surprisingly, the Irish went on to win, 7-0, the only touchdown coming on a short plunge by Joe Savoldi. Savoldi was one of many superb backs that year, the others being quarterback Frank Carideo, Jack Elder, and Larry "Moon" Mullins, all holdovers from 1928, and newcomers Marchy Schwartz and Marty Brill.

Rockne, who had gotten out of his sick bed to make it to the practice field the week before the Carnegie game, spent much of his time psyching up Savoldi, whose feelings had been hurt by one of the coaches in Rockne's absence. Just as Rockne sensed, Savoldi proved the difference against Carnegie.

Rockne attended one more game that season and it proved as tough as he had suspected. The Irish edged Southern California, 13-12, in Chicago. Rockne, who had used the pass infrequently that year, opened up more against U.S.C. One play was a typical Rockne surprise: Elder, the runner, threw the ball for a touchdown. Against Army, to complete the 9-0 season, Elder intercepted a pass by star Cadet Chris Cagle and returned it 96 yards in a 7-0 victory.

Rockne's last season was his best. The new stadium was built. He felt better. He believed he could have another perfect season. His hopes were based largely on his backfield of Carideo, Savoldi, Brill, and Schwartz. They were bigger, and better, than the Four Horsemen. All made All-America that year.

The Irish began rolling over opponents. One unusual, but temporary impediment, proved to be a Pittsburgh policeman who wouldn't let Rockne into the Pitt game without a ticket. The coach had predicted he would be recognized at the gate, only to be proven wrong one of the few times in his life. He was furious and had to be rescued by a Notre Dame business official, who hurried up with an extra ticket.

The day the Irish crushed Penn, 60-20, with Penn transfer Brill scoring three times for Notre Dame, began inauspiciously thanks to an overzealous Irish trainer, Scrapiron Young. Shortly into the game, the crowd of 75,000, which had overflowed the Franklin Field seats, began pressing around the Irish bench and Rockne ordered Young to clear the area.

Young cleared out everybody except one small, dapperly dressed fellow sitting on the bench in a smartly tailored overcoat, stovepipe hat, and a green Notre Dame blanket around his legs. Despite Young's growing anger, the man refused to budge or even pay the trainer the slightest notice.

Finally, Young literally picked him up, one hand on the collar of his overcoat, the other on the seat of his trousers. "Hold it, Scrap," cried Rockne. But it was too late. Young had pitched him into the air and he landed unceremoniously on his backside several yards away.

Rockne rushed over to the man, called over Young, and said, "Mr. Young, I would like to have you meet an old friend of mine —Mayor Jimmy Walker of New York."

In addition to possessing superb running and passing skills, Frank Carideo was a demon on defense. He intercepted five passes in 1929 and ran them back for a total of 151 yards. He also holds Notre Dame career records in number of punt returns and yards gained with punt returns, and added insult to injury by usually placing his own soaring punts beyond the reach of the opposition.

Rockne did not stint on conditioning, a fact readily apparent from the expressions on the faces of some of his straining squad members. This view of Rockne is exemplary; the bald head, thick, round shoulders, and slightly bowed legs could belong to no one else, except possibly Pat O'Brien.

Rockne skipped the Drake game to scout Northwestern, which he feared could ruin a national championship season for Notre Dame. But Drake hung close in the early going and when the Irish finally did pull away, assistant coach Hunk Anderson, perhaps recalling the 1926 disaster at Carnegie that Rockne skipped, kept the Irish front-liners in to the finish. There were several injuries and the team was tired coming into the crucial Northwestern game.

Some observers consider Rockne's halftime psych job against Northwestern his best ever. With the score 0-0, he gathered the team around him, then delivered a change of pace. He spoke quietly, explained patiently and calmly that they were having an off day, that they could do better, and that he was sure they would if they worked together. Simple enough, but convincing. Final score: 14-0.

For the next game, Army did Rockne a large favor by agreeing to shift the game from New York to Chicago's Soldier Field because the Irish had to play USC on the West Coast the following week and didn't want to travel East. This small problem arose despite the fact that in 1925 Rockne produced an entire manual on principles of scheduling.

When Notre Dame won that game, 7-6, on a touchdown run by Schwartz and point after by Carideo, and then won the last game easily over Southern California, 27-0, Rockne had reached the peak of his career. He could claim a fifth perfect season, 18 straight victories, an adoring nation, and more business offers than he could manage.

The last game Rockne coached was an exhibition game. He directed a group of Notre Dame all-stars against the New York Giants at the Polo Grounds on December 14, 1930. It was 15-0, Giants, at the half, when Rockne sent a message to the New York coach, Steve Owen, that said: "I came out here to help charity and at a lot of trouble. You are making us look bad. Slow up, will you? I don't want to go home to be laughed at." The Giants started their reserves in the second half and added only one more touchdown to win 22-0.

Shortly after that, Rockne, in a letter to New York columnist Joe Williams, related some of his feelings about his players and teams. Rockne hinted that his favorite quarterback was Frank Carideo from the unbeaten 1929 and 1930 teams. "He was cocky," Rockne wrote, "but I like to have my quarterbacks cocky, especially when they sincerely believe in themselves. Carideo did. When the game started, I let him run it.

"For real athletes," Rockne added, "you must hand it to the old Four Horsemen team. Somehow they seemed able to go to town whenever the occasion demanded. I've never seen a team that had more poise, mentally and physically. In their senior year, they had every game won before they played it.

"I can still hear Harry Stuhldreher saying to the fellows at the start of a game: 'Come on, let's get some points quick before these guys wake up and get the idea they can beat us.'"

Rockne said that team learned much from its 14-7 defeat by Nebraska in 1923. "Losing that game," he said, "did them a lot of good. It was a game they figured to win. They eased up. They thought they could win at any time. In short, they thought they were better than they were. It was a good lesson, a chastening, humiliating lesson. They never eased up again and they were never beaten again."

Three months after that analysis Rockne was dead, victim of a plane crash in Kansas. The date was March 31, 1931. He was 43. Ironically, the crash occurred not far from the farm of Jesse Harper, Rockne's predecessor and coach who was to be called out of retirement to serve again as athletic director.

Rockne had even considered the possibility of dying in a plane crash. He had told a friend, "I think each of us has a time to go and when that time comes, no matter where we are, it strikes. So I figure it might as well be in a plane as anywhere."

News of Rockne's death came as a shock. When he heard the news, the Army coach, Major Ralph Sasse, went to the player who had wept at the time his extra-point kick was blocked against Notre Dame in the 1930 game. According to *Army vs. Notre Dame: The Big Game, 1913–1917,* by Jim Beach and Daniel Moore, the coach told him, "I can honestly say that I am glad you missed that kick. If you'd made it, Rock wouldn't have won his last Army game." This, possibly, was Rockne's greatest knack: he could beat a team and still have it like him.

"Nothing has ever happened at Notre Dame that has so shocked the faculty and students as this tragic news," said Notre Dame's president, Rev. Charles L. O'Donnell.

"I can't believe it," said Hunk Anderson, Rockne's top aide who would succeed him. "Rock was a part of Notre Dame. It never can be the same without him."

"Rockne's dead! It doesn't seem possible," said Elmer Layden.

Little wonder then that it seemed a whole nation mourned. Life literally came to a standstill for miles around South Bend the day of the funeral. CBS broadcast the services. Rockne's coffin was carried by six stars of the 1930 team: Frank Carideo, Marchy Schwartz, Moon Mullins, Marty Brill, Tom Yarr, and Tom Conley.

"We who are here," said Father O'Donnell, "are but a handful of his friends." There were millions more. President Hoover said, "His passing is a national loss."

3 Frank Leahy

To all, he imparted his conviction that a man could win any battle he set his mind to winning.

—*From the eulogy to Frank Leahy,*
at his funeral
June 23, 1973

Three months before he died in the Kansas plane crash, Knute Rockne journeyed to the Mayo Clinic in Rochester, Minnesota, to have his phlebitis treated. He took with him one of his players, who needed a knee operation. One day Rockne encountered an old friend and introduced him to the player. Later he told his friend, "Someday that boy will be recognized as a great coach."

It was December 1930 when Rockne and the future great coach, Frank Leahy, lay in adjoining beds talking almost nothing but football. The more they talked the more convinced Rockne became that his assessment of the young man was correct: Leahy possessed an uncanny football mind; he was going to be an extraordinary coach.

Leahy wasn't so sure. He worried about the injury that had ended his playing career before the 1930 season began. His obscurity that year, he thought, might deprive him of an assistant coach's job that he wanted badly. Not so, Rockne reassured him. The master reached into his night table drawer and took out six letters. He flipped them onto Leahy's bed. Each letter was from a different college coach asking Rockne to send an assistant.

"You can have your choice," Rockne said.

So Leahy began a 10-year odyssey that ended with his return to Notre Dame in 1941, as head coach. By the time he was forced to resign after the 1953 season because of ill health brought on by the pressures of his job, Leahy had compiled a record and a tradition to rival Rockne's. In his first year, 1941, Leahy gave Notre Dame its first unbeaten season since Rockne's 1930 team. He went on to produce six undefeated teams in all, four national champions, and an 87-11-9 record that included a remarkable unbeaten string of 39 games that stretched across the post World War II years, from the first game of 1946 to the second game of 1950.

But the toll the job took on Leahy was awesome. When he retired, at the age of just 45, he was physically and emotionally spent. "He was a dishrag in his last year," a Notre Dame official said recently. He had collapsed and been administered the last rites of the Catholic Church at halftime of the 1953 Georgia Tech game. He was suffering from pancreatitis, the result of nervous tension and worry. He died in 1974, suffering from leukemia, arthritis, diabetes, and kidney complications. He lasted as long as he did only because of an unquenchable fighting spirit.

When Leahy announced his retirement in 1953, there was hardly a dry eye among Notre Dame followers. And little wonder. The Leahy spirit, his unrelenting desire to win not some of the games but all of them, produced a protracted drama of brilliant football and herculean deeds by the coach and those he inspired. These usually cardinal events were spiced with controversy and, just occasionally, a defeat of immense proportion.

What sort of man was this Francis William Leahy, who put a

new dimension on winning? He was rugged and handsome with blue eyes and a ready, charming smile. He could remember a face and the name that went with it. Once shy, he sought help from a Notre Dame public speaking professor and developed into an excellent speaker, and salesman, for Notre Dame.

But for many who sought a closer relationship than merely an exchange of formalities, Leahy could prove immensely frustrating. He did not socialize in the hearty, slap-on-the-back Rockne manner and seldom let all his inner feelings out. He spoke in a formal, even stilted manner, and reached for the polysyllable at every opportunity. Shortly after being named Notre Dame coach, he declared, "My vocabulary lacks the words to describe fittingly the monumental feeling of joy which permeated my entire body and soul." What he seemed to be saying was that he felt good about it.

Leahy referred to people he knew for years as "Mister" and never called his players by their nicknames but only their given ones. Czarobski, the great tackle, might be Ziggy to most, but to Leahy he was Zygmont. The players, in turn, called Leahy Coach. And well they might.

As a coach, Leahy was plenty tough, sometimes the epitome of the drill sargeant, who could make his wrath and sarcasm felt. "What was that, a blade of grass you tripped over?" he might yell to a fallen player. Or when Jim Shrader missed a point after touchdown that would have tied up a 1952 game with Pittsburgh, Leahy shouted, "Oh, Jim Shrader, you'll burn in hell for this." In more reserved moments he usually referred to his players as his lads. And almost always he forgave them their trespasses.

A staunch fundamentalist, he stressed blocking and tackling, and more. He reached to the personal lives of his players, showing a keen interest in all they were about, letting them know he cared. He cared what they wore, what they ate, if their shoes fit, what personal problem might be bothering them. He reasoned that a player couldn't do his best if something even minor was bothering him.

At the same time, Leahy's public stance was to approach every game with agonizing worry and a prediction of horrible things to come. Before the 1943 Navy game, he stated emphatically: "We can't keep Navy from scoring at least three touchdowns. We may score one on a lucky pass." Final score: Notre Dame 33, Navy 6. His orchestrated pessimism reached a depth of sorts before the 1953 season when he allowed, quite seriously, "I'll be amazed if we make a single first down in 10 games." The Irish never lost that year, his last.

But Leahy could laugh at his ways, too. He traced his perpetually dour outlook to his days as Boston College coach. He once predicted victory over rival Holy Cross only to have Holy Cross outplay B.C. The B.C. team managed to win by just 7-0 only after recovering a fumble in scoring position. "It was a close call," Leahy sighed. "From now on, pardon my pessimism."

Leahy made the T Notre Dame's regular formation. He uncovered marvelously talented quarterbacks: Angelo Bertelli, Johnny Lujack, Frank Tripucka, Bob Williams, Ralph Guglielmi. He produced great running backs as though they were carbon copies: Creighton Miller, Emil Sitko, Terry Brennan, Johnny Lattner, Neil Worden. No fewer than 42 players from Leahy's 9-0 1947 team went on to play professionally.

All the while, however, Leahy refused invitations by press and public to heap praises on his men. Once, he broke down the slightest bit and allowed of Lujack, who was taking over for the service-bound Bertelli in 1943, "I have high hopes for the youngster." A newspaper headline blared: "Extra! Extra! Leahy Admits Lujack Is Good."

Leahy preferred to downplay his athletes' talents for the twin purposes of rousing them while lulling the opposition. He would declare, evidence to the contrary, that Bertelli was no All-America candidate, to which one writer responded, "All Angelo Bertelli can do is pass, and all Rembrandt could do was paint."

But when it was all over in 1953 and the ailing Leahy had no choice but to resign if he wanted to live, he revealed some of his true thoughts about his players. He called his 9-0-1 1953 team his greatest; Lujack and Lattner his best all-round players; 1941 linebacker Bernie Crimmins his top defensive player, slightly ahead of tackle George Connor, and Bertelli his finest passer.

Not to be overlooked was the 60-minute, offensive and defensive giant, Leon Hart, one of Leahy's four Heisman Trophy winners, along with Bertelli, Lujack, and Lattner. Hart was a sensation from the start. Clearing his bench in a 1949 game, Leahy called for the huge freshman. The coach warned him not to be nervous, expressed confidence in him, patted him on the backside, and sent him in with a flourish.

His chin strap buckled, his heart racing with excitement, Hart wheeled and roared away from the sideline—and ran right over a halfback, Bob Livingstone, who was returning to the bench, knocking him out. "Nobody ever hit me that hard," said Livingstone, upon being revived. "Yeah," said the trainer, "but first he's got to learn that he's on our side."

There were a few players, just a few, who could get away with a little more than the others. Czarobski was a great wit. Once when an exasperated Leahy told his players he was going to start all over with fundamentals and said, "This, gentlemen, is a ball," Czarobski spoke up, "Hold it, Coach, not so fast."

"Creighton Miller," said longtime Leahy assistant coach Joe McArdle, "was the only player who could make Leahy seem almost thin-skinned. Creighton would have a tendency to open his mouth maybe when he should have had it closed. He was a great back, but he wasn't on scholarship, so you couldn't keep him in line as much." On one touchdown run, the talented Miller, mistaking the 5-yard line for the goal line, pulled up and almost was tackled before he could pick up speed again and get into the end zone. After the game, an exasperated Leahy marched Miller to the scene of his absent-mindedness and, pointing a finger, said, "This, Creighton Miller, is the 5-yard line. And this is the goal line. Do not ever mistake them again."

If he pushed all his players relentlessly, many to become the standouts that kept Notre Dame in the headlines every weekend and in the hearts of their followers every day, Leahy drove himself just as hard. He lived up to each of his pronouncements on coaching: the satisfied coach is a bad one; coaching is no profession for a lazy man; always expect the worst; always be tough on the field; victory can come only out of hard labor—sweat and tears and sometimes even blood; prayers work better when your players are big; always look

The last of the fabled Miller clan, Creighton Miller. His 911 yards gained rushing led the nation in 1943, and has been bettered just once by a Notre Dame ball carrier. His attitude and dedication were not always faultless, but he had to be handled carefully since he was not on scholarship.

for the storm, never the sunshine.

Indeed, these were stormy times, the Leahy years. He was criticized widely for the sucker shift and the feigned injury. He was charged with dirty play and censured by the NCAA for rule-bending recruiting practices. But, if some disliked him, more revered him. This was natural enough; he could be counted on to win games, as it turned out, almost as many as Rockne. Uplifted by Leahy in the Rockne tradition, the Notre Dame spirit could be felt around the country through the forties and into the fifties.

Leahy left nothing to chance, overlooked no detail, in his preparation of a team. For a game at Texas in 1952, he ordered 36 pith helmets. "Nobody knew what he wanted them for," former assistant McArdle recalled. And before anybody could figure out why, Leahy added another request. "He wanted to get our bench switched to the same side of the field as Texas," McArdle said. "I said, 'Hey, that's never been done before,' but he said it didn't matter that it had never been done. So I told the guy at the stadium that Dana Bible said it was all right. They were as afraid of Dana Bible down there as some people were of Leahy up at our place. So we sat on the same side with Texas and in the fourth quarter when we were in the shade we looked across the field and the sun was still beating down where we would have been.

"As for the pith helmets, they kept off the sun earlier in the game and we also put ice in them. So the players had air conditioning. It seemed to pay off because we had a lot left in the fourth quarter and that's when we won the game. That was one Texas should have won. They had the better team."

One time Leahy refused to halt a practice despite a driving rain storm, declaring with irrefutable logic, "You never know what might happen on a Saturday." Still, he was one of the first coaches to recognize the value of indoor practices. He emphasized the idea of surprise, including a deep pass when least expected, such as early in games. Mostly, he stressed hard work in the form of repetition. With the proper determination, he felt, Notre Dame would win over all.

He was always determined himself. As a high school junior in the aptly named town of Winner, South Dakota, he knew he wanted to go to Notre Dame and play football. But he wondered if he were good enough to make the team. He was persuaded to try by his older brother, Gene, and his high-school football coach and Notre Dame player of 1919-20-21, Earl Walsh. Once Leahy was convinced, there was no stopping him.

He was born in O'Neill, Nebraska, on August 21, 1908. His parents, who were homesteaders, moved shortly afterward to South Dakota. Leahy inherited a fighting spirit from his father, who gained mild fame by wrestling the legendary Farmer Burns. Young Leahy took up boxing, rode herd, and grew up capable of taking care of himself.

He played left halfback on the Winner High team and Earl Walsh recommended him to Rockne. But after graduating from Winner, Leahy went off to Omaha to live with his older brother, Gene, who had been a standout player for Creighton University there. Gene, who was given responsibility for Frank by their father, suggested to his younger brother that he stay out of college one year so that he would be more mature when he got to Notre Dame.

One of Notre Dame's best and most versatile backfields, from left to right: Johnny Lattner, Neil Worden, Joe Heap, and Ralph Guglielmi. Lattner was a dangerous runner; Worden was a solid runner and blocking back; Heap led the team in pass receiving; and Guglielmi held Notre Dame passing records for more than a decade.

Right: Bill Fischer, a two-time All-America guard, went on to a celebrated career in pro football.

Left: Leon Hart was a unanimous All-America selection in 1949, the same year he won the Heisman and Maxwell trophies.

Though he had no high school eligibility remaining, Leahy went out for the Central High team anyway. The coach, noting the player's lack of speed, switched him to tackle, where he played so superbly that word of his talent spread. Word also got back from South Dakota that Leahy had no business playing. By that time, he had gotten in most of the season. It was also in Omaha that Leahy boxed with the celebrated "Nebraska Wildcat," Ace Hudkins. Leahy did so well that Hudkins and his friends tried to get him to become a professional boxer. But Leahy never lost sight of his goal.

In September 1927, he enrolled at Notre Dame. The second day there he lost his wallet, with his total earnings of $19 in it. But the day was not a complete loss because he met Rockne. "Leahy, eh? Earl Walsh wrote to me about you." Rockne sized him up. Leahy stood in awe.

Leahy enrolled in physical education, a course that curiously included a number of pre-med subjects. To earn money, he worked at several odd jobs, including waiting on tables and cleaning up locker rooms. He was well liked by his classmates and was elected freshman class president. In football, he labored as a second-string tackle on the freshman team.

One day Rockne came over to the corner of the field where the freshmen practiced and, among other pronouncements, suggested, "How about trying Leahy at center for a while." Leahy, enthusiastic at being noticed, even if he had never played center, borrowed a ball from the team's trainer and practiced snaps in his dormitory corridor. Inevitably, this plan came to an unhappy ending when, practicing with a colleague in simulated punt formation, he hiked the ball through a window at the end of the corridor.

Leahy made the 1928 varsity as a center but was switched back to tackle in 1929 when he made the first team, though not without the usual number of reprimands from Rockne. One day in practice Marchy Schwartz was running an off-tackle play, but Leahy repeatedly missed his block. Then, Leahy recalled, "Rock called me over and let me have it. He said, 'Leahy, I never knew how really fine a defensive tackle you were until just now. You've just succeeded in stopping three of our own plays while playing on offense.'"

Plagued often by injuries, Leahy once secured Rockne's permission to play in a game despite a dislocated elbow. "Let me see that elbow," Rockne demanded. Leahy showed him his good one.

In the final scrimmage before the 1930 season, Leahy tore up his knee throwing a downfield block. He lay writhing in pain, his career over. After shaking off his depression, he resumed going to practice, even on crutches, doing what he could to help out. He absorbed every Rockne coaching technique and learned more than he could have strictly as a player. Soon he was assisting line coach Hunk Anderson. Rockne rewarded Leahy with a trip to Los Angeles for the final game of the season against Southern California. Though it may be difficult to believe, Leahy further damaged his knee while playing tiddlywinks at the California home of his friend, running back Larry "Moon" Mullins.

So Rockne took Leahy to the Mayo Clinic for repairs and produced the letters from coaches seeking assistants. Leahy chose a job at Georgetown, in Washington, under Tommy Mills, who had coached him as a Notre Dame freshman. After a year, Leahy joined the staff of Jim Crowley, one of the Four Horsemen, at Michigan State. When Crowley shifted to Fordham in 1933, Leahy went, too; as line coach, he constructed the "Seven Blocks of Granite," one of whom was Vince Lombardi.

In 1938, Leahy became head coach at Boston College. He won 20 of 22 games, capped by a 19-13 victory over Tennessee in the Sugar Bowl. A crowd of 50,000 welcomed Leahy and the B.C. team at Boston's South Station upon their return from New Orleans. Leahy had forged a national power and become a coach in demand. He turned down three offers from other schools and signed a five-year contract with B.C.

Just then, Elmer Layden resigned as coach at Notre Dame. Notre Dame called Leahy, and Boston College released him from his contract. At the age of 32, Leahy became Notre Dame's football coach and athletic director. It was February 15, 1941.

"To carry on for Rockne, from whom I learned so much and whose memory I so revere, I felt was a call no man could refuse," declared Leahy in a statement issued to counteract criticism in the New England press over his sudden departure. The Notre Dame job was the one Leahy wanted. With it in mind, he had secured a verbal agreement from B.C. officials to release him from his contract should the Irish job come open. He simply didn't expect such a vacancy to occur almost literally before the ink had dried on his B.C. contract.

Having heard of Leahy's success in Boston, almost all of Notre Dame's 3,000 students turned out to welcome the new coach at a rally before spring practice. Leahy told them, "We will make no attempt to emulate Knute Rockne but will try only to match Layden's record." *Only* Layden's record? Elmer Layden of Four Horsemen fame had done exceedingly well as the Irish coach the previous seven years before resigning to become National Football League commissioner. His record was 47-13-3, a sharp turnabout from the Hunk Anderson years. As successor to Rockne, Anderson, former Rockne star player and top assistant coach, managed a modest 16-9-2 record in three seasons, the last being a 3-5-1 mark in 1933.

What Leahy seemed to mean in fixing Layden's record as his goal was what he got around to saying a few minutes later, "that the day of the undefeated Notre Dame team is over," that there would be no more seasons like Rockne produced. But one astute newsman who knew Leahy would be striving for nothing less than perfection wrote, "Everyone is patiently waiting to see him hoisted on his own petard of fabrication."

Despite his warnings to the contrary, Leahy hinted at the good times to come when he professed a liking for a wide-open attack. "At Boston College, we tried 'goofy' stuff," he told the students. "Quick opening plays, long passes and short passes. If we come up with a good passer here next fall, we'll really open up. We gambled at Boston College and we'll gamble here if we have a chance."

Even then Leahy must have suspected he had the passer he wanted: a tall, skinny youth from Massachusetts whom Leahy ironically had recruited the previous year for B.C. but failed to get. Angelo Bertelli, 6-foot-1, 168 pounds, from West Springfield, Massachusetts, the "Springfield Rifle," had chosen Notre Dame. Now he and Leahy were to make some interesting history together.

That summer Bertelli stayed on campus, taking a job painting which strengthened his arm. He also practiced passes with the team's right end, George Murphy, who lived in South Bend. It seemed reminiscent of Gus Dorais and Rockne practicing during the summer of 1913. The results were similar, too. As the angular Bertelli fired away, the Irish rolled over their first five opponents in 1941 by the combined point totals of 142-27, Leahy becoming again the instant success he had been in Boston.

Certain lineup changes Leahy had made also helped. He moved Bernie Crimmins, the same Crimmins he later named as his all-time defensive player, from fullback to tackle; Harry Wright, from fullback to quarterback; Wally Ziemba, from tackle to end, and Dippy Evans from tailback to fullback, making way for Bertelli.

Though his career reached epic proportions in the years following World War II, Leahy's coaching style was so fixed and plainly evident in 1941-42-43, before he went off to serve two years in the navy, that his superb lifetime record and eventual undoing because of failing health could almost have been predicted. He built his teams around an accurate passer. He assembled strong defensive lines. He worried constantly. He landed in the hospital an emotional wreck for the first time in 1942, just as he would in later years.

And so as his first crucial game neared in 1941, Leahy presented the portrait of an anguished coach that would soon become a

Angelo Bertelli, on the left, was Notre Dame's greatest passer, until the young man on the right, Johnny Lujack arrived. Bertelli was the first Notre Dame player to receive the Heisman Trophy; four years later, in 1947, Lujack won it.

familiar sight. Standing on the platform of the South Bend train depot, he addressed the assembled reporters, formally, as was his wont. The team was bound for New York and a date with Army in Yankee Stadium.

"This game," Leahy said, "presents the most interesting, and in a way the most fascinating, situation that I have ever encountered as a coach, and you can see it's got me jittery. It is of the greatest importance to me personally, to Notre Dame, and to the boys on the squad to win this game. I have never taken a team into New York before. I am longing for the boys to win it. I have never been so worried before. I don't know if we're better than Army or not, honestly. I'm afraid not, but I hope we are." This was classic Leahy, the pre-game worrier unable to calm himself.

There was another aspect to this game. Leahy and Army's new coach, Earl "Red" Blaik, were not particularly fond of one another. They operated within a built-in rivalry; the Army-Notre Dame series already was the biggest in the country. Moreover, the two men took charge at their schools in the very same year, 1941, thus sharpening the competition between them.

"Earl Blaik and I are in exactly the same position," Leahy told reporters. "Each has been called back to his old school and given what was left over to work with. He has been given more credit for what he's done than I, and justly so. That is not false modesty. His situation certainly was more difficult than mine. Now we both come up unbeaten to this game."

It was just five weeks before Pearl Harbor but Americans, not suspecting the impending war, pursued their normal routines. In New York, interest centered on the game. One paper printed a sketch of players in Yankee Stadium with a large, ghostly face of Rockne overlooking the scene. Another paper reported: "Every single holder of a precious ducat is keenly aware of the thrills it entitles him to witness in a game that never fails to exceed its quota." The same account referred to Leahy as a "suave apostle of victory."

It turned out that Leahy was neither suave nor victorious that day but disappointed and wet. It poured rain. In the locker room before the game, one Notre Dame player with a sense of humor, Harry Wright, took Bertelli's uniform and hid it. He laughed and told Bertelli, "Forget it, you passers don't play on days like this." And another player, Steve Juzwik, said to Bertelli, "Why don't you stay in here where it's warm and curl up with a good book? You won't be worth a nickel to us in that muck." How right they were. Bertelli managed to complete only three passes. But Leahy's stout defense stopped Army, too. The game ended 0-0, a preview of 1946.

The outcome made Leahy downright morose before the following week's game, against Navy. "Our chances for victory are hopeless," he declared. Not exactly. Bertelli enjoyed his best game of the season, passing for one score and setting up two others in a 20-13 victory. The Irish then edged Northwestern and Southern California by a combined total of three points that did nothing for Leahy's jangled nerves but gave him and the Irish an 8-0-1 record. Who said "the day of the undefeated Notre Dame team is over?" Bertelli, runnerup for the Heisman Trophy as a sophomore, finished the year with 70 completions in 123 attempts for 1,027 yards. He threw for 8 touchdowns and set up 7 others with his passes.

Was Leahy satisfied? Hardly. He had been voted coach of the year in a number of polls, but he had other things on his mind. Bertelli had been throwing from the halfback position in the old Rockne box formation. Everyone knew Bertelli was not a running threat. Late in the 1941 season, defenses began crashing in hard, disregarding the possibility of a run. Leahy planned to add deception to his attack for 1942 by dropping the Rockne box in favor of the T formation. He called in Bertelli and told him he would be switched to quarterback in the T. He would play right behind the center and handle the ball on every play. He could hand off or fake and fade to pass. Leahy would have the deception he wanted.

But it took all of his coaching genius to get Bertelli functioning as smoothly from the T as he had in the box. Fading to pass and looking for receivers, Bertelli took longer getting away his passes. Leahy put in countless hours having Bertelli repeat the unfamiliar procedure. Then Leahy discovered Bertelli was too shy to call his own number often enough in the huddle. In a brilliant stroke, Leahy turned the signal-calling over to Harry Wright, who had been switched to guard in the T after playing quarterback the previous year in the box. Wright had no compunction about calling Bertelli pass plays.

Leahy had been sold on the T formation since watching the Chicago Bears use it in 1941. Before installing it at Notre Dame, Leahy sought all the information he could about it from the experts: Bears' quarterback Sid Luckman, Bears' owner-coach George Halas, and Maryland coach Clark Shaughnessy, regarded as the inventor of the T. Shaughnessy told Leahy, "No coach should embrace the T who is afraid to work." Apparently, Shaughnessy hadn't heard about Leahy's habits.

Leahy began assembling his assistant coaches on campus as early as 5 A.M. to discuss the T. "We not only had a job of teaching the boys," Leahy recalled later, "but of teaching ourselves." Leahy was convinced his then-revolutionary course was right.

"The T," he said, "represents modern, streamlined football. I could be wrong, but I think it is not only the football of today but will be the football of tomorrow. We had it at Notre Dame years ago. But the contemporary T is distinctly new and different, offering more attacking possibilities, I think, than any strategic theory football has yet devised. One of its attractions is its extreme flexibility. For example, last year we had an end run and it was just that, an end run. Now we have the same basic end run but we run it eight or ten different ways. A slight change here in the blocking assignments, a slight change there in the deception, and it's a different play."

By the time Leahy got his T working, however, the Irish had been tied in their 1942 opener by Wisconsin and had dropped a 13-6 game to Georgia Tech. Leahy began to hear loud criticism from Notre Dame alumni for abandoning the box formation. "If it was good enough for Rockne," they said, "it ought to be good enough for Leahy."

It was all enough to send Leahy to the hospital. He was worn out. He also was suffering violent pains in his back. Yet he went reluctantly.

"I have reached the point physically where I am of no value to the Notre Dame team," he finally admitted. "I have fought against making this decision, but I am now convinced it is my only course for the best interest of the team and for my own health."

In a converse manner of thinking, Leahy reasoned that if he was veering in the general direction of ill health, or was already sick, it meant he must be doing something right. "In order to get yourself a good case of the miseries," he suggested, "you must work hard, overwork, in fact. Well, when you do that, when you've accomplished something, you don't want to give it up too casually."

He checked into the Mayo Clinic and there, along with exhaustion, he was found to have some arthritis of the spine, which was to cause him much suffering later in life.

With its coach ill and absent, the team responded in traditional Notre Dame fashion. The players sent Leahy a telegram telling him not to worry and went out and overwhelmed Stanford, 27-0. The substitute coach was Leahy aide Ed McKeever, who had played freshman ball at Notre Dame in 1930, but transferred to Texas Tech when he found himself a fifth-string fullback in the fall of 1931.

The lopsided victory over Stanford seemed to revive Leahy as much as any medical treatment. "I just can't tell you how happy it makes me," he told a hospital visitor. "It almost makes me forget about my back." He was allowed a phone in his room and was able to keep in contact with McKeever. "Otherwise," Leahy said, "I would have gone crazy."

As it was, he suffered more anguish having to miss the next game, against Iowa Pre-Flight, a group of outstanding players from various colleges assembled to prepare for war duty. The naval cadets were coached by Lt. Col. Bernie Bierman of University of Minnesota fame. The Iowa team was rated the best in the country.

"I just don't see how we stand a chance," said McKeever, sounding just like Leahy. "But it's funny how the kids sometimes get the idea they can't be beaten." One of the first grand-scale Notre Dame pep rallies helped the players' confidence. They won, 28-0, and McKeever was carried off the field, but quickly slipped off the players' shoulders and declared, "People seem to forget Leahy gave the squad its groundwork."

Leahy was so excited he sent a telegram to the players saying he would be with them for the Illinois game. The doctors wouldn't release him, however. The Irish won anyway and the following game Leahy was back on the sideline even though he was advised to take off one more week. But Navy and Army were coming up and the coach insisted on being there.

"I'm still a very sick man," he told the team before the Navy game in Cleveland, and no one doubted him. The day of the game came up rain and mud, but risking his health, Leahy made it to the stadium and coached the team to a 9-0 victory. "You don't know him if you think we could have kept him off that bench, even in all that weather," McKeever said. Leahy's only concession during the ordeal was to remain behind in Cleveland that night, when the team left by train for South Bend, and travel the next day.

Doctors' orders or not, Leahy continued to worry and pushed himself physically to prepare the team for Army. As the game grew near, he even went so far as to predict a Cadet victory by 7-0 or 14-13, and recalled for reporters his recent days at the Mayo Clinic.

"You know, one of the things they did to me was to stretch my neck," he said. "They took me in a place they call the hangman's room, put my head in a leather noose, and pulled on a rope which lifted me clear off the floor. It was pretty horrible and frightening.

"I don't know. Looking back on it, maybe I didn't realize how safe I was in the hangman's room every morning. When I get to thinking of what's going to happen in New York . . ."

It was time for practice. Leahy put on his hat, bade farewell to the writers, and marched out of the room. Looking back, he said, "Don't get the idea I'm trying to kid you. Pick Army."

If they picked Army, they were wrong. It was 13-0, and Leahy had his first victory over Earl Blaik. The Notre Dame alumni, who had criticized Leahy earlier, now were praising him. Yet there was one astute individual who suggested the Irish had not quite arrived with their T formation. He was none other than Hunk Anderson, the former line coach Leahy had played under and assisted who was filling in as co-coach of the Bears while George Halas was in the navy.

"It takes a long time to explore the possibilities of the T to the full, and Leahy is just starting out with it," Anderson said. "In all fairness, Notre Dame still has a long way, a very long way, to go." Anderson pointed out that the Bears used about 120 plays in a recent game while Notre Dame used only about 15 against Army. "The T is no good without a wide diversity of application," he added. "This is what Notre Dame lacks at the moment. As an old Green, I look forward to their game with Michigan this week with feverish fear. I think they're in for a smacking around. Boy, do I hope I'm wrong."

Anderson, however, was right. Michigan beat Notre Dame rather convincingly, 32-20, and before the season ended the Irish had another blot on their record, a 13-13 tie against the Great Lakes Naval Station. That left Leahy's second season at Notre Dame 7-2-2. But good play by Notre Dame in the second half of the Great Lakes game was a sign of things to come in 1943. Trailing 13-0 at the half, the outclassed Irish were given an angry lecture by Leahy, who still wasn't feeling well.

"So they call you the Fighting Irish?" asked the coach, contemptuously, according to one who was there. "We have had teams at Notre Dame which merited that title, but this isn't one of those teams. Real fighters don't quit, and it shocks me to learn in this, our last game of the year, that you aren't real fighters. I don't know what you're going to do in this second half, but don't let me hear any of you calling yourselves Fighting Irish. That's a sacred thing with Notre Dame teams."

The Irish comeback also culminated a pattern they had fallen into all season; they were better in the second half than the first. Leahy, who knew he still had plenty of work to do, attributed the mistakes early in the games to a lack of confidence in the T. Every week it was taking the players a full quarter to get reacquainted with the new formation.

But by September 1943, it was a different story. With Leahy relatively healthy again, Notre Dame, fully indoctrinated in the T, rolled over every opponent in sight. Nobody came close in the first eight games. The Irish outscored the opposition, 312-37. Michigan coach Fritz Crisler, one victim, called the 1943 Notre Dame team its

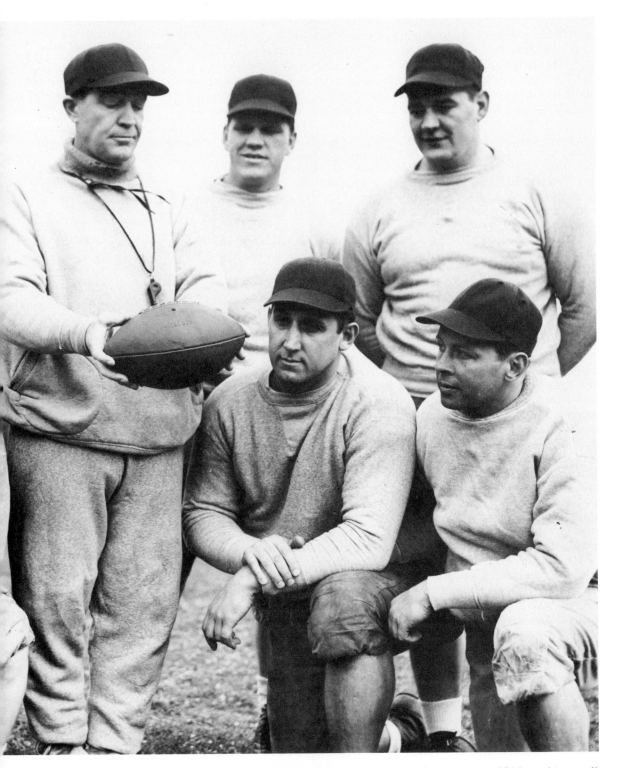

The master strategist Frank Leahy, shown here with his 1946 coaching staff; including (starting clockwise at the coach's left) Bernie Crimmins, Wally Ziemba, John Druze, Moose Krause, Joe McCardle, and Ed Doherty.

best ever. A newspaper headline, hailing a Notre Dame runner, said: "Mello Makes Jello of Michigan Line." Rip Miller, Navy's line coach and formerly one of the Seven Mules, said Leahy's team was Notre Dame's finest, better even than the 1924 and 1930 teams.

Not even Bertelli's departure in midseason to join the marines made any difference. In his final game, Bertelli threw three touchdown passes against Navy, then turned his position over to Johnny Lujack. Lujack literally filled Bertelli's shoes—the trainer passed them on to Lujack when the new quarterback remarked that his old ones were too tight. Then he went out and directed a 26-0 victory over Army, throwing for two touchdowns and running for another.

"We could have won that game by a lot more," said Leahy assistant Joe McArdle. "But Leahy never ran up a score no matter what some people said. After a while in that game we were under strict orders—no passing, no this, no that."

And how had Leahy forecast this glorious 1943 season? In his heart he may have known better, but for the record he had predicted only the worst:

"I'm afraid Pitt may surprise us." Final: Notre Dame 41, Pitt 0.

"Can't see us even coming close to beating that great Georgia Tech team." Notre Dame 55, Georgia Tech 13.

"I don't know why we are favored against Michigan. They're obviously too much for us." Notre Dame 35, Michigan 12.

"I'm afraid the boys are letting down too much and Wisconsin will take good advantage of it." Notre Dame 50, Wisconsin 0.

One writer chided Leahy for his "lachrymose lamentations."

Notre Dame finished the season with its first No. 1 national ranking under Leahy, despite struggles in the last two games against teams heavy with service-bound stars, many already professionals. The Irish edged Iowa Pre-Flight, ranked No. 2, 14-13, but lost the last game of the season, one of the classic games involving Notre Dame, by 19-14 to Great Lakes, ranked No. 6. Great Lakes won on a 46-yard pass play with 28 seconds remaining.

With that, Leahy joined the navy and Ed McKeever took over. Leahy spent most of 1944 and 1945 in the Pacific, organizing and supervising recreational activities at Midway, Tarawa, and Saipan, and later at St. Mary's (California) Preflight School. At Midway, he heard the broadcast of the 1944 Army-Notre Dame game. He couldn't believe it; 59-0 Army. Notre Dame had lost all but a few of its best players because of the war. "I went right out and drank myself into a stupor," Leahy recalled. Though the coach rarely drank, nobody doubted him in this instance.

Army added another humiliating victory over Notre Dame in 1945, 48-0, but Leahy returned for 1946. And so did more than a dozen of his players from 1943, including Lujack, who had served 11 months on a submarine chaser in the Atlantic. The Irish also added transfers from other colleges, including star lineman George Connor from Holy Cross, who had gotten his introduction to Notre Dame by taking his naval training there.

Not surprisingly, Leahy's team picked up where it had left off in 1943 and started an unprecedented 39-game unbeaten string that lasted into the 1950 season. The Irish crushed their first five opponents of 1946, outscoring them 177-18. Then came the long-awaited showdown with Army, which had won 25 straight and featured the

The archetypal hero: Johnny Lujack. Statistics do lie, for although Lujack holds no individual Notre Dame records, there are many who would say he was the greatest football player in the history of the school. During the time of 60-minute players, Lujack played defense with the same brilliance he displayed at quarterback.

NOTRE DAME 1947 NATIONAL CHAM

Line, left to right: Right end, LEON HART; right tackle, ZIGGIE CZAROBSKI;
WENDELL; center, BILL WALSH; left guard, BILL FISCHER; left tackle,
and left end, JIM MARTIN
Backfield, left to right: EMIL SITKO, right halfback; JOHN "Pep" PANELL
LUJACK, quarterback and TERRY BRENNAN, left halfback.

A sure way to spark a lively
argument is to volunteer one's
opinion on Notre Dame's
greatest team. This squad
would enlist an army of
supporters; the 1947 national
champions, undefeated in
nine games, and victorious by
a combined score of 291-52.

NS

guard, MARTY
RGE CONNOR

back; JOHNNY

1 Bagby Photo Co.

sensational running of Glenn Davis and Doc Blanchard.

Leahy brought the Irish to a frenzy. On the Notre Dame stadium locker room was hung a sign that said simply: "59-0 and 48-0." The Notre Dame student body, now grown to 4,500, assembled almost en masse at midweek and shook the old gymnasium with a pep rally the likes of which hadn't occurred there in some time.

The gym was jammed. So was its balcony. The doors had to be left open because the crowd was so big. And the roof seemed to some that it was being lifted off when Mrs. Knute Rockne was presented, stood up and took a bow.

Every member of the first team made a short talk. George Connor said, "All we know is that the Army players put their football pants on the same way we do. And when we finish with them, they'll wish they'd never put them on at all."

A Notre Dame student dressed as an Army cadet riled the audience by praising Army. A diapered effigy hung from the rafters with a note attached, "Time for a change." Said another sign; "End the meat shortage. Slaughter the Army mule." And another: "Let's have B-L-O-O-D."

Leahy himself got into the spirit. Though usually choosing stoic restraint at such times, the coach joined in the squad cheers after it was announced that Lujack and Gerry Cowhig would be co-captains for the game.

"Leahy," said an observer, "was just as pepped up about this game as his players."

Then came Notre Dame's great scare. Lujack fell to the ground in practice and turned his right ankle. For a few moments that seemed much longer, Leahy and the other players stood perfectly still, waiting, hoping for Lujack to get up. It was two days before the game.

Lujack, the hero from Connellsville, Pennsylvania, already had attracted attention when he first played against Army in 1943. West Point officials charged that Leahy had snatched Lujack from them. It was true that Lujack had an appointment to West Point if he wanted it, but he testified that Notre Dame always had been his first choice.

Now he was slowly getting to his feet and limping around heavily. His teammates gathered around. "Not since the days of the legendary George Gipp has such a tribute been paid to a Notre Dame player," one writer noted. And so the most often asked questions in the 48 hours leading up to the game were, "Will Lujack play?" and "How much will he play?"

"This is the football epic of the century," declared Army coach Earl Blaik. More than 1,300 Notre Dame students made the trip to New York. Another 2,000 from downtown South Bend joined them. The 2,000-member Cadet corps would be there. Hotel rooms were unavailable. Cots were moved into hallways, and some people had to go as far as Philadelphia to find accommodations.

Leahy was so keyed up his wife, Florence, did all she could to calm him. The two had met in New York, when Leahy was an assistant at Fordham. She was from Brooklyn, and was teaching school. Leahy took long subway rides to court her. They eventually had eight children.

Florence Leahy was at the South Bend train station to see the team off. What's more, she sent Frank, Jr., then 10 years old, with his father. "I have a notion," she told reporters, "that maybe young Frank can keep him from worrying too much."

The inevitable occurred—a 0-0 tie. Red Smith, writing in the New York *Herald Tribune,* summed it up: "It was like two Joe Louises standing face to face for six minutes, each letting go with the old Mary Ann on every play, each taking every punch full in the profile, and neither taking a single backward step. Perhaps the perfect mirror is the statistics sheet which shows that by rushing, passing and returning punts Army gained 276 yards and Notre Dame 271."

As for Lujack, he played, and brilliantly. Wrote Smith: "Lujack called every Notre Dame play, threw every Notre Dame pass, kicked every Notre Dame punt, ran the ball with speed and malevolence and tackled with hideous violence." One of those tackles was his famous game-saver, when he hit touchdown-bound Blanchard in the open field and brought him down.

This and another tie, 14-14 against Southern California in the final game of 1948, were the only blots on a perfect Notre Dame record until 1950. Leahy's Irish rolled through the rest of their 1946 schedule to gain the No. 1 ranking.

Incredibly, they repeated the act under Leahy in 1947 and 1948 and 1949. They were declared national champions again in 1947 and 1949 and finished No. 2 in 1948 because of the tie with U.S.C. Leahy thus had achieved four national titles in seven years at Notre Dame. And with a 41-7 victory over Navy in 1948, a typically one-sided Notre Dame game, Leahy surpassed Rockne's record of 22 straight unbeaten games.

George Connor played for a year at Holy Cross before transferring to Notre Dame, thus missing a chance to become Notre Dame's first three-time All-America.

This could be another version of the "gentlemen this is a football" speech that Leahy made in practice once after the ball had been dropped several times. This is the 1949 backfield, from left to right: Emil Sitko, Bob Williams, Bill Gay, and Larry Coutre.

Among the vanquished, cries arose to stop playing Notre Dame. Army did, and so did Wisconsin, for a while. Tulane officials wouldn't speak to their Notre Dame counterparts after a 59-6 beating in 1947. Notre Dame found it difficult to schedule new opponents, even though playing Notre Dame meant a big payday.

Rumors abounded that, because of adverse reaction to Notre Dame's victory streak and scheduling difficulties, Leahy offered to resign. In fact, he did offer. But Rev. John Cavanaugh, Notre Dame's president, announced, "Frank Leahy deserves unqualified credit for his coaching record which is just about the most impressive ever made by any coach in this country." The priest quoted a "nationally known coach" as saying, "Leahy deserves to be ranked along with the peerless Rockne." What finer tribute could a Rockne successor be paid?

All the while, Leahy kept the victories coming. Army was polished off, 27-7, in 1947, as that series was terminated for a decade. The game was televised and it was estimated that 175,000 people, remarkable for that time, watched it. In the stands at Notre Dame were Pat O'Brien, the Hollywood Rockne; Mrs. Rockne herself, and Jesse Harper, Rockne's coach. The victory gave Leahy a 3-0-2 record in his rivalry with Earl Blaik. "Gee, I feel good, gee, I feel good," Leahy kept repeating in the dressing room after the game. He called himself "the happiest Irishman in America."

He could have remained happy, had he permitted himself that luxury, because he kept good quarterbacks coming, which meant he had the keys to victory. Behind Lujack, whom Leahy arranged to have tutored by none other than Bears' quarterback Sid Luckman in the spring of 1947, came Frank Tripucka, of whom Leahy admitted, "He is nowhere near the passer Lujack is, but he throws very nicely, at that." And behind Tripucka came All-America Bob Williams.

But with the victories, the pressure on Leahy built. The strain of trying to keep the string intact while knowing that one day it would be broken was immense. That day almost came with the 1948 opener, against Purdue, but Notre Dame survived on what has come to be known as the luck of the Irish. Even though his name was Al Zmijewski, the reserve, and largely unknown, tackle was declared a son of Erin for the day when he intercepted a fourth-period pass and ran for a touchdown that put the game out of reach. A last touchdown left Purdue short, 28-27.

Two years later the streak ran out against Purdue, 28-14. There was every indication the sad day was coming. Opponents were having better success recruiting by telling prospects they would have more of an opportunity to play for them than if they went to Notre Dame. The Irish suffered heavy losses at 1949 graduation, Bob Williams being one of the few remaining first-stringers left. In the spring of 1950, the Irish lost a football game to their alumni, 25-7.

Still, Leahy was "shocked" by the Purdue loss, according to Leahy assistant Joe McArdle. "You knew it was coming, but when it finally did you couldn't believe it," he said. "Leahy always worried, but that was up until the kickoff. After that, he didn't feel there was anybody who could beat him. I remember feeling a little sheepish when we lost. I went out the back door."

Thus, 1950 proved Leahy's most bitter year. The streak was over, the team managed just a 4-4-1 record, the only year Leahy failed to produce a winner. The coach set out to correct his problems. He issued a warning to alumni: there would be no more seasons like 1946-49 if they didn't help with recruiting. "Offers of regular scholarships are no longer sufficient to attract the really top-flight boys," he said. "They just laugh at us and go elsewhere." He told of one player, set to go to Notre Dame, who changed his mind when slipped ten $1,000 bills by an enemy recruiter. Leahy urged Irish alumni to combat these tactics with some good, friendly persuasion. In this regard, Leahy set the example.

The subject was Johnny Lattner, out of Chicago. A four-sport star in high school, Lattner was the focus of scouts' attention for miles around when Leahy sat down with the youngster and talked to him about the merits of attending Notre Dame. Leahy then clinched their understanding by getting Lattner a summer job. Lattner said he needed one and Leahy obliged by setting him up as a laborer in an atomic energy experimental laboratory near Joliet, Illinois. It was a top-security place, and guards that surrounded it shut off all recruiters who would have Lattner change his mind.

Leahy built his 1951 comeback team around halfback Lattner, who could run, kick and pass in a style reminiscent of Lujack, and Gipp, too. A 60-minute sensation, Lattner made a quick impression before his sophomore season by scoring three touchdowns in the spring alumni game of 1951 and excelling on defense as well. The Irish were on the rebound, producing 7-2-1 seasons in both 1951 and 1952. What followed was Leahy's most dramatic season.

He sensed that he had one of his best teams for 1953. What he

Johnny Lattner was one of the most sought after high-school seniors in 1950, but chose Notre Dame when Leahy landed a summer job for him. He became one of Notre Dame's most memorable superstars. He appeared almost frail in pictures, but packed nearly 200 pounds on a raw-boned, six-foot, two-inch frame.

didn't know was that it would be his last. He didn't have the quantity of players he once did; but the quality was there. Ralph Guglielmi was the quarterback. Recalling Guglielmi as a sophomore in 1952, Leahy said, "He was harum-scarum and erratic. He was only 18 years old then. Now he's grown up. He's 19 and beginning to act like a veteran quarterback." Then there was Lattner and his running mate, Neil Worden. They had combined for a mile-and-half in yardage the two previous seasons.

"I only wish we were big like Ohio State or Purdue, or fast like Michigan State or Oklahoma," Leahy lamented. "But we lack both

the size and the speed, so we have to do the best we can with what we have."

And he did—at great personal cost.

The fateful day came on October 24, which was supposed to be a happy occasion. After all, it was Johnny Lattner's birthday. But that was forgotten as the afternoon of the big game with Georgia Tech unfolded. All the pressures of the years caught up with Leahy. He collapsed in the dressing room at halftime. He was given the last rites of the Catholic Church—the first of seven times in his life.

When the team came out for the second half, Leahy was miss-

Lattner was a lightning fast outside runner, could pass accurately from a dead run, kicked, played defense, and caught passes, as he is doing here in the Navy game of 1952. It was good for 51 yards and the Irish went on to win 17-6. Number 30 of Navy is Joe Gattuso, in futile pursuit.

ing. Herb Juliano, then one of the Irish radio broadcasters, slipped out of his booth upstairs to investigate. "I talked my way past a guard and into the dressing room," he recalled. "The trainer told me he didn't know if it had been a heart attack or not, but the coach was in bad shape. But you won't tell anybody, will you?"

"No, it's just between us," said Juliano, who might have added us and the thousands of radio listeners on the independent Irish football network that went to 115 stations in the United States and overseas. When he got back to the booth, Juliano carried the first news of the coach's condition, and let everyone know about it.

It was not a heart attack. But Leahy nevertheless thought for a while that he was dying. His condition was diagnosed as acute pancreatitis and fatigue. He was hospitalized, but had no intention of retiring. "I'm confident," he said in a statement from his sick bed, "that my health will permit me to finish this season and the remaining two years of my contract. After 1955, I'll await the pleasure of the officers at Notre Dame. They always have treated me exceedingly well."

From the hospital, Leahy watched practice on closed-circuit television. One day the players were lined up in front of a camera in the back of the TV truck parked at the practice field, waved to Leahy, and gave off a "get-well-soon" cheer.

After 12 days, a weakened Leahy forced himself back to his office, then journeyed to Philadelphia for the game with Penn. He was obviously sick. Before the game, Leahy watched groundskeepers sweep snow off the Franklin Field tarpaulin and prepare the field. Unable to stand, he sat on the 30-yard line marker. During the game, he paced the sideline, but now and then slumped into a chair. After the game, he told reporters in the dressing room, "I've never been so tired and completely exhausted in my whole life. During the game the excitement kept me going. But once it was over and I got in here I felt that I might collapse again."

There followed still more agony for Leahy. Controversy arose over feigned injuries. In the Iowa game, with time running out in the first half and the Irish out of time outs, tackle Frank Varrichione faked an injury to get the clock stoped and with two seconds left Ralph Guglielmi threw for a touchdown pass. Then, in the final seconds of the game with the Irish again out of time outs, Art Hunter and Don Penza both collapsed in an act reminiscent of Varrichione's and got the clock stopped, allowing Guglielmi time to throw another touchdown pass, with just six seconds remaining.

Leahy had managed a tie, 14-14, but set off a national controversy as he had the previous year with his so-called sucker shift to draw opponents offside. The fake injury dated even to the years before Rockne faked his limp in the 1913 Army game. Leahy pointed out he was doing nothing new, nothing other teams didn't do. Nevertheless, criticism did not abate. That Notre Dame would stoop to such deceit could not be condoned, many reasoned.

Emotionally battered, Leahy could not muster the strength to make it to the next game, against U.S.C. on the West Coast. But Lattner and Guglielmi and the rest made life as bearable as they could for the coach with victories in that game and the last one, a 40-14 thrashing of S.M.U. that gave Notre Dame a 9-0-1 record. Up on the players' shoulders after that, his last game, Leahy looked wan.

Just prior to the trip to Dallas for the storied 1949 S.M.U. game, these key Irish performers, from the left: quarterback Bob Williams, end Leon Hart, and tackle Jim Martin, were photographed while picking up their uniforms.

His face was drawn. His hair fell across his forehead. He had achieved his sixth unbeaten season. But he would not be back.

No question, he wanted to be back. "I figured we were bounced out of there," said assistant coach McArdle, adding of his mentor, "He'd never admit the truth." A less harsh assessment is that university officials, fearful mainly because of his health but also mindful of the criticism, persuaded him to resign.

On January 31, 1954, he bowed out saying: "It's a tremendous weight off my mind to get out of the game, as much as I love it." So he left Notre Dame, but left his heart there.

In the next 19 years, Leahy became involved in a number of business ventures, some of them notably unsuccessful. A low point in his life occurred in 1959 when he admitted "a lot of stupidity on my part" to the Securities and Exchange Commission, which conducted an investigation of transactions he made of certain stock.

Leahy returned to football for one year, in 1960, as general manager of the Los Angeles Chargers of the American Football League. Then he re-entered the insurance business, moving to Lake Oswego, Oregon, a Portland suburb. He suffered increasingly poor health and friends noted a number of times a man with less determination would not have lived as long as he did. He died June 21, 1973. He was 64.

4 Ara Parseghian

He ranks right alongside Rockne and Leahy
        —Ed "Moose" Krause, on Ara
        Parseghian
        February 13, 1976

Most men die never having reached their goal. This cannot be said of Ara Parseghian. When it came to coaching football, this intense, emotional man of Armenian and French extraction and native of Akron, Ohio, made it to the very top of his profession. In 11 seasons at Notre Dame, he won more games than anyone other than Rockne.

Yet if all these victories, 94 of them, ranked Parseghian with such legends as Rockne and Leahy, one victory alone certified his greatness. It happened on the night of December 31, 1973. Notre Dame defeated Alabama, 24-23, in the Sugar Bowl. The Irish, having achieved their first perfect season since 1949, stood alone as the nation's No. 1 team.

A banner was raised in the stands that night as the game ended that read: "God Made Notre Dame No. 1." It was only partially correct. Ara Parseghian helped. And God, no doubt, would agree. Parseghian had led Notre Dame to an undefeated season and national championship once before, in 1966. But that season was marred by a 10-10 tie with Michigan State and criticism of Parseghian for running out the clock.

That night in the Sugar Bowl Parseghian gambled to erase, as much as he ever could, the memories of that historic tie and establish without question Notre Dame's top ranking and his own lofty standing among the coaching immortals. It happened in one brilliant moment near the end of a dramatic struggle between two undefeated teams straining for the national championship.

Alabama, trailing by a single point, had Notre Dame backed up close to its goal line. It was the Irish ball, third and eight at their two. A fourth down punt could set up an Alabama field goal. Parseghian, risking an interception or safety that would lose the game, ordered his quarterback to pass.

This quarterback was hardly the most glamorous of those Parseghian helped make famous—*Time* cover boy Terry Hanratty or Joe Theismann or John Huarte, who led Notre Dame's turnabout in Parseghian's first season. This quarterback was named Tom Clements; what he did was help make Parseghian famous, nudging him up among those coaching greats once and for all.

Clements did it with a play still etched in Parseghian's mind. Clements faked a handoff and dropped into the end zone to pass. "From the sideline the pass appeared overthrown," Parseghian recalled, "but then I saw Clements had led Weber perfectly." These were fleeting seconds that take much more time than that off a coach's life. Tight end Robin Weber made the catch, strangely not one of the best known in Notre Dame history, yet one of the most important. It was a 35-yard gain and the Irish were out of trouble; they ran out the clock and unlike 1966 were widely applauded for doing so.

Notre Dame was not No. 1 in 1974, but the Orange Bowl victory, dedicated to Parseghian, was a sweet and exciting triumph. This was Ara's last victory ride, and even in this moment of jubilation, his face shows the strain and exhaustion that accompanied his last months as head coach.

Tight end Robin Weber? Why he was a second-stringer who had caught only one pass all year. And he wasn't even the primary receiver. Shades of Johnny "One-Play" O'Brien. Clements to Weber: A modern-day example of the classic desperation Rockne often got by with when he wasn't winning by outrageous margins. And if anybody cared to think God played a part, few would argue the point.

When Parseghian was lifted to the shoulders of his players that night, he literally had reached the top of his profession. It had taken a decade of work days that sometimes stretched to the ultimate 24 hours, plus all the joy and pain that went with it. Parseghian had orchestrated instant success in 1964; the ecstasy and agony that were the national championship and the tie with Michigan State in 1966; a bowl game for the first time in 45 years, only to lose; Cotton Bowl retribution; a perfect season. The Sugar Bowl victory was the crowning achievement.

Less than a year after that momentous victory Parseghian would announce his retirement, leaving Notre Dame supporters shocked. They might have known, though, the toll the job was taking. "It was killing Leahy and it was killing Parseghian, too," said a longtime Notre Dame observer. "Parseghian had the good sense to get out on his own."

So ended the 11-year Era of Ara. He had taken over a 2-7 outfit from 1963 and turned it into a near championship 9-1 team; produced Notre Dame's first national title in 17 years in 1966; guided Notre Dame to a top-ten finish in nine of his 11 years; led the Irish into five bowl games; coached 40 first team All-Americas, and amassed uncounted coaching honors.

Parseghian accomplished all of this the only way he knew how: with a weekly build-up of emotion that often moved him to tears or close to it, an unswerving drive to win over all, and the ability to transmit that intensity to his players. These characteristics developed slowly in Parseghian's very early years but apparently had taken shape enough by his senior year of high school for his yearbook editor to predict: "He will become football coach at Notre Dame."

Parseghian's mother rooted for a girl, not a successor to Knute Rockne or Frank Leahy. Having had Ara, named for a ninth century Armenian king, she kept him in dresses until he was big enough to know better. And, thinking football a nasty game, she forbade Ara to participate until finally he sneaked off to play it anyway.

His mother, Amelia, came from France. His father, Michael, a native of Turkish Armenia, fled to Greece during the 1916 Armenian massacres, then to the United States. He joined the army, went to France, and met his future wife. They settled back in the United States, in Akron.

Ara was born May 21, 1923. Sheltered by his mother, he played few sports as a youth and he and his brother Gerry generally were pushed around by their peers. When their father found out, he advised them to take no insults from anyone, and the toughening of Ara Parseghian began.

Not that football was suddenly embraced by the elder Parseghians. Not until his junior year at Akron South High School did young Parseghian go out for the team—even then without his parents' permission. It took some friendly persuasion from older brother Gerry to keep Ara on the team. He played guard that year, fullback as a senior.

He also displayed the temperament that later would be his trademark—he reached such an emotional peak over a playoff game his senior year that he broke down and cried on the field when his team lost.

In 1942, he enrolled at Akron University, then dropped out to enter the navy. He played under Paul Brown at the Great Lakes Naval Training Station, then under Sid Gillman when he enrolled at Miami of Ohio after the war. Under Gillman, Parseghian first thought of coaching and switched his course of study from business administration to education.

He left Miami before graduation—though he later returned during off-seasons to get his bachelor's and master's degrees in education—to play professionally for the Cleveland Browns, but an injury abruptly ended his playing career. He returned to Miami of Ohio as asistant to Woody Hayes in 1950, succeeding Hayes as head coach in 1951.

In five years, Parseghian's teams won 39 games, lost only six and tied one, and won two Mid-America Conference championships. In his first year, his team upset a Big Ten team, Indiana, 6-0, a game marked by Parseghian psychology. He ordered two sets of uniforms to be taken to Indiana, old tattered ones and brand new ones. The day before the game Miami worked out in the old ones. The Indiana fans who watched spread the word that though the Miami team was considered a small college power it would pose no threat to their team. The next day, however, Miami dressed fit to kill and played as though it might do just that.

It wasn't surprising then that a Big Ten school would hire Parseghian. Northwestern needed him in the worst way and he responded with a 36-35-1 record in eight seasons there, including a 7-2 record in 1962, Northwestern's best since 1948. For a while that season, Parseghian even had the Wildcats ranked No. 1 nationally but didn't have the depth to stay there.

His most notable achievement at Northwestern was beating Notre Dame four times in four games, in 1959 through 1962: 30-24, 7-6, 12-10, and 35-6. So Notre Dame officials were well acquainted with Parseghian when he called to inquire about a possible coaching job. Yes, Notre Dame was looking. It had not had a winning season since 1958.

Since Leahy retired, the Irish had fallen to mediocrity. At first, the school officials had turned to Terry Brennan, 25-year-old star halfback under Leahy. It seem like an enlightened choice when the Irish rolled up 9-1 and 8-2 records. Then came 1956, when many of the players recruited by Leahy had graduated. The record fell to 2-8. Two more mediocre seasons followed and Brennan was released.

His successor, Joe Kuharich, became the first and only losing coach in the history of Notre Dame football: three 5-5 records and a 2-8. Hugh Devore, who had filled in while Leahy was in the service in 1945, served again as interim coach in 1963, a 2-7 season. Devore bowed out graciously, saying, "I am happy to serve Notre Dame in any capacity. I have been a Notre Dame man since I came here under Knute Rockne in 1930. Anything that Notre Dame does in the best interests of its football program I will serve."

Parseghian was not a Notre Dame man, a rarity for a head coach at the school. But he knew what needed to be done and his talents as a football salesman who could persuade the right players to enroll and then get the most out of them was immediately perceived by Rev. Theodore Hesburgh, the university president, and Rev. Edmund Joyce, executive vice president and chairman of the faculty board in charge of athletics. "We had to go for the best man available," Father Hesburgh said. "We had to pick an ambitious young man who already had proven he could win in the kind of competition we meet."

What the arrival of the 41-year-old Parseghian meant to the typical Notre Dame student was described by one, Terry Wolkerstorfer, writing in the *Scholastic*. It was the morning of December 4, 1963. He was a passenger in a car bound for Christmas vacation and was dozing when the news came on the radio.

"I awoke with a start, ripping my pants on the door handle. My class has never seen a winning football season at Notre Dame, has the worst four-year record in history, and in fact, is the only class to have witnessed two-win seasons twice.

"Having suffered through four disastrous years, I received the news of Parseghian's hiring in much the same way as I imagine Americans must have received news of V-J Day after suffering through World War II."

An incident that indicated times were changing occurred a few days later. Parseghian, it seemed, was determined to be his own man. It was arranged for him to proceed to South Bend, sign his contract, then hold a press conference. Reporters and television crews assembled in large numbers at the Morris Inn on campus. Then, unexpectedly, Parseghian refused to sign the contract and stormed through the hotel lobby and out the door. He wanted full control to run the football program.

And if that independence was applauded, so was the coach's confidence. "Under Father Hesburgh Notre Dame has made great progress academically," Parseghian said after he did sign. "Our job is to restore Notre Dame's football image, to keep Notre Dame's athletic progress abreast of its academic progress. Although there is too much balance in college football for any team to dominate the

Victimized by a recruiting lull and unable to apply pro coaching techniques at the college level, Joe Kuharich became the only coach in Notre Dame history to compile a losing record. He is posing here with Daryle Lamonica, on the left, who led the team in passing in 1962, and Frank Budka, who set the passing pace in 1961 and 1963.

game as Notre Dame did in the forties, I can promise you that if hard work means anything at all Notre Dame will have winning football—beginning this fall.'"

And so a battle cry arose: "6 and 4 in '64." George Connor, the former great Irish tackle, declared: "If Notre Dame comes in with a 5-5 record in 1964, it will be a magnificent achievement." As for Parseghian, he would not commit himself with an exact prediction of the record but he did declare, "I am not deaf and I am not naive. The students think this will be a new era for Notre Dame football and they are right. I am determined it will be a winning era."

To that end, Parseghian began by shuffling his personnel. It was just what Leahy had done when he arrived at Notre Dame. Parseghian would later declare, "You've got to put the right man in the right job." His biggest problem was finding a quarterback. There hadn't been an outstanding one since 1956, Paul Hornung's last season.

John Huarte was the answer. Huarte had languished for two years and not even won a letter. He had played only a total of 40 minutes. Parseghian watched him during spring practice. "I knew he could pass," the coach recalled. "I watched his ability to handle his body, his quickness with his feet and his hands, and I thought he'd be a great ball handler."

Then there was Jack Snow. What good would a passer be without someone to throw to? Parseghian moved Snow from tight end to split end. "I liked his speed," Parseghian said, "the quickness with his maneuvers. He has that sense of knowing where daylight is, of finding what we call the open seam."

Knighted by Parseghian, Huarte and Snow became Notre Dame's winning combination. Snow caught two touchdown passes in a 30-23 victory over the alumni to conclude spring practice, a game Huarte missed because of a separated shoulder. Still, Parseghian saw the possibilities: if he could improve the pass defense, if Huarte got well, if the team speed was good enough . . .

Lack of speed worried Parseghian. "We have size and a semblance of depth," he said at the time. "But our mobility, our forward movement and our pursuit capacity, are not what I would like to have." As Parseghian drilled his men, a motto among them evolved: "We are engaged in life, liberty, and the happiness of pursuit."

Like Leahy, Parseghian worked his players relentlessly, and himself, too. His philosophy: "A baseball manager has 162 games to operate in. He can lose in April or May and still come out on top. But in football you have only nine or ten games. Every Saturday is do or die." His players ran so much, sprints and long distances, most weighed considerably less than they did before Parseghian arrived. They picked up speed, which he liked.

And when one player challenged his authority, refusing to carry out an assignment in spring practice, Parseghian banished him from the team. There was no mistaking who was boss.

One thing for sure: after so many lackluster seasons, the players were ready to be led. And so the Era of Ara opened—with a resounding 31-7 victory over Wisconsin. "This team was hungry," Parseghian said. "It was a team which really wanted to win. Notre Dame had won only one game in the last ten against Big 10 teams."

There was something else about this team, too. It exuded confi-

dence. "The first day he met us," said one of the players, Jim Carroll, "he told us we were good." And he gave them goals, extraordinary goals. He put up a huge sign in the locker room that said "Pride." He circled the number of points, 24, scored against the 1946 Irish team during the entire season and asked, "Can you match this?" They couldn't, but the 77 points they did give up were the fewest since 1947.

So if he worked the players like Leahy and applied the psychology of a Rockne, Parseghian still mixed in his own personal ingredient of passion. His spirit was infectious. He worked out with the players at spring practice. He did calisthenics with them. He always seemed to be in a hurry, a man with a purpose. He would prowl the sideline, throwing his head in disgust at a bad play, leaping up and down at something good. "His enthusiasm rubs off on everybody," said athletic director Ed "Moose" Krause.

Not to be overlooked, of course, were Huarte and Snow. Said the losing Wisconsin coach, Milt Bruhn, after Parseghian's opening-day victory: "What really hurt us was that we ran into one of the finest passing combinations I have ever seen with Huarte and Snow."

Those two had been discovered by Parseghian, who displayed a flare for shoring weaknesses that few coaches could match. "He goes after weak spots like a surgeon," one Notre Dame observer said. "He evaluates talent like a computer and this will be as much a part of Notre Dame's rise as any other factor."

Another thing, Notre Dame came on strong in the second half against Wisconsin, something previous Irish teams had not often done. "There has been a lot of criticism over the years about Notre Dame not being a second half team," Parseghian said after the game. "But our conditioning showed up and we wore them down. It really feels good."

The pieces had all come together for Notre Dame and Parseghian. One after another, opponents were beaten: Purdue, Air Force, U.C.L.A., Stanford. The 1964 team became the first since Leahy's 1953 team to win its first five games. Irish rooters no longer were chanting "6 and 4" but were calling for a national championship.

Even Frank Leahy showed up on campus again. The man who had been critical of Terry Brennan and Joe Kuharich for failing to instill a winning spirit went so far as to predict an Irish victory on the eve of the Stanford game. "You never talked that way on Friday nights when you were coach, Frank," Moose Krause responded.

Leahy didn't seem to mind the kidding so taken was he with the new winning Irish. "It really is a pleasure to see Notre Dame play this season," he said.

Parseghian was responsible. As Leahy had once done, the new coach worked and worried through every week. Up at 5 A.M. Watching films and formulating strategy. Practice in the afternoon; a harsh word here, a kind one there, moving in and out among the players, saying just the right thing in just the right tone to each individual. Increased worry as the week progresses. By Thursday nights, it would be hard for Parseghian to sleep.

All the while, school spirit, for so long dormant, bubbled over again. The majority of the 6,800 students were now jamming into the ancient field house for the weekly pep rallies. Their object of affection was Parseghian. They wore buttons that read, "The Era of Ara" and "Aradicate the Enemy," and they cheered at the very sight of the coach.

Unlike the 1966 squad, overpowering in talent and numbers, Parseghian's 1964 team was strung together tenuously, as the coach himself knew only too well. "Our whole offense is built around Huarte," he cautioned. "Without him, we just don't go. We have one excellent defensive unit and one real good offensive unit, but we have a lack of depth behind either. We've got to stay healthy because each time we win from now on makes us more and more a marked team."

Still, the Irish kept winning: Navy, Pittsburgh, Michigan State, Iowa. It was 34-7 against Michigan State, which had won its previous eight games against Notre Dame. "If there is any better team in the world, I'd sure hate to play them," said State's coach, Duffy Daugherty. The Irish were 9-0 and ranked No. 1.

The last team in its way to a remarkable 10-0 season and national championship was Southern California, the game to be played in Los Angeles. U.S.C. would always mean trouble for Parseghian; his Notre Dame teams would manage only a 3-6-2 record against the Trojans. Parseghian was to endure some painful second halves against them.

The 1964 game started similarly to the others that season. The Irish took a 17-0 halftime lead. Parseghian exhorted his players with a pep talk just before they came out to play the second half. *Life* magazine recorded the coach's words:

"Let's have your attention up here. Thirty minutes stands between us and the greatest sports comeback in history. Thirty minutes! You gotta go out there and play this second half, boys— a 60-minute football team. This is the way we started this football season and this is the way we're gonna finish, you understand? I want that defense down there knocking them on their butts. You go after it, understand? I mean, really gang tackle 'em. You did a damn good job in there and I'm real proud of you. I want to be prouder of you when you come back here after that second half, boys. Let's really go out there and give them thirty more minutes of Notre Dame football!"

What happened was that U.S.C. rallied to win, 20-17. But there was one pep rally left. About 7,000 students and Notre Dame fans showed up at the field house. "I have been down the last few days," said Parseghian, getting up to speak, "but to come back to this . . ." The cheers made further talk useless. The team set 27 school records. Every play Huarte was involved in gained 8.5 yards, second only to the standard set by George Gipp himself. Snow had caught nine touchdown passes, still a Notre Dame season record. A few days later Parseghian was given a new five-year contract.

Displaying a characteristic of any successful coach, Parseghian did not pause long to look back on 1964. He spoke of the future. First, there was the long range. Recruiting was already coming easier. "We have a pretty good selling point going for us in the '64 season," he said, "and we've found, happily, that the youngsters are much more receptive to us than they were just a year ago." As for 1965, he needed a quarterback and receiver to succeed the departed Huarte and Snow.

"You don't replace players like Huarte and Snow overnight," he said in what turned out to be a prophetic remark. There simply was no passer to match Huarte on campus—with the exception of two freshmen ineligible for the varsity, Terry Hanratty and Coley O'Brien. Parseghian would have to alter the Irish game to a running one, and wait for 1966.

So run the Irish did, for 72 points against the alumni. Only nine passes were thrown and Parseghian noted, "It would be a great mistake trying to force a successful 1964 offense on a 1965 team. We'll be a position and possession team." But Notre Dame discovered more stubborn opponents that autumn than the Irish alumni. That Notre Dame finished with a 7-2-1 record was testimony to Parseghian's talents. The team peaked with a 28-7 revenge victory against U.S.C.; it ended by failing to score a touchdown in its last two games when its running-oriented attack was shut down.

The sight of Hanratty and O'Brien throwing spirals in spring practice was enough to brighten Parseghian's outlook for 1966.

Up until very recently, Jack Snow was putting this kind of distance between himself and NFL defenders. These Navy backs didn't have a chance. Snow grabbed Huarte's perfect pass and completed a 45-yard touchdown play in Notre Dame's 40-0 win over the Midshipmen in 1964.

Paired with sophomore receiver Jim Seymour and meshed with such veterans as Nick Eddy, Alan Page, Kevin Hardy, Jim Lynch, Pete Duranko, either Hanratty or O'Brien would be an absolute godsend. Parseghian could pick either one. A national championship was being forecast for Notre Dame.

Parseghian chose Hanratty. Although O'Brien had more polish, Hanratty was bigger and more durable and could throw longer. Such decisions never arise for most coaches. Hanratty to Seymour became a throwback to Huarte to Snow. The new duo passed its way into the hearts of alumni everywhere and onto *Time* magazine's cover.

This surge to still new heights in Notre Dame history began against Purdue. The rest was easy—until Michigan State. Hanratty's first pass was a mere 42-yard completion to the 6-foot-4 Seymour. Then an 84-yard pass play, same combination, for a touchdown. And a 39-yarder for another touchdown. And a 7-yarder for still another. Final: 26-14 over a Bob Griese- and Leroy Keyes-led Purdue team.

From there, the Irish rolled up such scores as 35-0, 32-0, 38-0,

40-0, and, poor Duke, 64-0. On to Michigan State. The long-awaited battle for No. 1; 76,000 fans in Spartan Stadium; a national television audience; Parseghian's biggest game.

It began horribly for the Irish. Star runner Nick Eddy slipped on the train steps at East Lansing, reinjuring his shoulder and knocking himself out of the game. Center George Goeddeke separated his shoulder on the first series. Then Hanratty, running a quarterback draw play that was brought in mistakenly by a lineman, was hit by George Webster and finished off by Bubba Smith. Result: another separated shoulder, Hanratty's.

Down by 10 points and three of their best players, the Irish ralled with reserves Coley O'Brien and Rocky Bleier. O'Brien threw to Bob Gladieux for a touchdown and Joe Azzaro kicked a field goal. The 10-10 final would not soon be forgotten: Parseghian elected to run out the clock and preserve the tie and No. 1 national ranking.

Just prior to the 1966 "game of the decade" with Michigan State, Nick Eddy, on the left, injured his shoulder, and thus deprived his team of the sort of vital skills that might have meant a decisive victory for the Irish. Pictured here with Eddy is Kevin Hardy, a six-foot, five-inch, 270-pound defensive tackle.

No wonder Bob Gladieux looks so content. He doesn't have to run against Alan Page, a monstrous defensive end who still stacks up ball carriers for the Minnesota Vikings. Gladieux led Notre Dame in rushing in 1968.

In the dressing room, Parseghian gathered his players and, according to Bleier, in his book "Fighting Back," said:

"Men, I'm proud of you. God knows, I've never been more proud of any group of young men in my life. Get one thing straight, though. We did not lose. We were No. 1 when we came, we fell behind, had some tough things happen, but you overcame them. No one could have wanted to win this one more than I. We didn't win, but, by God, we did not lose. They're crying about a tie, trying to detract from your efforts. They're trying to make it come out a win. Well, don't you believe it. Their season is over. They can't go any-where. It's all over, and we're still No. 1. Time will prove everything that has happened here today. And you'll see that after the rabble-rousers have had their day, cooler minds who understand the true odds will know that Notre Dame is a team of champions. There will be moments when you'll want to blast out at something, or someone. But when we open these doors to the press and to some of our so-called well-wishers, remember one thing: Whatever you do, whatever you say, reflects on us, on your parents, on the team, and on Notre Dame."

Ten years later Parseghian still found himself defending what he had done in the final seconds. But he continued to point out that only the very last play of the game represented a concession, not the five runs that preceded it.

One play of the series that began at the Irish 30-yard line was a draw to Bleier that, Michigan State coach Daugherty acknowledged some time later, almost worked well enough to give Notre Dame position for a field goal. It took a good tackle by George Webster to stop the play.

On fourth and one at the 39, Parseghian points out, the Irish went for a first down rather than give up the ball. Then, in what might have been a pass, O'Brien was sacked by Bubba Smith. With time for one play, Parseghian said he rationalized, "The hell with it. There's no sense putting it up and taking the chance."

The week after the Michigan State game Notre Dame trounced U.S.C., 51-0, to insure the national championship. The Trojans' coach, John McKay, declared that he would never be beaten that badly again and did everything he could to atone for it the following year—including bringing O. J. Simpson with him to Notre Dame.

Simpson ran for 150 yards and two touchdowns as U.S.C. won, 24-7, one of two defeats suffered that year by the Irish. The other, in an 8-2 season, was 28-21 to Purdue. Notre Dame had lost eight All-Americas from the 1966 team, including runners Nick Eddy and Larry Conjar, and didn't possess quite the ground game to balance the passing. The absence of Alan Page and Jim Lynch on defense didn't help.

Hanratty and Seymour completed their record-breaking careers during a 7-2-1 1968 season, though Hanratty suffered a knee injury and missed the final three games. Then emerged still another prominent Irish quarterback, Joe Theismann, who would eventually break most of Hanratty's records.

Parseghian's 1968 problems were mainly defensive ones. The team gave up more points, 170, than any of his Notre Dame teams. He could see his problems coming, predicting before the season, "We'll be seriously taxed on defense early. We couldn't have drawn two more offensively talented teams to start off the year." He meant Oklahoma, which fell, and Purdue, with Keyes, which didn't.

Parseghian became the target of a demonstration by black Notre Dame students. They carried signs that read "All-white backfields are a thing of the past," and "How about O.J. Simpson and Leroy Keyes?" The coach called the protest "dissent without having all the facts."

There was other dissent. Some students, who probably wouldn't have been understood in what might be called simpler times, declared that football was irrelevant. And there also was that segment of the faculty that considered the athletic reputation of the school a drawback to its academic accomplishments. But the Notre Dame football tradition not only survived, it thrived.

Back on the field, the defensive unit, which had struggled early in 1968, continued to improve. Anchored by the huge Mike McCoy, it began matching the Theismann-led offense by the end of the year and maintained that level throughout an 8-1-1 1969 season. This happy development couldn't have come at a more propitious time. The university was looking for new ways to raise money just as major bowl representatives were viewing the Irish as a means to raising money themselves.

Another member of the overpowering Irish defense was Tom Regner, who teamed with Alan Page, Kevin Hardy, and Don Gmitter to form an almost impenetrable front four.

Another player who made Parseghian's early years at Notre Dame easier was Dick Arrington, an All-America offensive guard in 1965. He was also a heavyweight champion wrestler, a fact not lost on most of his opponents.

Father Joyce made the announcement that the Irish would abandon their policy of declining bowl invitations, which they had done since 1925, by accepting to play in the Cotton Bowl on New Year's Day, 1970. "The crucial consideration," he said, "was the urgent need of the university for funds to finance minority student academic programs and scholarships. Notre Dame's share of bowl game proceeds will be dedicated to this pressing university need." The date in Dallas proved a profitable way to usher in a new decade; Notre Dame received a check for $340,000.

Only the 21-17 score wasn't satisfying. Still, a Notre Dame policy barrier against post-season play had been broken, and Parseghian liked that. A strong advocate of playing in bowls, the coach said, "It's a great way to pit the top teams in the country against each other. And I think in the Cotton Bowl we proved we were a better team than most people gave us credit for being." Then, too, Parseghian had been given the clear sign by university officials that another bowl appearance just might be a possibility.

History repeated itself the very next New Year's. The Irish,

having been led to a 9-1 season by the senior Theismann, found themselves back in Dallas, facing Texas once again in the Cotton Bowl. This time they hooked the Horns, 24-11, the first time in 30 games Texas had lost. Parseghian had constructed what he termed an "invert defense," which allowed defensive players to pursue the several potential ball-carriers in a play developing from the Texas Wishbone T offense. "The object of the invert," summarized one player after the game, "is to tackle everybody. Somewhere in there will be the man with the ball. It's a beautiful defense for a team like Texas."

The game capped a career in which Theismann set 20 major school records that he still holds and proved to any doubters that Parseghian was quite capable of winning what could be considered a "big game." The victory lifted Notre Dame to No. 2 nationally, higher than it had been since 1966. But the pressure to be No. 1 remained just as intense as ever.

"I think there is a great deal of pressure for every member of the Notre Dame football squad," Parseghian told one of the many South Bend gatherings he addressed. "When people expect you to be 10 and 0, you can't improve on it. You can only get worse. If you lose one or two, it's not a good season.

"We recognize that everyone wants to beat Notre Dame, that they can make a season out of beating Notre Dame. Our objective, of course, is to avoid that if we possibly can. It will not be an easy chore."

That was before the 1971 season. Parseghian would have to wait two more years for his 10-0 season. The years 1971-1972 brought identical 8-2 records and more All-Americas, among them Walt Patulski, Clarence Ellis, and Tom Gatewood. But 1972 ended in

Tiptoeing around in the secondary, waiting for a misdirected pass is Clarence Ellis, one of Notre Dame's speediest defensive backs. In 1969, he broke up 13 opponent pass plays, and over a three-year career from 1969 through 1971 he batted away 32; both are Notre Dame records.

agony for Parseghian. The Irish were beaten badly in the final game of the season by U.S.C., 45-23. Then they were humiliated in the Orange Bowl, 40-6, by Nebraska. It was January 1, 1973, an unlikely beginning to what would be Parseghian's most unforgettable year.

That night in the Orange Bowl Parseghian was an obviously depressed man. He answered questions briefly, without emotion. Then someone asked him if such a one-sided defeat would mean a Notre Dame absence from future bowl games. Characteristic of his determination, Parseghian flared up in response.

"No," he said, "I would suggest to you that it would be just the opposite. That we would want to come back. That we would want to prove that we're a better football team than we showed tonight."

Walt Patulski, co-captain of the 1971 Irish, and a unanimous All-America selection that year. In 1970 he stole 112 yards from the opposition by making 17 tackles that resulted in minus yardage.

Now here's a friendly Irishman you wouldn't want to go out of your way to antagonize. Even in a publicity photo, where feigned ferocity was fashionable, Mike McCoy looks particularly awesome.

Ara Parseghian / **107**

And so 1973 would become almost a vendetta. A master of organization, Parseghian got his priorities together for the new season. At the top of the list was a basic change in his football philosophy. On offense, he became less conservative. More significantly, on defense, he focused on faster players, preferring speed to size. Of the 30 players he recruited for 1973, 21 had played defense in high school. Parseghian was intent on bolstering the 1972 defensive team, which had given up 152 points, the second highest total of any of his Irish teams.

"I'm hopeful that freshmen can fill some of the holes on defense," the coach said. Shortly, he was rewarded beyond his expectations. The 6-foot-3, 220-pound Ross Browner was big enough to plug any hole, and fast enough to help plug other gaps. One of Parseghian's finest recruits, Browner was moved in immediately at defensive end and Parseghian was moved to remark: "Browner fits in beautifully for what we want to do defensively." This meant putting pressure on opponents with a quick rush line rather than being limited with one of sheer beef.

Looking around for speed, Parseghian could find plenty in running backs Eric Penick and Art Best, two of Notre Dame's fastest runners in years. Penick, as a sophomore, had gained 727 yards, the most by an Irish back in 17 years. The trouble was he fumbled 16 times. So Parseghian prescribed a rigorous weight lifting program resulting in an additional 20 pounds of muscle for Penick. At 215, he discovered he could deal punishment as well as absorb it. His confidence increased and his fumbling decreased.

The 1973 team, Parseghian's best, would not be led by a classic passer such as Hanratty or Theismann but by Tom Clements, described by Parseghian as one possessing "accuracy" who could "throw long enough to keep you honest." The Irish of 1973 would be a running team—fullback Wayne Bullock would be the workhorse—with occasional play-action passes from Clements. Quickness would be the keynote on defense.

Tom Clements quarterbacked Notre Dame from 1972 through 1974 and directed his teams to a combined 29-5 record. He was a good runner, as well as an accurate passer. The pass he completed from his own end zone in the final seconds of the 1973 Orange Bowl game was one of the most exciting plays in Notre Dame history.

The season would turn on the games with Purdue and U.S.C., two traditionally stubborn foes. Purdue would be easier. Best loosened up the Boilermakers with a 64-yard run. Two long drives, engineered by Clements, resulted in two touchdowns, by Best and Bullock, and Bob Thomas kicked two field goals, for a 20-7 victory. And what about that young, agile Notre Dame defense? Purdue gained only 78 yards rushing. Enough said.

U.S.C. had not been beaten by a Parseghian team since way back in 1966. The defending national champion Trojans had the nastiest habit of messing up perfect seasons by Parseghian, which they did in the final games of 1964 and 1970. It was time for a bit of the Rockne touch. Parseghian assembled his team for a highly emotional talk the Monday night before the U.S.C. game. He warned his players repeatedly that U.S.C. had been intimidating Notre Dame teams, something the Irish should be doing to the Trojans. The little talk set the tone for the week.

There was another Rockne touch, the bolstering of a key player's confidence. Field goal kicker Thomas had been suffering a slump since the Purdue game. At practice, Parseghian was dropkicking field goals, mixing with his players as usual and with Thomas in particular. After one kick, Thomas recalled the coach turning to him. "He told me not to worry, that I would beat Southern Cal with my field goals. Can you imagine how great that made me feel?"

Parseghian, the team, and almost the entire student body reached fever pitch together. The Irish band marched around campus every day playing the Notre Dame victory march. Other enterprising students plastered pictures of U.S.C. star Anthony Davis on campus sidewalks so that he could conveniently and symbolically be stepped on. Below his picture was the word: "Remember." The previous year Davis scored six touchdowns against the Irish. "Do you realize until last year no one had run back a kickoff for a touchdown against Notre Dame since I became coach here in 1964?" Parseghian noted to a reporter. "And Davis goes and runs back two in one game to whip us."

Defensive tackle Steve Niehaus was out for the season with a knee injury but an ad for a pep rally in the campus paper, which was calling that day for the impeachment of President Nixon, said, "Steve Niehaus will be there on crutches; what about you?"

In the interests of self-preservation, it was necessary for reed-slim Joe Theismann to scramble occasionally, as he is doing here in 1970 against Northwestern. But he made the most of his scrambles and was an outstanding passer. He holds most of Notre Dame's all-time total offense and passing records.

"The students seem to enjoy the games as much as ever," noted Parseghian, observing their proper frame of mind with suitable satisfaction. "Davis scored six touchdowns against us last year," linebacker Greg Collins told a cheering mob of students at the pep rally. "This year he'll be lucky to gain six yards. He'll be on his knees, but it won't be in the Notre Dame end zone." "We're going to beat the —— out of Southern California," predicted Penick.

And so it came to pass that the Irish did just that, 23-14. The difference was three field goals kicked by the once doubting Thomas. For U.S.C., it was the first loss in 24 games; for Davis, a mere 55 yards in 19 carries. Speedy Penick got off an 85-yard touchdown run and Notre Dame rolled up 404 yards.

Nobody came close to the Irish after that; they crushed four more opponents for a 10-0 season, Parseghian's first perfect one. But, at Notre Dame especially, perfection begets only more pressure and so Parseghian had to reach back and rally himself and the squad one more time, against Alabama in the Sugar Bowl.

"It's very similar to the '66 game with Michigan State," said Parseghian, still unable to forget that debacle. "But one significant thing is we don't have to rely on anybody else. We can determine our place in the national rankings on our own performance here." In other words, with a victory No. 3 ranked Notre Dame could replace No. 1 ranked Alabama.

Parseghian's big problem was defensing Alabama, a Wishbone T offensive team stimilar to the Texas Wishbone team the Irish had beaten three years before in the Cotton Bowl—with one exception. Alabama could pass better than Texas.

"Texas was very patient," Parseghian told reporters who clamored to learn his plans. "They would run the fullback 18 times in a row if you let them. We tried to get them out of this habit and make them do things they didn't want to do, like passing. But Alabama's not afraid to throw."

Alabama coach Bear Bryant was quoted as saying this was "the biggest game in the South's history." This was, of course, the game in which God, Parseghian, and Clements—maybe not even in that order—combined to do in Bryant and the Crimson Tide, 24-23, as Notre Dame finished with a perfect season and gained the No. 1 national ranking. The South had lost another one. Parseghian's rebuilding job was responsible. The porous defense of 1972 rose to No. 2 nationally in 1973.

The transition from the 1973 to 1974 seasons offers possibly the most poignant example of the emotional roller coaster that is the Notre Dame head coaching job. Once where there was great joy, there was immense grief. Parseghian, in the summer of 1974, had to face up to a scandal that made embarrassing, shocking headlines. Six players, who would have been sophomores, were dismissed from school for the 1974-75 academic year after being found with a woman in a dormitory room.

Parseghian fought hard—not to let the players remain on the football team—but to keep them in school on the basis that they would be subjected to far more attention in the press than non-athletes. He went to the administration and pleaded their cases. He shed tears over the situation. But, in the end, he lost his battle. For weeks afterward, he was depressed.

A crisis also occurred in Parseghian's family life. He had always worked hard not to let his job detract from his life with his wife, Kathleen, whom he had met when both were students at Miami of Ohio, and their two daughters, Karan and Kristan, and son Mike.

But now daughter Karan had scheduled her wedding for September 7, and when the Georgia Tech game was rescheduled from later in the season to September 9 to satisfy the demands of television, Parseghian faced an extraordinary amount of pressure working up to the two events of that weekend. What made the wedding all the more significant was the fact that Parseghian's daughter suffered from multiple sclerosis but was determined to lead as normal a life as possible.

"The week before the wedding she was worried she wouldn't be able to make it down the aisle," said Notre Dame publicist Roger Valdiserri. "Ara sat down with her and discussed the problem and then said, 'Okay, let's go over to the church and try it.' He wanted everything to be just right for her."

Parseghian, in fact, had made dozens of appearances and appeals around the country fighting against the disease. Parseghian's sister had contracted it, his wife's brother had died from it, and at the age of 17, his daughter had gotten it. Parseghian became a member of the National MS Society's board of directors and served on numerous committees.

Everything turned out fine that weekend in September, thanks in no small part to Parseghian's preparations all summer. "Everybody in the church cried," recalled Valdiserri. "I think it was the most emotional experience Ara ever had." Winning a football game was easy by comparison and two days later Notre Dame overwhelmed Georgia Tech, 31-7.

The Irish made it 2-0 against Northwestern, a victory that enabled Parseghian to tie Leahy in total Notre Dame victories with 87. Some even predicted another perfect season despite an unusual number of injuries, 22 in all before the season opened, and the loss of the six suspended players, four of whom were starters. But an old nemesis, Purdue, which had ended Notre Dame unbeaten streaks of 39, 13, and 12 respectively in 1950, 1954, and 1967, broke a string of 13 Irish victories with a 31-20 upset at Notre Dame.

By the end of the eighth game, a 14-6 victory over Navy, Parseghian decided to retire. He made the decision flying back to South Bend from Philadelphia, long before a 55-24 loss to U.S.C. to complete a 9-2 season. What a painful loss that was, admitted Parseghian, looking back at it from retirement.

"With everything that had gone wrong that crazy season—the injuries, so many injuries it was ridiculous; the dormitory trouble; two close friends of mine died that fall; Van Patrick died the day after I did his last show with him; my daughter's wedding—with all of that, we had only lost one game, we were leading U.S.C. at the half, we still had an outside chance for the national championship. I thought we were going to do it. Then came the momentum shift in the second half. . ." His voice trailed off.

His announcement a week after the U.S.C. game came as a shock.

That Hardy could nimbly move his huge body is shown in this picture of Purdue's Bob Griese getting a pass off despite Hardy's leap. Notre Dame won this 1966 game 26-14, and Hardy went on to All-America laurels, along with ten of his teammates.

"I am not leaving Notre Dame at this time to take any other coaching position, either on the college level or in the professional ranks," Parseghian said. "I just feel that I should get away from coaching for at least a year, after which I will review my coaching future. I just need the time to rejuvenate physically and emotionally."

By his own admission, Parseghian at the age of 51, was physically and emotionally spent. "The last two seasons coaching became less fun for him" a colleague said. Actually, the beginning of the end came with the final two games of the 1972 season, 45-23 and 40-6 defeats. They so affected Parseghian an assistant was moved to remark, "No one knows just how much he suffered. You had to be there, on the field, to see it. You had to see him suffer as his team was beaten like that." Then came the all-out crusade of 1973 leading to the national championship. And, finally, all the crises of 1974.

"It would be impossible to enumerate all the contributions Ara Parseghian has made to this university both as a coach, a leader of young men, and as a representative," said Father Joyce, executive vice president. "We are all indebted to him for the excellent manner in which he has carried on the tradition and spirit of Notre Dame football. He has indeed been a very real asset to Notre Dame because of his extreme integrity, moral leadership, and his unfaltering loyalty." Father Joyce added, "We understand fully and appreciate his concern for his health and for the welfare of his family."

"I've been exhausted for two years," Parseghian explained further. "The pressure is terrific. I'm intelligent enough to know what the job has been doing to me. For my health, and my family's sake, I decided I couldn't go on. I remember what these pressures did to Frank Leahy, who also was here 11 seasons. But Frank had two years away from coaching during World War II. I have to get away for a while."

"He was taking pills for high blood pressure, pills to sleep at night, and tranquilizers," said Valdiserri. "Here was a guy who wouldn't take an aspirin for a headache. He said, 'This is no way to live.' Toward the end he would ask me about Leahy and how he came to lose his health."

The same day Parseghian announced his retirement, athletic director Moose Krause went to the coach's home and, in a dramatic gesture that fits appropriately into Notre Dame lore, offered to resign as athletic director and hand the job over to Parseghian.

"We embraced," said Parseghian. "It was an emotional experience. He was willing to make that sacrifice on my behalf. But I rejected the idea. I've never been interested in an athletic directorship."

And, too, all those stories that Parseghian was about to take a professional coaching job had no foundation. True, he had opportunities. According to Valdiserri, he was offered the position of general manager with the Cleveland Browns; owner Art Modell wanted him to run the operation. And at $100,000 to $125,000 a year. But the truth was Parseghian had to get away from football. That is, after one more game—a rematch with Alabama, this time in the Orange Bowl.

Meanwhile, Notre Dame named Dan Devine to succeed Parseghian. Devine, a success at the University of Missouri but something

Tight end Dave Casper poses with Ara. Casper was one of the tri-captains of the 1973 Irish, the team that made possible Parseghian's first and only perfect season as Notre Dame coach.

less than that as a pro coach at Green Bay, had been considered by Notre Dame officials once before, when they settled on Parseghian. This time Devine made it and was awarded a five-year contract.

Predictions, which were numerous, that he would have difficulty succeeding Parseghian came true in 1975. An 8-3 record drew criticism. And so did Devine's quiet manner. Unlike the emotional, hard-driving Parseghian, Devine came on toward those Notre Dame rooters accustomed to something more fiery as a shy, even aloof, man. After one season, no one was predicting Devine would become another Notre Dame legend.

Before his last game, Parseghian resisted any inclination to ask his players to win one for him. It was a request that went without saying, anyway, because the players recognized the significance of a happy ending to the Parseghian story.

Most of the elements of the previous year's bowl game with Alabama remained. The Notre Dame-Alabama rivalry was just as keen; most of the key players were returning. Alabama, every bit as good, had just completed another 11-0 season. Again, Alabama went into the game ranked No. 1.

And again, Alabama came out with a defeat. This time Notre Dame doubled its victory margin from the previous year to two points, 13-11. The Irish took a 13-0 lead and hung on. Alabama was driving toward field goal range at the end when defensive back Reggie Barnett preserved Notre Dame's victory with an interception.

The Era of Ara had ended. Parseghian entered the locker room, crying. "I've never seen him so happy," one player said. Athletic director Krause declared: "We've won football games for Rock and the Gipper and Leahy. We won this one for Ara."

5 Ecstasies

As a junior in 1955, Paul Hornung led Notre Dame in scoring, passing, pass interceptions, and punting. In 1956 he finished second in the nation in total offense, and won the Heisman Trophy, despite his team's dismal 2-8 record. This picture was taken during the 1955 contest with Miami, a game won by the Irish 14-0.

Michigan was the stepladder by which Notre Dame today mounted the dizziest heights in its football history, the Catholics downing the Wolverines by a score of 11 to 3.
—*The Chicago Inter-Ocean*

Notre Dame 11, Michigan 3

November 6, 1909

This victory would earn for Notre Dame, which had begun football in 1887, recognition as champions of the west.

The Irish players and coach, Frank C. "Shorty" Longman, seemed confident of victory. Michigan, regarded for years as a national power, did not appear to take Notre Dame too seriously.

And for good reason. Though Notre Dame had been rolling up scores regularly, the Wolverines also had been winning by extraordinary margins, possibly against better opposition.

The Irish arrived in Ann Arbor to find the place still celebrating a 43-0 victory from the previous week. So what they accomplished was positively stunning to the local folks. When it was over, the Chicago *American* reported: "All Michigan is in mourning this afternoon."

The Irish thoroughly fooled Michigan with a number of short passes. The Wolverines were aligned to stop longer ones and took much of the first half trying to adjust.

Notre Dame also presented a successful running game, led by Harry "Red" Miller. The first touchdown, worth five points, was scored on a short run by Pete Vaughan. Legend has it he broke the goal post when he hit it with his head. Vaughan later established he would have been little good the rest of the game had he done that, but said he did break the post with his shoulder.

A crucial play followed. With Notre Dame leading 5-3, Michigan lined up for a field goal after being stopped for two plays near the Notre Dame goal line. Wolverine coach Fielding "Hurry Up" Yost said after the game, "They only had a yard to go, and a place kick was not the proper play."

The Michigan quarterback, Wasmund, took much blame for calling the play but apparently it was the Michigan captain and kicker, Allerdice, who was responsible. Though Yost was unhappy about a field goal attempt, Allerdice made a sound judgment by current thinking. A second field goal by him would have put Michigan ahead, 6-5.

The kick, however, was blocked. The ball bounced back up the field, Notre Dame recovered, and marched to its second touchdown. Billy Ryan scored on a 30-yard broken-field run. It was 11-3 and it might have been worse.

Miller almost broke loose for another score, but Wasmund tackled him. And Miller lost a pass in the sun from Vaughan that would have been a touchdown.

The game also marked the successful use of the onside kick. Walter Camp reported: "This play is one that nobody can figure out.

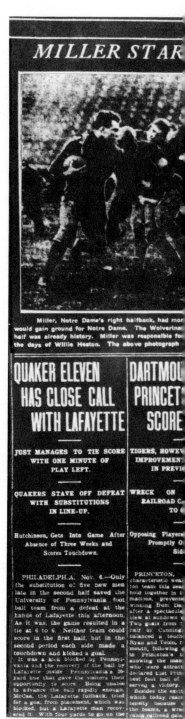

MILLER STAR

Miller, Notre Dame's right halfback, had mor would gain ground for Notre Dame. The Wolverine half was already history. Miller was responsible for the days of Willie Heston. The above photograph

QUAKER ELEVEN HAS CLOSE CALL WITH LAFAYETTE

JUST MANAGES TO TIE SCORE
WITH ONE MINUTE OF
PLAY LEFT.

QUAKERS STAVE OFF DEFEAT
WITH SUBSTITUTIONS
IN LINE-UP.

Hutchinson, Gets Into Game After
Absence of Three Weeks and
Scores Touchdown.

PHILADELPHIA, Nov. 6.—Only the substitution of five new men late in the second half saved the University of Pennsylvania football team from a defeat at the hands of Lafayette this afternoon. As it was, the game resulted in a tie at 6 to 6. Neither team could score in the first half, but in the second period each side made a touchdown and kicked a goal.
It was a kick blocked by Pennsylvania and the recovery of the ball by Lafayette inside Pennsylvania's 20-yard line that gave the visitors their opportunity to score. Being unable to advance the ball rapidly enough, McCaa, the Lafayette fullback, tried for a goal from placement, which was blocked, but a Lafayette man recovered it. With four yards to go on the

DARTMOU PRINCET SCORE

TIGERS, HOWEV
IMPROVEMEN
IN PREVI

WRECK ON
RAILROAD C
TO O

Opposing Player
Promptly O
Sid

PRINCETON,
characteristic was
hold together for a
mations, preventa
winning from De
after a spectacula
blew at sundown
Two goals from
half by Cunning
balanced a touch
Ryan and Tobin, r
mount, following th
in Princeton's
snowing the man
who were attract
declared that Prin
best foot ball of
served a victory.
Besides the exhi
which today resu
tensity because
the teams, a wh
vania railroad dela

If it bounds one way the kicking side is likely to recover it and make a touchdown. If it bounds another the defending team may gain a big advantage. It so happened that on two occasions Notre Dame recovered the ball at times when it meant much to that team and counted heavily against Michigan."

OIT, MICHIGAN, SUNDAY MORNING, NOVEMBER 7, 19..

G ON ONE OF HIS LONG RUNS

eating Michigan yesterday than any other man. It was Miller who, by great interference or marvelous running, wn good tackling ability a week before, seemed powerless to stop this human plough till part of the second Dame's touchdowns and he showed himself to be the best half man seen in a back field on Ferry Field since rting on one of his runs, aided by good interference.

NOTRE DAME, PLAYING GREAT FOOT BALL, BEATS MICHIGAN; SCORE, 11-3

"SHORTY" LONGMAN FIRST OF YOST'S FORMER PUPILS TO WHIP THE "OLD MAN" WITH HIS OWN TACTICS.

Wolverines, Showing Lack of Judgment, Fail to Seize Opportunity Which Should Have Scored Touchdown and Won Game.

By HAROLD TITUS

ANN ARBOR, Nov. 6.—Frank Longman, the pupil, defeated Fielding H. Yost, the teacher, on Ferry field this afternoon. Notre Dame, the dark horse of western foot ball, humbled Michigan with an 11-to 3 score. Allerdice and his men were outplayed at every point of the game, with the exception of punting.

Longman, who learned his foot ball under Yost, sent against Michigan a day 10 splendid players and a man named Miller. They outgeneraled, outtackled, out-blocked Michigan. They were faster, fought harder and their knowledge of the game made that possessed by the Michiganders seem small.

And, in spite of this fact—in spite of Notre Dame's great strength and splendid execution of plays—Michigan might have won had someone seen the opportunity and grasped it.

Somebody Blunders.

Worn out by their grilling work, the Catholics weakened toward the end of the game. It was Michigan's ball on their six-yard line, third down, and less than two to go. Allerdice attempted a place kick. The Indians men blocked the attempt.

That tells the whole story. At that time the score stood 6 to 3 against the maize and blue eleven. A touchdown would have put them in the lead. The failure took their heart. Yost used everything he had taught his men. Forward passes failed, carefully planned trick plays were broken up, straight foot ball was futile. The Michiganders could not drive back their opponents in time to win.

Notre Dame refused to be stopped. They hammered the ends, struck off tackle, pounded the guards, used the forward pass, split plays and delayed passes. They fought, fought, fought, refusing to be denied.

Miller, of Notre Dame, carried the ball scores of yards during the afternoon, without interference, without aid from his teammates. And when the other backs took the ball it was Miller who opened holes for them and left a wake of sprawling Michiganders.

Michigan First to Score.

Now and then Michigan would break up, but the bracing never lasted more than a few minutes at a time. It was well toward the end of the period of play before the Wolverines began to fight as they fought against Syracuse a week ago today. Desperation drove them down to the Notre Dame goal, and when the ball bounded away from the Indians into who tore through the line to block the attempted place kick, the ball left Michigan. There was no time to remedy their mistake.

Michigan was the first to score. Dave Allerdice sent the ball spinning between Notre Dame's goal posts and over the cross bar as the whistle ticked off the eighteenth minute. Ten minutes later Miller, backed by his entire eleven, broke the opposition and scored a touchdown. In the second half Ryan, protected only by Miller, skirted his left end for a 30-yard run to the Michigan goal.

First to Best Yost.

Longman was wild with joy. For years Yost's pupils have worked to develop a team that would humble Michigan. Year after year they have failed. Now and then Hernstein or McGugin would give the Michigan coach a hard battle. But Michigan always triumphed. It was "Shorty" Longman who battled so hard for Michigan against the conference team four and five and six years ago, who first triumphed over his former teacher.

Notre Dame won by Yost tactics. They had the speed for which Yost begs. They tackled as Yost would have men tackle. Their forward pass formations were essentially like those used at Michigan. Their defense was the Yost defense. But the Indiana players and Miller were better men than...

FOOTBALL SCORES

Local.
D.A.C. 19, D.U.S. 0.

State.
At Lansing—M. A. C., 51; DePauw, 6.
At Lansing—C. of M. Freshmen, 6; M. A. C. Freshmen, 3.
At Olivet—Olivet 40; Hillsdale, 6.
At Fenton—Fenton, 0; Ithaca, 6.
At Coldwater—Coldwater, 28; Hudson, 0.
At Muskegon—Muskegon, 23; Benton Harbor, 6.
At Ypsilanti—Ypsilanti, 17; Mt. Pleasant, 0.
At Traverse City—Traverse City, 11; Manistee, 0.
At Reading—Reading High, 1; Webb Academy of Grand Rapids, 5.
At Plainwell—Plainwell, 5; Dowagiac, 0.
At Davison—Flint Mutes, 11; Davison High, 0.
At Saginaw—Ann Arbor High, 16; Saginaw, 0.
At Port Huron—Port Huron, 6; Detroit Eastern, 0.
At Port Huron—Port Huron Reserves, 5; Richmond, 0.
At Jackson—Jackson, 6; Adrian, 0.
At Battle Creek—Battle Creek High, 5; Albion, 0.
At Saginaw—Saginaw High, 0; Ann Arbor High, 0.
At Alma—Alma Reserves, 22; St. Louis, 0.

West.
At Ann Arbor—Notre Dame, 11; Michigan, 3.
At Lincoln—Kansas, 6; Nebraska, 0.
At Chicago—Chicago, 34; Northwestern, 0.
At Columbus—Case, 11, Ohio State University, 0.
At Cleveland—Oberlin, 20; Western Reserve, 0.
At St. Louis—Missouri, 6; Washington, 0.
At Des Moines—Drake, 17; Iowa, 16.
At Jackson—Mount Union, 5; Hiram, 0.
At Champaign—Illinois, 3; Indiana, 0.
At Lafayette—Ind.—Wabash, 13; Purdue, 0.
At Richmond, Ind.—Earlham college, 10; Wittenberg college, 0.
At Terre Haute—Rose Polytechnic, 18; Butler College, 0.
At Galesburg, Ill.—Knox, 17; Beloit, 0.
At Ames—Ames 18; Cornell college, Ia., 6.
At Manhattan—Kas.—Kansas Agriculture, 18; Creighton university, 0.
At Denver—Denver University, 5; Colorado School of Mines, 0.
At Lexington—State University, 0; St. Mary's, 0.
At Lake Forest—Lake Forest, 7; Lombard, 0.
At Berkeley—University of California, 12; University of Nevada, 3.
At Culver—Culver Military academy, 4; Benton Harbor College, 3.
At Colorado Springs, Colo.—Colorado Col...

South.
At New Orleans—Tulane, 6; University of Cincinnati, 0.
At St. Louis—St. Louis University, 22; Miami College, 0.
At Atlanta—Auburn, 5; Georgia Tech., 0.
At Nashville—Vanderbilt, 0; Tennessee, 0.

East.
At New York—New York University, 11; Rutgers, 3.
At Middletown—Wesleyan, 6; Williams, 0.
At Exeter—Phillips Andover, 5; Phillips Exeter, 0.
At Hartford—Trinity, 64; Storrs Agricultural, 0.
At Syracuse—Syracuse, 5; Tufts, 0.
At Worcester—Worcester Academy, 11; Harvard Freshmen, 0.
At Manchester—New Hampshire State College, 17; Massachusetts Agriculture, 0.
At Rochester—Colgate, 11; Rochester, 0.
At Schenectady—Union, 15; Middlebury, 0.
At Clinton, N. Y.—Hamilton, 12; Lawrence, 5.
At Mercersburg—Mercersburg Academy, 17; University of Pennsylvania, Freshmen, 3.
At Haverford—Lehigh, 9; Haverford, 0.
At Gettysburg—Gettysburg, 39; Susquehanna University, 0.
At Washington—Carlisle, 9; George Washington, 0.
At Morgantown, W. Va.—University of Pittsburg, 0; West Virginia University, 0.
At Philadelphia—Pennsylvania State College, 31; Bucknell College, 0.
At Swarthmore—Villa Nova, 19; Swarthmore, 0.
At Pittsburg—Carnegie Technical School, 0; Franklin and Marshall, 0.
At Annapolis—Navy, 0; Washington and Jefferson, 0.
At Hoboken—Stevens, 0; Ursinus, 40.
At Virginia—Virginia Military Institute, 0.
At Lexington, Va.—North Carolina A & M College, 3; Washington and Lee, 0.
At Richmond, Va.—Virginia Polytechnic Institute, 15; University of North Carolina, 0.

NAVY IN DRAW GAME.

Fails to Defeat Washington and Jefferson; Neither Scores.

ANNAPOLIS, Md., Nov. 6.—Navy and Washington & Jefferson this afternoon played each other to a scoreless standstill when during 50 minutes of actual play, neither side could cross the other's goal line. Navy was the heavier and was further aided by Dalton's wonderful punting. Washington and...

"THEY OUTPLAYED US, BUT SHOULD NOT HAVE WON"

COACH YOST ALSO SAYS HE'S SICK AND TIRED OF THE WHOLE BUSINESS.

"TWO BAD MISTAKES PREVENTED MICHIGAN FROM WINNING, 9 TO 5."

"Hurry Up" Man Takes Off His Hat to the Irishmen; All Praise "Red" Miller.

By ROBERT CLANCY

ANN ARBOR, Mich., Nov. 6.—Ann Arbor, Michigan's college town, last week celebrating a 44 to 0 victory over the Syracuse eleven in a hilarious fashion, resembles the deserted village tonight. It has been years since the little town has taken on such a gloomy aspect.

All week Michigan has figured on beating Notre Dame with ease, holding Pennsylvania to a close score and probably beating them on "cleaning up" on Minnesota, thereby landing the championship of the west.

Hopes were shattered this afternoon, but not from the direction where the blow might be expected to come.

True, Notre Dame was expected to

WEST HAS A NEW BACK FIELD STAR

"RED" MILLER

Notre Dame 35, Army 13

November 1, 1913

Notre Dame coach and athletic director Jesse Harper had been looking for a game in the East that would help establish the Irish as a national power. Army, in answer to a Harper letter, accepted the challenge because it had an open date. It had been playing Yale but had stopped because it was absorbing too much punishment before its big game with Navy.

Enter Notre Dame. The Irish rode the train; the regulars got to sleep in the lower compartments. The players carried their own equipment and sandwiches. For them, this was a crusade. The Army team and corps of cadets viewed the game as a curiosity; they had heard about this western team but not all that much.

They had not heard about the forward pass that Harper had had quarterback Gus Dorais and end Knute Rockne practicing over the previous summer—just for this occasion. In the first period, Dorais tried two passes, but both fell incomplete. The Cadets huddled in concern—but the concern was small. They were beating Notre Dame physically, rushing hard and tackling hard.

Then Rockne faked a limp. The defenders lost interest in him. Surprise! He got behind everybody, and running smoothly, caught a touchdown pass from Dorais. Army ralled for two touchdowns but Notre Dame came back with Dorais throwing long to Rockne and short to halfback Joe Pliska. Then, as Army spread out on defense, Dorais sent Pliska through the middle of the line for a touchdown. Notre Dame led, 14-13.

Early in the second half, Notre Dame put on a goal-line stand that included a sharp tackle by Rockne and an interception by Dorais. The rout was on. Dorais completed a string of passes. Army spread out more on defense. Then Notre Dame ran the ball. And so it went. There was no stopping the Irish as Dorais completed either 14 of 17 passes or 15 of 17—accounts vary—for 243 yards. Fullback Ray Eichenlaub plunged for the last two touchdowns.

Army eagerly agreed to another game the following year and the Irish returned to the Plains every season after that through 1922. The series gained momentum because Army was anxious to pull ahead in victories. But it never did. The series continued uninterrupted until 1947.

At the top of the pile is Joe Pliska, whose runs up the middle of the Army line set the stage for the Dorais-Rockne passing show.

Notre Dame 27, Army 17

October 30, 1920

This was George Gipp's greatest game. The Army knew about him but was helpless to stop him. And this was a good Army team. So good, in fact, that the week before the Notre Dame game the first-stringers took off and scouted Navy against Princeton while the rest of the Cadet squad beat Tufts. A crowd of about 10,000, a veritable throng in those days, jammed Cullum Hall Field.

It didn't help Army morale for the Cadets to contemplate Notre Dame's 13-game winning streak. And what transpired before the game was a bit unnerving. Drop-kicker Gipp engaged in a duel with Army kicker Red Reeder, but Reeder dropped out at the 40-yard line. Gipp walked to the 50, called for four footballs, calmly kicked two over one crossbar, then turned and kicked the other two over the other bar. Any questions?

Future leaders that they were, the Cadets refused to cave in at the sight of such goings on. They took a 7-0 lead after a long drive. But Gipp passed the Irish into scoring range, then added the point with a drop kick to make it 7-7. Gipp returned a punt, then passed to Roger Kiley for a touchdown and kicked the point. A long Army punt return by Walter French made it 14-14. Then French kicked a field goal to give Army the lead at the half.

What transpired in the stands at intermission eventually would evolve into sufficient reason to interrupt the series after 1947. Gambling was observed between student cadets and Irish fans, who had made their way up from New York City, The Irish subway alumni were just beginning to be heard.

Near the end of the third period, Gipp led a Notre Dame drive that featured his runs and passes. On the go-ahead touchdown play, early in the fourth period, Gipp faked taking a handoff while Johnny Mohardt scored. Gipp added the point, making it 21-17. Following a long punt return and pass completion by Gipp, Chet Wynne scored the clinching touchdown.

Gipp ended with 332 total yards with his rushing, passing, and kick returns. The performance solidified Rockne's opinion, stated often in later years, that "Gipp was the greatest natural athlete I have ever seen."

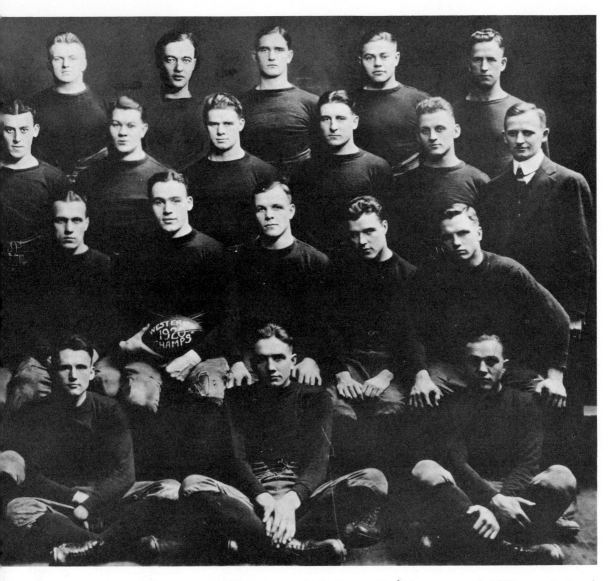

Called the Western champions, Notre Dame's superb 1920 team featured George Gipp (top row center).

Notre Dame 13, Army 7

October 18, 1924

"Outlined across a blue-gray October sky, the Four Horsemen rode again today. . ."

Immortalized by Grantland Rice, the four men had come to Notre Dame for various reasons: Harry Stuhldreher's older brother, Walter, already was there; Don Miller was following three older brothers to South Bend; Jim Crowley, from Green Bay, was talked into it by Curly Lambeau, Packers' coach and Notre Dame alumnus, and Elmer Layden was recommended by Davenport, Iowa, high school coach Walter Halas, brother of the Chicago Bears' George.

Rice's words made the four inseparable. They reached their peak in 1924, an undefeated season. They had to be at their best to beat Army. A crowd of 60,000 filled New York's Polo Grounds. With quarterback Stuhldreher mixing his plays, the other three Horsemen took turns running until Layden finally scored on a short plunge in the second period. In the third period, Crowley ran around end for 18 yards and a touchdown and made the point. It was 13-0, Notre Dame.

Army drove to make it 13-7 in the fourth period and Notre Dame needed a spectacular play by Adam Walsh to hold on. Playing with not one but two broken hands, one he took into the game and the other suffered in the first period, Walsh leaped to make an interception at the Army 35.

After that, Layden missed a drop kick field goal attempt. But the Irish held Army, then ran out the clock. This was one of two narrow victories by the powerfull, 9-0 Notre Dame team of 1924. For Stuhldreher, Miller, Crowley, and Layden, it was their date with destiny, courtesy of Grantland Rice.

Walsh eventually got so tired of hearing about the Four Horsemen he concocted a name for the line, the Seven Mules. These, for the record, were Ed Hunsinger and Chuck Collins at ends; Joe Bach and Rip Miller, the tackles; Noble Kizer and John Weibel, the guards, and Walsh at center.

Walsh mentioned the nickname for the first time as the train carrying the Notre Dame team to the 1925 Rose Bowl made a rest stop along the way. People at the station were clamoring for the Four Horsemen. Walsh assembled the linemen and declared, "You're looking at the best part of the team, the Seven Mules."

Don Miller completing a 22-yard gain in the second quarter, minus his helmet. The Notre Dame player on his knees to the left is Chuck Collins. This was one of the runs that inspired Grantland Rice's lead in the *Herald Tribune* the following morning.

Notre Dame 27, Stanford 10

January 1, 1925

Rockne had wanted to make a trip to the West Coast for some time. Having finished the 1924 season with a 9-0 record, he accepted Stanford's invitation to play in the Rose Bowl. It would be the first time Notre Dame appeared in the Far West.

The Pasadena stadium was then a horseshoe holding 53,000. A wooden fence enclosed the open end. At halftime, the crowd pressing against the fence while peeking through the cracks in it knocked it down and poured inside. So several thousand more than the official number watched the game.

That everyone was eager to see this game was understandable. It was truly a national championship game, Rockne and his Four Horsemen matched against Stanford's illustrious coach, Pop Warner, and famed running back, Ernie Nevers. But the day belonged to another running back, one of the Horsemen, Elmer Layden.

A Notre Dame fumble in the first period set up a Stanford field goal. But on the first play of the second period, Layden burst through the middle for seven yards and a touchdown. Jim Crowley's kick was blocked and it was 6-3.

Nevers tried a screen pass but, thanks to former Irish player Slip Madigan's scouting, Layden was ready for it. Playing extra wide as a linebacker, Layden picked off a deflected ball in the air and sprinted 80 yards to score. After Crowley's kick, it was 13-3 at the half.

In the third period, Layden punted, the ball was fumbled, and one of the Seven Mules, Ed Hunsinger, picked it up and ran 20 yards to score. Crowley's kick made the score 20-3. But a Harry Stuhldreher pass was intercepted by Nevers, who shortly passed for a Stanford touchdown. 20-10, Notre Dame.

Nevers then led Stanford down the field, all the way down, in fact, to Notre Dame's 1-foot line. Nevers plunged and . . . Stanford players and fans claimed he scored; Irish players insisted otherwise. The officials said he didn't. The Irish had held Stanford for four downs from their 2-yard line, one of the most important Notre Dame goal line stands ever. The last stop was made by a reserve tackle, John McMullen, an explosive but erratic defender whom Rockne figured would hit Nevers as hard as anybody if he hit Nevers at all. Rockne figured right.

Later in the fourth quarter Nevers was taking Stanford down the field again when Layden stepped in front of another screen pass and ran 70 yards for the clinching touchdown. Stuhldreher, it was learned, had played with a broken bone in his foot and Crowley ended up in a hospital suffering from heat exhaustion. There, he heard about Stanford fans making much of their team's 17 first downs to the Irish seven, 164 to 134 rushing yards, and 146 to 48 passing yards. "Yeah," said Crowley, "and next year they're going to award the National League pennant to the team that has the most bases on balls."

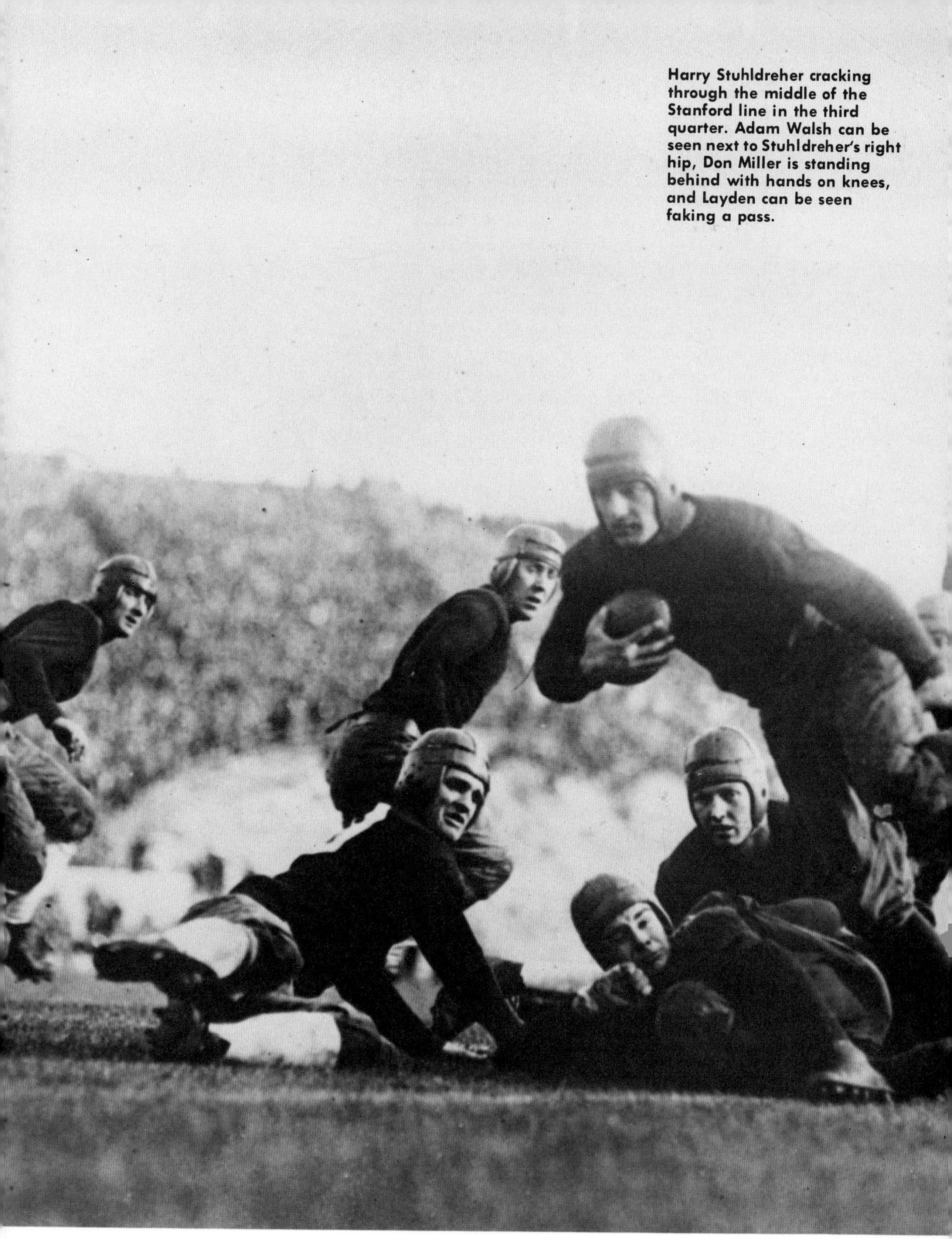

Harry Stuhldreher cracking through the middle of the Stanford line in the third quarter. Adam Walsh can be seen next to Stuhldreher's right hip, Don Miller is standing behind with hands on knees, and Layden can be seen faking a pass.

Notre Dame 12, Army 6

November 12, 1928

This was the game Notre Dame won for the Gipper. Rockne ordered the doors to the Yankee Stadium locker room shut and related George Gipp's supposed deathbed request. Rockne's words lifted the Notre Dame players to an emotional peak.

Emotion is precisely what Rockne wanted from his players. They needed it because they were struggling with injuries and had already lost twice and managed to win two others only by one touchdown. It was not a typical Rockne team.

Army, which had won six straight games and was gaining consideration as the nation's No. 1 team, boasted the best all-round player on the field, Chris Cagle, a great two-way back. Notre Dame had a back of its own who merited watching, Jack Chevigny; he became particularly inspired by Rockne's Gipper speech.

The first half ended, 0-0. The only scoring opportunity came in the second period when Notre Dame drove to the Army 2-yard line, but fumbled away the ball.

Cagle, in the third period, set up the game's first touchdown with a 40-yard pass to the Notre Dame 14-yard line. The Cadets drove to within the 1-yard line, from where John Murrell scored. The point after was missed.

Notre Dame struck back. The Irish marched to the Army 2-yard line and Chevigny scored from there. The kick was missed, leaving the score 6-6.

Early in the fourth period, Chevigny attempted a 50-yard field goal, but was short. Shortly, the star runner who was to be killed at Iwo Jima set up the game's winning touchdown. He ran 13 yards to the Army 30. Notre Dame then drove to the 16 only to have a bad pass from center sail back to the 32. But Chevigny fell on the ball, then much of the Army team fell on him, knocking him out of the game.

During the ensuing time out, Rockne made two substitutions, including a little known sophomore end named Johnny O'Brien. On third-and-26 from the 32, John Niemiec faded to the 43 and threw a long pass toward the goal line. O'Brien ran under it, faking out Cagle, of all people, on the way, dived, and, while outstretched, grabbed the ball while falling across the goal line.

For that play, O'Brien became known as Johnny "One Play" O'Brien. The kick was missed. It was 12-6, Notre Dame.

Cagle struck back. He ran back the kickoff 55 yards, then ran 25 yards to the Notre Dame 10. He then passed incomplete, was hit, and, almost exhausted, had to be taken out. A pass was completed to the 4-yard line. A run moved the ball to the Notre Dame 1. Army lined up. But time ran out. Exciting enough?

Winning one for the Gipper. The partially obscured figure in the middle of the picture is Jack Chevigny, lugging the ball for seven yards against the Cadets. Chevigny scored Notre Dame's first touchdown.

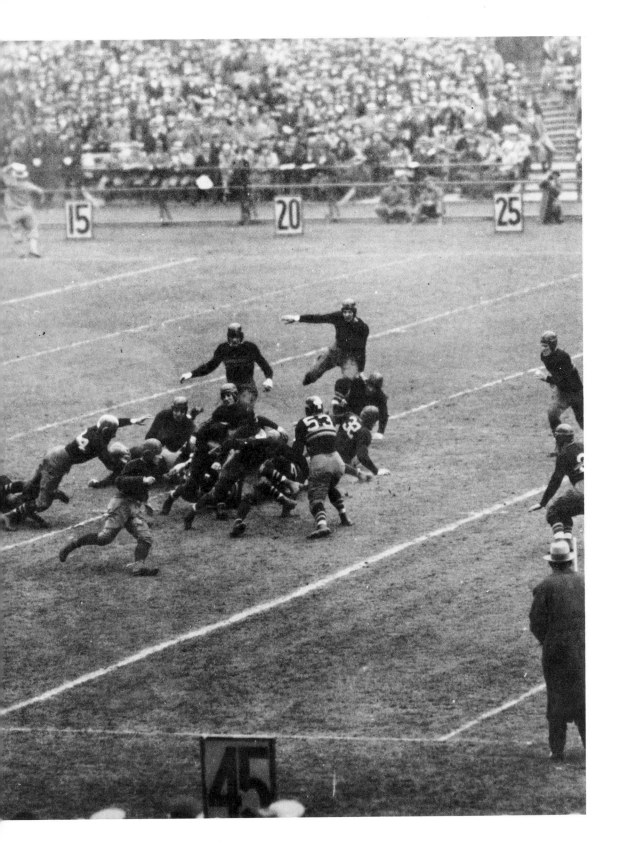

The Notre Dame-Carnegie Tech rivalry was hot during the twenties and thirties. Nearly 70,000 saw the 1929 game at Pitt Stadium. This picture shows a Notre Dame pass falling incomplete. The player on the right is wearing a primitive face mask.

Notre Dame 7, Carnegie Tech 0
October 26, 1929

Not even a severe phlebitis condition could keep Knute Rockne from this game with Carnegie Tech, which had defeated the Irish in their previous two meetings. Rockne was assisted to the field in a wheel chair and had to be carried into the locker room to make one of his patented fiery speeches.

Subsequent events produced a smile on the haggard face of the man in the wheelchair by the Notre Dame bench. After a scoreless first half, Jack Elder got off a 33-yard run on a punt return to the Carnegie Tech 7-yard line. Joe Savoldi hit the line four times after that, producing gains of three yards, two yards, one yard, and on fourth down at the one, the necessary one yard. Frank Carideo kicked the extra point.

Carnegie responded with its only offensive success of the afternoon. It moved the ball for three first downs, its total for the game. But it couldn't drive far enough against the stubborn Notre Dame line. Murray Armentrout, the halfback who tackled Elder to delay the Irish touchdown, made the longest run from scrimmage for Carnegie, a mere eight yards.

Jack Cannon, Eddie Collins, Johnny Law, and Marty Brill were the defensive standouts for Notre Dame. On offense, Elder and Savoldi were the heroes as the Irish had to make every yard count. They managed only eight first downs themselves and completed no passes in five attempts.

The crowd of 66,000 was the largest until then to see a football game in Pittsburgh.

One of Rockne's most melodramatic ploys to fire the will of his team: the wheelchair ride to the bench before the Carnegie Tech game. Naturally, it worked. Notre Dame won 7-0 on a run by Joe Savoldi.

Ecstasies / **131**

Notre Dame 60, Penn 20

November 8, 1930

Marty Brill, who had transferred to Notre Dame from the University of Pennsylvania, returned with the Irish to Philadelphia's Franklin Field and heaped embarrassment on the overwhelmed Red and Blue with touchdown runs of 66, 36, and 25 yards.

Brill, a Philadelphia lad, had been rebuffed in his efforts to make the Penn varsity, switched to Notre Dame, and sat out a year of ineligibility because of the transfer. He then proved good enough to find a place in the backfield with Frank Carideo, Joe Savoldi, and Marchy Schwartz, a backfield many observers considered superior to the Four Horsemen.

Until the game with Penn, Knute Rockne had used Brill primarily as a blocker but the coach knew well how Brill felt about Penn and fully intended to turn him loose. For his first touchdown, Brill, out of the Notre Dame box formation, faked to Savoldi, then to Schwartz, spun, and cut between guard and tackle, and was gone. Brill carried only 10 times in the game, but three went for touchdowns.

While running up the 60-20 rout, Notre Dame gained 567 yards against a respected Penn team. The other touchdowns were scored by Carideo, Schwartz, Savoldi, Moon Mullins, Bucky O'Connor, and Mike Koken. Brill also was the standout on defense for the Irish. Penn managed its three scores against the Notre Dame substitutes.

Had Grantland Rice waited six years he might have more appropriately dubbed these brutes the Four Horsemen. This was the Notre Dame backfield, just before the 1930 Penn game. (L-R) Frank Carideo, Joe Savoldi, Marchy Schwartz, and Marty Brill. Marty ran for three touchdowns against the Quakers, to settle accounts with the school that had ignored him.

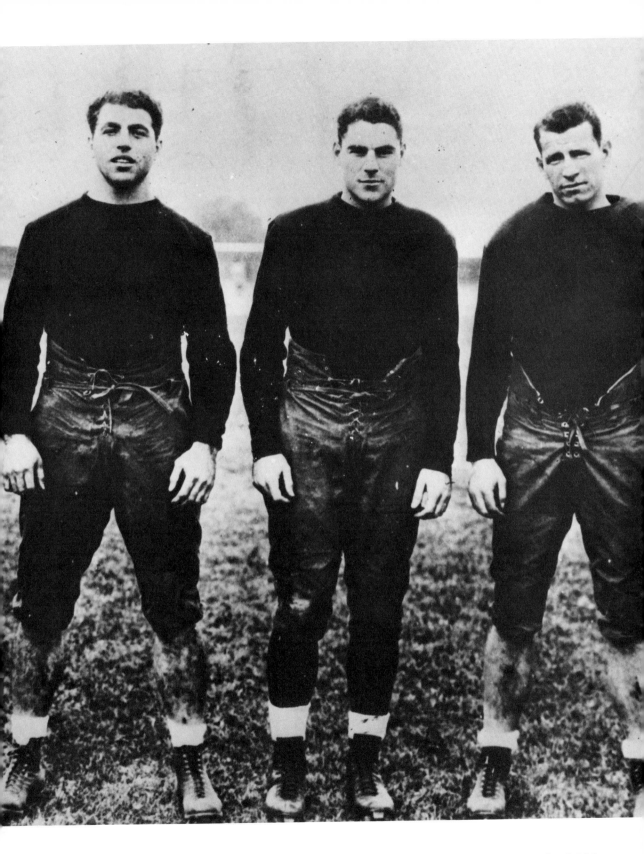

Notre Dame 18, Ohio State 13

November 2, 1935

By all standards, this was one of the best games of football ever played. Sportswriters voted it the most thrilling football game for the first half of the 20th century.

With both teams undefeated, Notre Dame at 5-0 and Ohio State at 4-0, it was billed as the game of the century. The Irish coach, Four Horseman Elmer Layden, used a bit of his mentor Rockne's psychology before the game, telling writers Notre Dame would be lucky to hold the Buckeyes to 40 points. The newspaper headlines that bannered his feigned concern proved incentive enough for the Irish.

Still, they were no match for Ohio State in the first half. With 81,000 looking on at Ohio State, the Buckeyes unveiled razzle-dazzle lateral plays. One worked for a touchdown and another, involving two laterals, set up a second score. It was 13-0 and it stayed that way until the final period. Then Notre Dame's Steve Miller scored from the 1-yard line after a long punt runback by halfback Andy Pilney to the Ohio 13 and a pass by Pilney to the 1. But Wally Fromhart missed the point after.

Notre Dame got the ball back and marched downfield only to fumble at the Ohio goal line. The game looked lost for the Irish. Only three minutes remained when they got the ball back on their own 21. But Pilney worked the halfback pass, first to Fromhart at the Ohio 38, and three plays later to Mike Layden, the coach's younger brother, for a touchdown. It was 13-12. Fromhart again missed the point.

There were 90 seconds left. Notre Dame tried an onside kick but Ohio managed to get it at midfield. Surely, then, the Irish had lost. But no. Ohio's Dick Beltz, trying an end run, was swarmed under and fumbled. Hank Pojman, a second-string center, touched the ball last before it rolled out of bounds. It was Notre Dame ball at its own 45.

Pilney, trying to pass, found the receivers covered, and ran. He weaved through Ohio players to the Buckeyes' 19. When he was hit, his left knee was mangled and he was carried from the field on a stretcher, his career ended.

He was replaced by Bill "The Bard" Shakespeare. There were 50 seconds left. Shakespeare passed and the ball went in and out of the arms of Ohio's Beltz. Almost an interception. Forty seconds left. Layden sent in the next play with reserve quarterback Dick McKenna. The ball went back to Shakespeare and the ends crossed paths downfield.

Wayne Millner jumped for the ball in the end zone and caught it. It was 18-13. The point was missed again. The Irish kicked off. Ohio tried one desperation pass. The game was over. It took Red Barber, who was broadcasting the game, ten minutes to learn who had caught the winning pass. The Notre Dame spotter had run wildly from the radio booth when Millner made his catch.

Notre Dame spotted Ohio State 13 points and then got busy in the fourth quarter. This is their first touchdown, scored by Steve Miller from the one-yard line.

Notre Dame 0, Army 0

November 9, 1946

The two greatest college football teams of the post-war era battled to a scoreless tie in a game that transfixed almost an entire nation in anticipation and left it replaying the outcome even to this day.

When the Army-Notre Dame game of 1946 is mentioned, one play in particular is usually recalled: Johnny Lujack of the Irish tackling Army's Doc Blanchard in the open field. It was a game-saving stop in the third period at the Notre Dame 36-yard line after a 21-yard rumble by Blanchard.

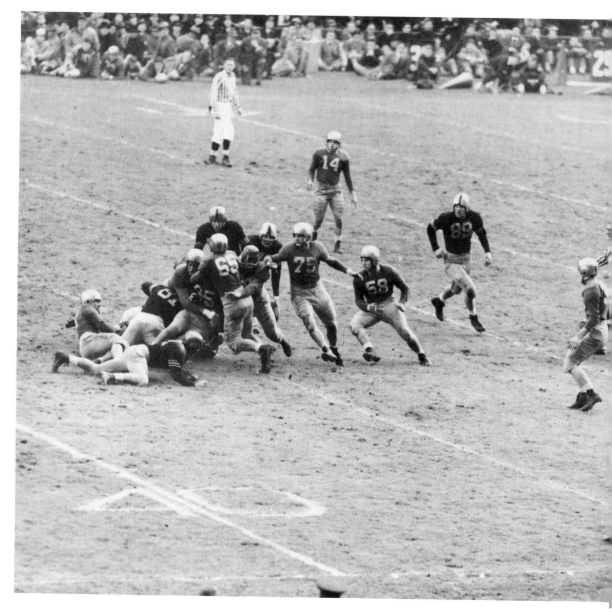

It was the dramatic highlight of a game witnessed by 74,121 at Yankee Stadium. They were the lucky few. More than one million ticket requests had to be turned down. Little wonder that $3.30 end zone seats were selling for as much as $200 on the street the day of the game.

Army got its first chance to score in the first period when Emil Sitko fumbled at the Notre Dame 24. Glenn Davis ran to the 18 but three straight plunges by Blanchard left Army a foot short of the first down near the 14-yard line, and the Irish took over.

Notre Dame got off an 85-yard drive in the second period, the most impressive drive of the game. Lujack, mixing his plays deftly, engineered the march. He started it with a keeper for a first down. He later passed 25 yards to end Bob Skoglund to the Army 41. Co-captain Gerry Cowhig ran 19 yards to the Army 12, where Army quarterback Arnold Tucker made a touchdown-saving tackle of his own. A short pass and a run up the middle put the ball on the four. Lujack sneaked to the 3.

On fourth down, Lujack pitched out to Bill Gompers around Notre Dame's left end. But Army end Hank Foldberg dropped Gompers inches short of the first down. On the play, Notre Dame was charged with clipping Davis. But Army declined the 15-yard penalty that would have given the Irish another play, and took the ball.

Terry Brennan fumbled late in the half at the Notre Dame 35. But Tucker had three passes batted down by the Irish, who took over. Army got the ball back for one final first-half effort; this time Tucker ran the ball. He broke free over tackle for 30 yards before being denied a touchdown by Lujack, with a sensational tackle on the last play of the half.

In the third period, Tucker intercepted a Notre Dame pass at his 10-yard line and ran it back 32 yards. On the next play Blanchard got loose for his famous run, which ended with a head-on tackle by Lujack. A pass to Foldberg moved Army to the Notre Dame 15, but Brennan ended the drive with an interception off Tucker at the Irish 5.

There was another Irish crisis early in the fourth period. Sitko intercepted a deep pass at the Notre Dame 5, then fumbled, but Lujack recovered. Then Cowhig fumbled to Army's Jim Enos but Army failed to move in four tries. Notre Dame punted, but only to its 38. There, Jack Zilly hit Tucker, trying to pass, and Jim Martin fell on Tucker's fumble. The rest of the game was played around mid-field.

When they left the field, the players seemed mired in disappointment. Most witnesses seemed satisfied that they had seen the "world's greatest football game."

The extent to which Blanchard and Davis were throttled can be seen in this picture of Blanchard in the clutches of three Irish defenders. Identifiable are Jim Mello (65), John Mastrangelo (75), Marty Wendell (58), Emil Sitko (14), and Johnny Lujack (32). Later in the game Lujack made an open field tackle of Blanchard that cut down a sure touchdown.

Notre Dame 27, S.M.U. 20

December 3, 1949

"Southern Methodist has the greatest football team we've played all season and that Kyle Rote is the most underrated back in football." That was a relieved Frank Leahy speaking after his Irish survived an S.M.U. scare to finish with a 10-0 record, their fourth straight undefeated season.

It wasn't supposed to be much of a contest. The Irish were unbeaten over 37 games. S.M.U. had already finished a lowly fifth in the Southwest Conference. Moreover, the Mustangs were suffering from several key injuries, among them Doak Walker, no less, who was unable to play against Notre Dame. "I'm glad you were not in there," Leahy told Walker afterward.

Notre Dame dominated the first half, taking a 14-0 lead. Nothing seemed changed in the second half—for a while. Then, with Notre Dame leading 20-7, Rote, running wild, added his second and third touchdowns as the Mustangs pulled into a 20-20 tie.

Guided by Bob Williams, Notre Dame drove 57 yards for the winning touchdown. Short but consistent runs by Emil Sitko, Bill Barrett, and end-turned-fullback Leon Hart carried the drive, with Barrett scoring the winning touchdown with eight minutes to play.

But S.M.U. came back, pushing to the Irish 5-yard line with Rote leading the way on a nine-play, 75-yard drive. But Hart knocked the wind out of Rote, who had to leave the game, and S.M.U. failed to score.

The Mustangs got one last chance. With Rote back in the game, they moved to the Irish 40 on passes to Rote and John Champion by sophomore Fred Benners. But time ran out.

Two earlier close calls also were fresh in Leahy's mind as he hailed S.M.U. after the game. On one of the rare occasions he was stopped, Rote, in the first period, had been downed at the Irish 1-yard line as S.M.U. failed to score. Meanwhile, one Irish touchdown, a pass from Williams to Ernie Zalejski, came only after three S.M.U. defenders had surrounded Zalejski and appeared to have batted the ball away only to have it hit an S.M.U. player's knee and bound into the hands of the surprised receiver.

"I'm sorry I didn't get a chance to play against the greatest Notre Dame team of all time," Doak Walker told the Irish players in a visit to their dressing room. But none of them was.

"God bless you, everyone," Leahy told his men.

One of the most remarkable individual performances in college football history was produced this day by Kyle Rote, up to that point somewhat in Doak Walker's shadow. His running and passing nearly upset the heavily favored Irish. He is seen here finishing another profitable run, with Jim Mutscheller (85) about to stop him.

Notre Dame 7, Oklahoma 0
November 16, 1957

Oklahoma had amassed the longest winning streak in the history of intercollegiate football—47 games. Notre Dame hadn't even come close to winning its games of the previous two weeks. Terry Brennan was fighting for his coaching job following a 2-8 season.

In front of 62,000 fans in Oklahoma, the Irish did the improbable, impudently holding the Sooners scoreless through three periods. In the fourth quarter, they threatened to do the impossible. They drove 80 yards, largely on the rushes of Nick Pietrosante and Pat Doyle, to the Oklahoma 3-yard line, where quarterback Bob Williams pitched out to halfback Dick Lynch, who circled the bunched-up Sooner line for the touchdown.

As they had the entire game, the Irish stopped Oklahoma's famous run-pass option play to hold their 7-0 lead, and even dared to throw a couple of long passes near the end when some people thought they should have been a trifle more conservative.

At the final gun, Notre Dame became the first team to beat Oklahoma since the opening game of 1953 when Frank Leahy's last Irish team beat the Sooners, 28-21. Terry Brennan finished the season with a 7-3 record and saved his job for one more year. Oklahoma coach Bud Wilkinson declared that he felt "no relief" that the streak was over. Give him a win anytime, he seemed to be saying.

This was not just any great day for the Irish: it was one of the greatest.

Oklahoma running back Carl Dodd's progress downfield has just been abetted by Denny Morris's block on Nick Pietrosante. Dodd was shoved out of bounds five yards further. Coming up too late is Dick Lynch (25), this Saturday's hero.

Notre Dame 24, Texas 11

January 1, 1971

Texas was supremely confident of a second straight Cotton Bowl victory over the Irish. And no wonder. The Longhorns had won 30 straight games, the third longest winning streak in college history. It included a 27-17 victory over Notre Dame the previous year.

Texas was installed a six-point favorite, but it might have been a 60-point favorite the way Longhorn fans were reacting. They roared into Dallas from all over the state, predicted victory, and began celebrating. "We're ready to take it to them," said Texas tackle and co-captain Bobby Wuensch.

The Irish, at first, weren't even sure they wanted to be there. A players' straw vote taken before the end of the season revealed they preferred the Orange Bowl. Clearly, that's what the Notre Dame band preferred, too. "My God, what are we doing here?" asked one band member to another in a downtown Dallas hotel lobby. "Yeah," said another, "everyone wanted to go to Miami."

But Ara Parseghian won over his players' hearts and minds. He pointed out that the Irish, ranked sixth nationally, had an outside chance to be No. 1 in the Associated Press poll. (The United Press poll had closed and Texas already had been voted champion.) That slim hope to be No. 1 and revenge for their defeat by Texas the previous year motivated the Irish.

They went out and won one, not for the Gipper, but themselves. They hit so hard they caused nine Texas fumbles and recovered five of them. Texas fans watched in disbelief, their cries of "Hook 'em Horns" silenced. The big Longhorn backs, Steve Worster and Jim Bertelsen, were stopped.

All the scoring occurred in the first half, Notre Dame's 24 points being more than any team had scored against Texas in an entire game in three seasons. Joe Theismann got the Irish started, directed a Texas-style, time-consuming 80-yard drive capped by a 26-yard scoring pass to Tom Gatewood. Theismann added two more touchdowns with runs of three and 15 yards.

When both Theismann and Gatewood were slowed by injuries, Parseghian called on reserve quarterback Jim Bulger, whose first pass ever for the Irish was a 37-yard completion to Clarence Ellis, star defensive back who switched to offense to make the catch. The play set up a field goal that completed the scoring.

"This," Parseghian said afterward, "is one of the big moments in Notre Dame football history." The Irish finished No. 2 behind Nebraska in the AP poll.

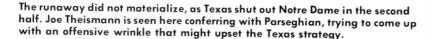
The runaway did not materialize, as Texas shut out Notre Dame in the second half. Joe Theismann is seen here conferring with Parseghian, trying to come up with an offensive wrinkle that might upset the Texas strategy.

Notre Dame 23, U.S.C. 14

October 27, 1973

Remember, Anthony Davis did have a junior year. In between scoring six touchdowns against the Irish as a sophomore and four as a senior, the fleet Southern California back was virtually halted in his only appearance in South Bend.

Not that he was stopped altogether. He still managed 55 yards on 19 carries and one touchdown, a 1-yard run—a good enough day's work for most, but not Anthony Davis. Slow him up and U.S.C. could be beaten. That is what the Irish tried to do, and they succeeded.

The Notre Dame offense did its part, too, slugging its way for 404 yards with Eric Penick running 85 yards for one touchdown, quarterback Tom Clements one yard for another, and Bob Thomas adding field goals of 32, 33, and 32 yards. Penick ended up with 118 yards on 13 carries.

The defeat for the Trojans was their first in 23 games. "Notre Dame outplayed us," U.S.C. coach John McKay told reporters after the game and walked out of the stadium, no kidding, humming Notre Dame's "Victory March."

The Irish scored first on a Thomas field goal. U.S.C. marched 65 yards for a 7-3 lead as Davis got his lone touchdown. Another Thomas kick cut the margin to 7-6. With 30 seconds left in the first half, Clements sneaked over on fourth down at the end of another long drive for a 13-7 Notre Dame lead.

Penick got off his 85-yard run on Notre Dame's first play from scrimmage in the third period with the help of blocks by Frank Pomarico and Gerry DiNardo. That made it 20-7, Notre Dame.

Two passes from Pat Hayden to Lynn Swann and an Irish personal foul resulting in Reggie Barnett's ejection from the game led to U.S.C.'s second touchdown. From the Notre Dame 27-yard line, Hayden lofted a pass over Barnett's replacement to Swann, 20-14.

But another Notre Dame drive, later in the third period, resulted in the clinching points, Thomas' third field goal. Two fumbles, one by Davis, hurt U.S.C.'s chances of catching up.

Parseghian was carried off the field by his jubilant players and fans. The Irish went on to an 11-0 season and No. 1 ranking.

Eric Penick, on his way to an 85-yard touchdown run in the third quarter. Penick finished the afternoon with 118 yards gained, 50 more than the entire U.S.C. running corps could manage. This run broke open a tight game and gave the Irish a 13-point lead.

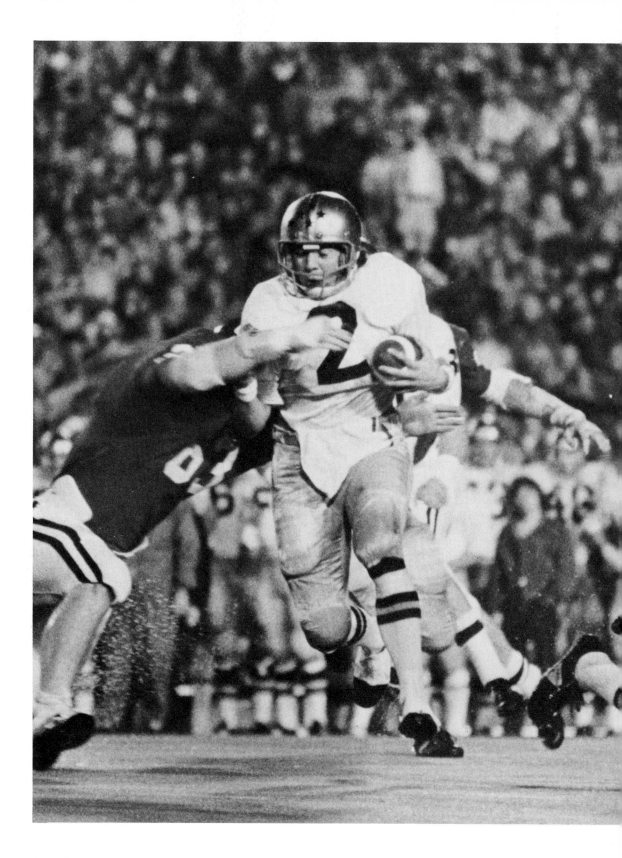

Notre Dame 24, Alabama 23

December 31, 1973

Ever since 1966, Ara Parseghian had had to live with the reputation of having played for a tie against Michigan State. More people remembered that than the fact Notre Dame went unbeaten in 1966 and won the national championship.

Against Alabama, in the Sugar Bowl, Parseghian gained redemption. This was the first meeting ever between the schools as well as the coaches, Parseghian and Paul "Bear" Bryant. Both teams were undefeated. The national championship was at stake.

As often happens with the stakes so high, the game was filled with mistakes; but also with big plays and excitement. Notre Dame, the underdog, fought back three times to win.

Freshman Al Hunter ran a kickoff 93 yards to nudge the Irish ahead, 14-6. Alabama took the lead and lost it again before regaining it, 23-21, on a halfback-to-quarterback pass, passer Richard Todd making the catch for the touchdown from halfback Mike Stock.

Tom Clements directed the winning drive for Notre Dame, carrying the ball three times himself and throwing a 30-yarder to Dave Casper to set up the winning field goal by Bob Thomas from the Alabama 9-yard line.

Yet, improbably, the most excitement of all occurred after what would be the final score already had been posted. This occurred when Parseghian ordered Clements to risk a dangerous pass from the Notre Dame end zone after Alabama had backed up the Irish at their 1 with a 69-yard punt by Greg Gantt.

On third down at the two, Clements hit reserve tight end Robin Weber alone at the sideline, ironically near Bear Bryant. The play enabled the Irish to run out the clock.

"When we had them backed up on the 1-yard line, if I'd been a betting man I'd have bet my life we were going to win," Bryant said afterward.

"Coach Bryant had every right to feel that way," said Parseghian, "because had we punted from our end zone and had our punter gotten off a good kick of 40 yards, Alabama would still have been in excellent position for a game-winning field goal.

"Thus, the decision for the pass play seemed the only way out of the dilemma."

The victory gave Notre Dame the national championship, according to the Associated Press poll, and its first perfect season since 1949. "It was by far the most exciting challenge I had ever faced as a football coach," said Parseghian.

Tom Clements engineering the 79-yard, fourth quarter drive that set up Bob Thomas's winning field goal. This run was stopped after only a three-yard gain, but moments later Clements lofted a perfect pass to Dave Casper on the Alabama 15-yard line.

Notre Dame 13, Alabama 11

January 1, 1975

What a way to go. "This game ranks right up there among the greatest in my career," said Parseghian, a happy, weeping victor in his final game as coach of Notre Dame.

The Irish went into this Orange Bowl game against Alabama as nine-point underdogs and seeking to rebound from a humiliating 55-24 defeat by Southern California. Like the previous year in the Sugar Bowl, Alabama was coming into the game undefeated with another opportunity to be recognized unequivocally as the national champion.

Alabama coach Bear Bryant, who had not won a bowl game since 1966, would have to wait longer. This particular night the Irish won one for their departing coach.

The Irish jumped to a 13-0 lead. Al Samuel recovered a fumbled punt at the Alabama 16-yard line. Wayne Bullock scored on a four-yard run. Later, the Irish drove 77 yards, with Mark McLane scoring on a 9-yard run.

With time running out in the first half, Alabama drove 56 yards, with the help of two crucial passes from Richard Todd, to a field goal that cut Notre Dame's lead to 13-3.

A Notre Dame victory seemed assured late in the fourth period but Alabama's Todd, on fourth and five, threw to Russ Schamun, who outran the Notre Dame defenders for a touchdown with 3:21 to play. It was 13-11, Notre Dame, after Todd completed a two-point conversion pass to a diving tight end, George Pugh.

The Notre Dame defense saved the victory. First, it was 6-foot-3, 215-pound sophomore safety John Dubenetzky, who had been harrassing Alabama with blitzes much of the game. He intercepted a pass at the Notre Dame 10-yard line to stop one Alabama drive.

Then, with 68 seconds remaining, senior defensive back Reggie Barnett, intercepted another pass, enabling Parseghian to retire from Notre Dame with a victory.

Praising his players for "playing in pain," the coach declared: "I have nothing but admiration for these kids who played their hearts out when normally they could have been on the sidelines with legitimate injuries."

Eric Penick gliding into the swirling action at the end of scrimmage. Blocking for him are Al Wujciak (66) and Wayne Bullock (30). Bullock may have been taking a well deserved breather; he carried the ball 24 times in the game for 83 yards and one touchdown.

6 Agonies

Agony for Ara in 1974 as U.S.C. scores the touchdown that ruined Parseghian's dream of a perfect debut season.

U.S.C. 16, Notre Dame 14
November 21, 1931

We expect to put up a fight and hope to make the contest more interesting than last year," said Southern California coach Howard Jones as he brought his West Coast champions to Notre Dame. The previous year, in Knute Rockne's last game as Irish coach, Notre Dame had won easily, 27-0.

This game marked the final South Bend appearance of several Irish stars, among them Marchy Schwartz, who had never suffered a defeat. U.S.C. had lost once, to St. Mary's. The game was rated even.

Notre Dame broke on top, 14-0, with touchdowns by Steve Banas and Schwartz and points after by Chuck Jaskwich. The Irish maintained the lead going into the fourth quarter. But U.S.C. was starting to move.

In the final minutes of the third period, U.S.C. drove from Notre Dame's 48-yard line after a punt to the Notre Dame 14. A pass interference penalty against the Irish started the U.S.C. drive. On the second play of the final period, an end-around moved the ball to the 1. Gus Shaver, who alternated between quarterback and full-back, scored on a plunge. Johnny Baker's kick was blocked.

U.S.C. drove again when it got the ball back. An interference call against the Irish on a long U.S.C. pass moved the ball to the Notre Dame 24. Quarterback Orvil Mohler and Shaver picked up 14 yards on one run each. Then Shaver took a pitch out from Mohler and ran 10 yards around end for the score. Baker's kick made it Notre Dame 14, U.S.C. 13.

U.S.C. got the ball again on its 28-yard line with four minutes to play. Shaver completed deep to the Notre Dame 40, then pass interference—the third such call against the Irish during the U.S.C. rally—put the ball on the Notre Dame 17. There were two minutes remaining.

Notre Dame drew a five-yard offside penalty. An end-around play lost one. A pass failed. It was third down at the 13, the ball in the middle of the field. U.S.C. called for a field goal from Baker, from the 23. The crowd of 52,000 leaned forward anxiously.

Baker, a senior guard, kicked perfectly to end Notre Dame's unbeaten string at 26. The Notre Dame *Scholastic* concluded: "It was just one of those things." The Irish went on to lose their final game of the season, 12-0, to Army, finishing the season under new coach Hunk Anderson at 6-2-1.

For the U.S.C. team, a ticker tape parade was staged in Los Angeles. A crowd estimated at 300,000 attended.

The first Irish touchdown was scored by Steve Banas, who is seen here later in the game being grappled down by Southern Cal's captain, Stan Williamson.

Great Lakes Naval Training Station 19, Notre Dame 14

November 27, 1943

A Notre Dame victory in its final game of 1943, against the strong Great Lakes service team, would give the Irish their first perfect season since 1930 and Frank Leahy's second undefeated season in three years. This game, played before an audience of 22,000 navy recruits at Great Lakes, would be Leahy's last coaching appearance before his two-year service stint.

Twice in the course of the game it appeared that Notre Dame would win. The Irish moved easily after taking the opening kickoff, driving 67 yards to score as Johnny Lujack mixed runs and passes into the flat. Jim Mello and Creighton Miller did most of the running, while Lujack scored on a quarterback sneak on fourth down. The Irish made the 7-0 lead stand up for the first half.

Great Lakes, however, drove 71 yards to score after taking the second-half kickoff. The touchdown came on a 24-yard end run by Emil Sitko, who had been a freshman at Notre Dame the previous year and would become an Irish star after the war. Former Irish standout of 1939-41, Steve Juzwik, attempted the point after touchdown, but it was blocked.

Notre Dame managed to hold its 7-6 lead until near the end of the third period when Dewey Proctor of Great Lakes broke between guard and tackle, took off down the sideline, and scored at the end of a 51-yard run. Juzwik missed the kick but Great Lakes led, 12-7.

Late in the fourth period, Notre Dame executed the best drive of the game, 80 yards, to go ahead 14-12 and seemingly win the game. Mello, Miller, and Bob Kelly carried the ball most of the time during the 20-play, eight-minute march. On fourth and two at the Great Lakes' 28, Mello swung end for four yards and a first down. Miller scored from the 1.

Only 1:06 remained when Great Lakes got the ball back at its 38-yard line, where Notre Dame purposely kicked out of bounds, which was then legal. On the first play, left halfback Steve Lach passed out of the single wing to end Cecil Pirkey to the Notre Dame 46. On the next play, Lach faded, scrambled to his left, noticed quarterback Paul Anderson running deep and unguarded, and threw to Anderson, who caught the ball at the Notre Dame 5-yard line and trotted into the end zone with just 33 seconds remaining. This time Juzwik made his kick, as if it mattered. It was 19-14, Great Lakes.

Lujack tried desperately to save the game for Notre Dame but a deep pass was intercepted by Sitko on the last play.

Despite the defeat, Notre Dame's 9-1 record and 340 total points, one of the highest offensive outputs in the school's history, merited the Irish the No. 1 national ranking.

After his freshman year at Notre Dame, Emil Sitko joined the Navy, and in a Great Lakes Naval Training Station football uniform, helped ruin his old school's perfect season. Here he is being tackled by John Yonakor and Herb Coleman.

Time has mercifully run out on the worst defeat in Notre Dame history.

Army 59, Notre Dame 0

November 11, 1944

Army had waited years for this. Thirteen to be exact. The Cadets had not beaten the Irish since 1931. They hadn't even scored against Notre Dame since 1938. This time they were ready like never before.

Led by Glenn Davis, "Mr. Outside," and Felix "Doc" Blanchard, "Mr. Inside," Army had crushed six straight opponents before taking on Notre Dame. The Cadets had scored 360 points in those games while Davis had amassed 13 touchdowns in just 26 carries. Blanchard had added six more touchdowns.

Notre Dame, defending national champion, had been decimated by graduation and loss of players to the armed services. For this wartime team, only five lettermen returned; these were supplemented by trainees in a V-12 program that had been set up on campus.

Frank Leahy had joined the navy and Ed McKeever had taken charge of the team. He had done well, winning five of the first six games and would finish the season with an 8-2 record. But most of those opponents also were weakened by the war. A 32-13 defeat by a strong Navy team the week before the Army-Notre Dame game suggested the Irish might be no match for either service school in wartime.

In addition to Davis and Blanchard, Army boasted Doug Kenna at quarterback, one of the Cadets' best backs in years; halfback Max Minor, a sprint star from the University of Texas, and guard Joe Stanowicz, intercollegiate wrestling champion in the unlimited weight class. This Army team, which would win the national championship, had 14 All-Americas and was one of the strongest college teams ever.

The Irish were overwhelmed. Kenna was largely responsible for a swift start by the Cadets. He ran for the game's first touchdown at the end of a 44-yard drive the first time Army had the ball. He intercepted a pass, setting up the second touchdown, scored by Minor. Kenna then passed for a third score. It was 20-0 and Davis hadn't even gotten into the game yet.

When Davis got his chance, he made the most of it. He intercepted a pass, returned it 41 yards to the Notre Dame 6-yard line, then ran for the touchdown on the next play. Shortly, he scored again from the 6, and it was 33-0 at the half.

Taking a punt return at his own 40 in the third period, Kenna reversed to Minor, who ran all the way to score. Kenna threw a short touchdown pass to make it 46-0. Davis scored his third touchdown, a 64-yard run after taking a direct snap through the quarterback's legs. A startled Army tackle, one Harold Tavzel, scored the last touchdown when he could not help but intercept a pass that went directly to him just a few strides from the Notre Dame goal line.

"If there was anyone to blame for the size of the margin," said Doc Blanchard, "it was Notre Dame, which fired our desire to win with its long humiliation of Army teams."

Army 48, Notre Dame 0

November 10, 1945

Army continued to be awesome in 1945. Going into the Notre Dame game, the Cadets had rolled up 773 points to their opponents' 68 since the start of the 1944 season. They were seeking their second straight win over Notre Dame, something never accomplished by Army.

Hugh Devore, filling in for Frank Leahy, had done an admirable job. The Irish had won their first five games against war-depleted squads like their own, then surprised Navy with a 6-6 tie. They would finish the season with a creditable 7-2-1 record.

Devore bravely predicted Army didn't stand a chance of repeating its 59-0 victory of the previous year. Events proved him right, though not by much.

The outcome again was quickly evident. The Cadets scored the first time they got the ball, on a Notre Dame fumble. Glenn Davis ran 26 yards to score. In the second period, Davis took a pass from Arnold Tucker along the sideline at the Notre Dame 20-yard line, faked out two defenders, and ran for his second touchdown. Doc Blanchard scored on a 1-yard plunge to give Army a 21-0 halftime lead.

Davis and Blanchard did it again in the third period. Reversing his field and shedding tacklers, Davis ran 21 yards to score. Then Blanchard intercepted a George Ratterman pass and ran 36 yards for still another touchdown. It was 35-0 and getting worse.

Then the Army substitutes ran up the score. They marched 71 yards for a touchdown, then in the closing seconds put the ball in the air against the outclassed Irish. A touchdown pass was executed with only 17 seconds to play.

The Cadets thus outscored Notre Dame 107-0 in two years. They finished the season with 18 straight victories and a second straight national championship. Like the 1944 Cadets, Army of 1945 was one of the strongest teams ever.

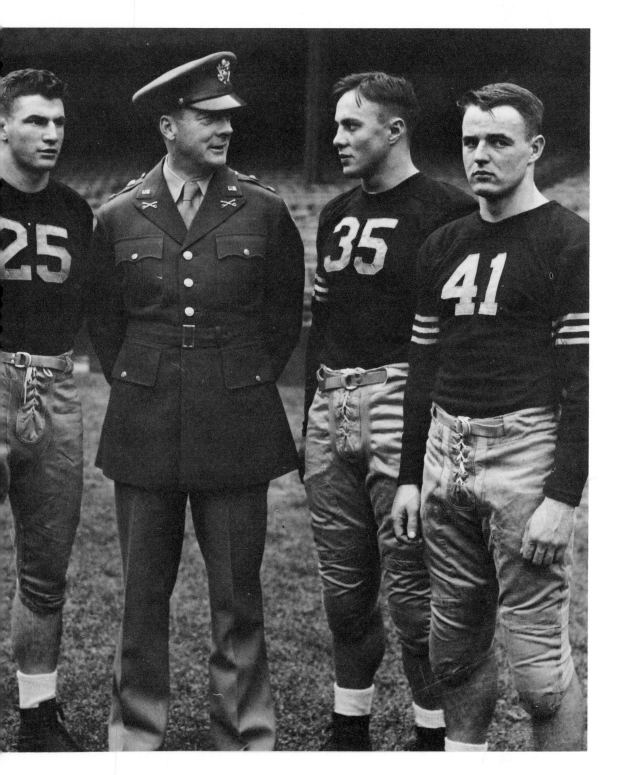

Army coach Red Blaik with his magnificent 1945 backfield, from the left: Arnold Tucker, Tom Williams, Doc Blanchard, and Glenn Davis. They had another enjoyable afternoon at the expense of Notre Dame.

Purdue 28, Notre Dame 14

October 7, 1950

Purdue, a 20-point underdog and dominated by sophomores, pulled one of the great surprises in modern football history with a one-sided 28-14 victory that ended Notre Dame's 39-game unbeaten streak. The Boilermakers did it in most convincing fashion: rolling to a 21-0 halftime lead, holding off a late Notre Dame rally, and doing it all at Notre Dame Stadium.

The hero for Purdue was 5-foot-9 sophomore quarterback Dale Samuels. He merely threw three touchdown passes in the first half that stunned most of the crowd of 56,716. On top of that, Purdue might well have scored three more touchdowns. Drives were stopped at the Notre Dame 1 and Notre Dame 7 and an 86-yard Purdue touchdown run was called back on a penalty.

At the half, Leahy told his players the obvious, that he had never addressed a team at halftime that was trailing 21-0. "If you can come back you will probably be remembered as the greatest fighting team in Notre Dame's colorful gridiron history," Leahy told them.

They did come back fighting. Bob Williams passed to Jim Mutscheller for a touchdown in the third period and John Petitbon ran 10 yards for a second score as the fourth period opened. But 21-14 was as close os the Irish were to come.

Samuels did it again. He connected with Mike Maccoli on a pass play covering 56 yards. It was 28-14, Purdue.

"We weren't especially geared up for the game," said Purdue coach Stu Holcomb. "The reason is because we didn't think we could win."

It was Notre Dame's first defeat since the final game of 1945 and its first loss at home since 1942.

Leahy told the players: "The entire world will be watching how we take adversity. It is a real test of real people to lose like champions."

There would be more defeats that year. The Irish finished with a 4-4-1 record, the only time Leahy did not produce a winning season.

Mike Maccioli stepping off long yardage against Notre Dame. All afternoon Purdue backs scampered around and between the seemingly entranced Irish.

Iowa 14, Notre Dame 14
November 21, 1953

Those who saw this game at Notre Dame Stadium would never forget it. By twice gaining time outs on feigned injuries, Notre Dame managed two desperation touchdown passes that gained a controversial 14-14 tie with Iowa.

The Irish stormed 57 yards on eight pass plays to get their second touchdown with only six seconds showing on the clock. Ralph Guglielmi threw nine yards to Dan Shannon for the score that matched an Iowa touchdown that came with only 2:06 to play.

An 11-yard Guglielmi-to-Shannon pass as time ran out in the first half gave Notre Dame its first touchdown at the end of a 12-play, 59-yard drive, equalizing a first-period touchdown by Iowa.

But both Notre Dame touchdowns followed faked injuries, which stopped the clock and gave the Irish the precious time they needed.

With 20 seconds left in the first half, and Notre Dame at the Iowa 6-yard line, Guglielmi was trapped and thrown trying to pass on the 11. With no more time outs available, Notre Dame seemed destined to watch the clock run out along with everyone else until an official spotted tackle Frank Varrichione stretched on the ground. Time was called.

After Varrichione had trotted off the field, Notre Dame lined up without a huddle and Guglielmi got off his pass to Shannon for the touchdown. Time had run out when Don Schaefer added the extra point.

History repeated itself two quarters later. As time in the game was running out, with Iowa winning, 14-7, Guglielmi again passed the Irish into scoring position. Johnny Lattner took a pass at the Iowa 9-yard line, struggled to get out of bounds, but couldn't with 30 seconds and no time outs left.

Then, more chicanery. Both Art Hunter and Don Penza "collapsed" on the ground and officials called time out. After both were "revived" and told they had to leave the game, Guglielmi twice passed incomplete in the end zone to Joe Heap, then hit Shannon with only six seconds to play.

"You can't beat the Fighting Irish for resourcefulness and preparedness for any and all eventualities and emergencies," *The New York Times* reported. However, rather than praising Leahy and the Irish, many sharply criticized such tactics, calling them unsportsmanlike and worse, and Leahy was not to hear the end of it for the rest of his days.

The tie, the only blemish on an otherwise perfect season, Leahy's last, cost the Irish the national championship, leaving them No. 2.

A dejected Frank Leahy along the sidelines, apparently unwilling to watch the futile efforts of his team. Iowa was leading 14-7 when this picture was taken.

U.S.C. 20, Notre Dame 17

November 28, 1964

All that stood between Notre Dame and its first perfect season in 15 years was an average U.S.C. team that had already been beaten three times. Though Ara Parseghian had kept repeating in his first year at Notre Dame that perfect seasons no longer were possible, nine consecutive victories put the coach in the position of being called something less than a prophet. The Irish were installed 11-point favorites to finish perfectly.

Things went according to the oddsmakers—at first. John Huarte connected on a 21-yard pass to Jack Snow following a field goal to make it 10-0, Notre Dame. Then Bill Wolski ran around end to make it 17-0 at the half. All was well for the Irish.

But then came one of those patented second-half U.S.C. rallies. The first time the Trojans got the ball they drove 68 yards in nine plays to cut the advantage to 17-7. Then two breaks hurt the Irish badly: a fumble ended a Notre Dame drive at the U.S.C. 9 and a touchdown was called back on a holding penalty.

On came the Trojans. Starting from their 8-yard line, they marched all the way to the Notre Dame 23 with the help of passes by Craig Fertig to Fred Hill and Rod Sherman and darting runs by Mike Garrett. From the Irish 23, Fertig hit Hill in the end zone to make it 17-13 with only 4½ minutes left.

U.S.C. held and got the ball back at the Notre Dame 40. A run went nowhere. Two passes failed. On fourth down, Fertig threw a desperation pass toward Sherman, who made the catch and danced into the end zone. That made it U.S.C. 20, Notre Dame 17 with 1:35 left.

A Huarte pass was intercepted, but Notre Dame held and took over for one last gasp. As time ran out, Huarte threw a long pass into the end zone toward Snow, who leaped with four U.S.C. defenders. The ball fell to the ground.

Notre Dame's 9-1 season was good for No. 3 national ranking. But this was a game Parseghian would have trouble forgetting.

Sherman looking back, perhaps in disbelief, perhaps to make sure no flag has been dropped. He's over the goal line and U.S.C. has sprung one of its most painful upsets in a series marked by startling reversals.

Michigan State 10, Notre Dame 10

November 19, 1966

Rarely, except for events such as Pearl Harbor, has a nation come to attention as it did for this game. Two of the best teams ever assembled—Notre Dame, an 8-0 record, ranked No. 1, coming off 40-0 and 64-0 victories, and Michigan State, 9-0, ranked No. 2, winner of 19 straight regular-season games. The Irish boasted the incredible total of 11 All-Americas, more than any squad in their history. They were 4½-point favorites.

There was organized fury under the golden dome on the Notre Dame campus as students worked into a frenzy for the game in East Lansing. Bedsheet banners, hung from dormitory windows, included a 50-foot inscription to Spartan coach Duffy Daugherty: "Duffy's Fate: Second Rate." A 50-foot high numeral "I," constructed by a student, collapsed.

Sports writers swarmed the football offices. Ara Parseghian held court beneath a portrait of the legendary Rockne. Linebacker Pete Duranko declared, "Saturday is the end of a dream." End Jim Seymour, *Time* Magazine cover boy along with quarterback Terry Hanratty, wondered why all the excitement. Just a sophomore, he was too young to understand, some of his elders realized.

Then unfolded some of the strangest doings in college history, ending with Parseghian's highly controversial decision to run out the clock, play for a tie, and preserve the No. 1 ranking and right to a national championship. The coach was widely criticized for taking the easy way out. "What's he do in the future—tell them to tie one for the Gipper?" asked a critic.

Things started to go wrong for Notre Dame when star halfback Nick Eddy, upon arriving in East Lansing, slipped on the steps of the Irish train and fell on an already injured right shoulder; he was out of the game. Then Michigan State's huge Bubba Smith, reacting to large buttons worn by Spartan supporters that read "Kill, Bubba, kill," finished Hanratty with a separated left shoulder.

Michigan State roared off to a 10-0 lead to the delight of most of the 80,011 watching. But Coley O'Brien, Hanratty's diminutive and diabetic backup, saved the Irish. He threw a 34-yard scoring pass to Eddy's backup, Bob Gladieux, and directed a 70-yard drive to set up a tying field goal.

At the finish, Parseghian ordered several running plays in Notre Dame territory, fearing an interception would put Michigan State's barefooted kicker, Dick Kenney, in winning field goal position. State players taunted the Irish, calling them sissies and calling time-outs as well in an effort to get the ball back. "We couldn't believe it," said Spartan co-captain George Webster of the Irish strategy.

Neither could a lot of people. Parseghian got his national championship, though his conservatism cost him may votes in the AP and UPI polls. "Time will prove everything that has happened here today," Parseghian told his players in the locker room in defense of his strategy. But people have not forgotten.

Before he joined the list of injured regulars that included Hanratty, Eddy, and George Goeddeke, Bob "Rocky" Bleier tried the middle of the Michigan State line with only modest success. George Webster (90) and George Chatlos (82) combined to make the tackle.

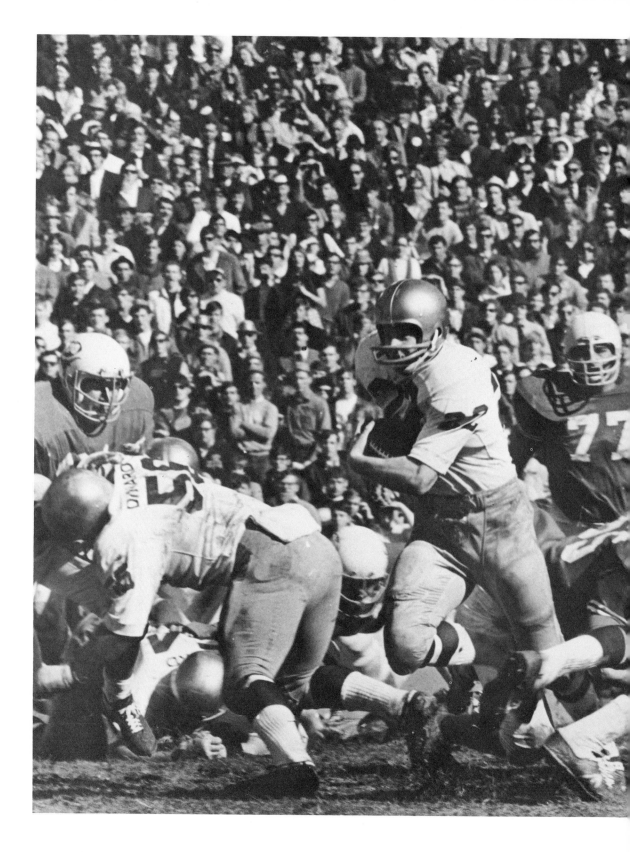

Texas 21, Notre Dame 17

January 1, 1970

This was Notre Dame's first bowl appearance since 1925. It was the 34th Cotton Bowl and No. 1 ranked Texas was a seven-point favorite. Texas had won 19 straight games since James Street had taken over as quarterback. The Irish had finished their regular season 8-1-1. One reason they accepted the bid was money. The Notre Dame treasury would be fattened by about $340,000 from game revenues. The money was earmarked for construction of academic facilities for minority groups and scholarships.

For added support, Notre Dame took along three of the Four Horsemen, all then living. In the week leading up to the game, the coaches tried to out-dirge each other. Parseghian bemoaned the lack of practice time, injuries to offensive players, and the immense size of the Texas players. His counterpart, Darrell Royal, fretted about the prospect of a slippery field.

All that was forgotten amid a twelfth man episode that might have cost Notre Dame the victory. The controversial play came late in the first half with Texas leading 10-7. With Texas putting the ball in play on its own 12-yard line, a Longhorn lineman came running on the field, waving his arms wildly. Before he reached the line of scrimmage, the ball was snapped, Street fumbled, and the Irish recovered at the Texas 6-yard line. Or so they thought.

The late-arriving Texas lineman claimed he had called time out before the snap and was upheld by the officials, thus denying Notre Dame a scoring opportunity just before the half. "It was one of those crazy, unusual plays," said a dejected Parseghian after the game. "But it's history now and there's nothing we can do about it."

Then, too, the Irish had their chances. They took a 10-7 first-half lead on the arm of quarterback Joe Theismann, who completed 10 of his first 13 passes. But in the third period, the Longhorns shut down Theismann while their Wishbone T offense, directed by Street, asserted itself. Eighteen straight running plays produced a 14-10 Texas lead.

Notre Dame roared back for a 21-17 advantage but Texas staged still another rally in the game's final minutes. Led by Street, who worked the triple option to perfection, the Longhorns used 15 running plays and two key passes to preserve their No. 1 national ranking.

Former President Johnson offered locker room congratulations to Texas, condolances to Notre Dame.

Taking the play away from the ball-control Texas wishbone, Notre Dame ground out yardage in the first half, behind solid blocking such as seen here, in advance of Denny Allan's 19-yard first quarter gallop.

U.S.C. 55, Notre Dame 24

November 30, 1974

How could it be possible that any team not equipped with knives or guns score 55 straight points on the Fighting Irish? Yet it happened. After Notre Dame took a 24-0 lead, Southern California positively blackened Ara Parseghian's last regular-season coaching day with a blitz of points that prompted second thoughts by the coach about retiring—until he recovered from the immediate shock.

As far as forgetting the disaster entirely, that remains beyond Parseghian's capacity. He, and Irish followers everywhere, will never forget it. In just 17 minutes, U.S.C. scored eight touchdowns and 55 points, 26 by Anthony Davis, who finished his career with 11 touchdowns against Notre Dame. There are whole teams that have never scored 11 touchdowns against Notre Dame.

Actually, the game was not as close as the score indicated. This was because it appeared that U.S.C. would go on scoring forever until coach John McKay pulled out his first stringers. Mass substitutions insured that U.S.C. would fall just four points short of the most ever run up against Notre Dame, by Army in 1944.

It started out a perfect day for the Irish in the Los Angeles Coliseum. Quarterback Tom Clements directed them to three touchdowns, including a 29-yard play, and a field goal. Nobody suspected a thing when U.S.C.'s Davis took a short pass from quarterback Pat Haden for a touchdown in the final seconds of the first half.

But then Davis returned the second-half kickoff 102 yards for a touchdown. Then he ran six yards for a touchdown. Then four yards for a touchdown after a Notre Dame fumble. Then two yards for a two-point conversion. That made it U.S.C. 27, Davis 26, Notre Dame 24. And the Trojans weren't finished. Haden added two more touchdowns on passes to the coach's son, Johnny McKay, and another scoring pass to Shelton Diggs. When Charles Phillips intercepted his third pass and returned it 58 yards to score, coach McKay called off the slaughter.

"The greatest, most incredible game," Davis said afterward. "We had some magic. We turned into madmen."

"We've never played a good second half out here," said Parseghian, who went on to suggest that because the U.S.C. game on the West Coast usually comes at the end of the season the Irish have to prepare as best they can in extremely cold weather. "The cold weather seems to thicken the blood or something," said the coach, adding that he favored October meetings on the Coast for the future.

"I still don't know what happened," U.S.C. coach John McKay told reporters in the dressing room. "I can't understand it. I'm going to sit down tonight and have a beer and think about it. Against Notre Dame? Maybe against Kent State. But Notre Dame?"

Orchestrating the rout was John McKay, who made it plain that the 51-0 loss to Notre Dame in 1966 made every subsequent game against the Irish an opportunity for revenge.

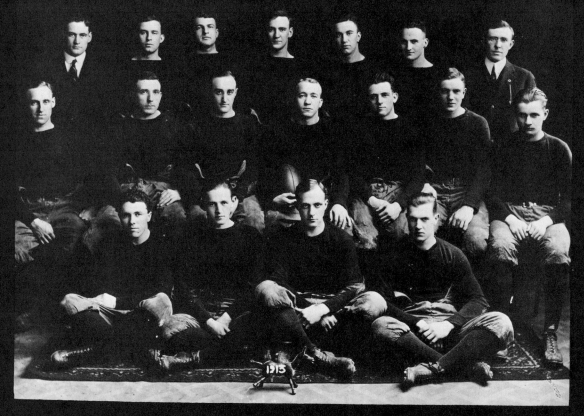

The interlopers from the West: the 1913 Notre Dame football squad. In front (left to right) are Mal Edward, Al Bergman, Bill Cook, and Arthur Larkin. Middle row (L-R), Ralph Lathrop, Keith Jones, Joe Pliska, Captain Knute Rockne, Charley Dorais, Fred Gushurst, and Al Feeney. Top row (L-R), Cap Edwards, Emmett Keefe, Ray Eichenlaub, Al King, Freeman Fitzgerald, Charles Finegan, and Coach Jesse Harper.

A review of each season follows, including scores of all games, names of captains and coaches, playing sites, notations as to unusual weather conditions, upsets, and in the case of last-second heroics, the time remaining when the decisive score was made. Also listed are the recipients of major awards, and players named to All-America teams. Notre Dame's annual UP and AP rankings are also given. The AP team, named by sportswriters, began in 1936; the UP rankings, voted by college coaches, first appeared in 1950. Players indicated with a dagger † were unanimous first team selections.

Notre Dame
All-Time
Football Record

KEY TO ABBREVIATIONS

AA	All-America Board
AP	Associated Press
C	Walter Camp (In *Collier's* magazine in 1925)
COL	*Collier's* magazine (Walter Camp's selections to 1925; Grantland Rice 1925-47; American Football Coaches Association 1948-56)
CP	Central Press (1963-70 only)
FBW	*Football World* magazine
FC	American Football Coaches Association (In *Collier's* 1948-56)
FN	*Football News*
FW	Football Writers' Association (In *Look* magazine, 1946-71)
INS	International News Service (merged with United Press in 1958)
L	*Look* magazine (Football Writers' Association selections from 1946)
LIB	*Liberty* magazine
NA	North American Newspaper Alliance
NEA	Newspaper Enterprise Association
NW	*Newsweek* magazine
SN	*Sporting News* (unofficial from 1965)
T	*Time* magazine (unofficial)
UP	United Press (merged with INS in 1958)
UPI	United Press International (merger of INS and UP in 1958)
WCF	Walter Camp Football Foundation
S-O-N-D	Month: September, October, November, December
W-L-T	Game won, lost or tied
H	Home game
A	Away game, played at opponent's home stadium
N	Game played at a neutral site; see footnote for city
Nt	Night game
YS	Game played at Yankee Stadium, New York
HC	Homecoming game
TH	Game played on Thanksgiving Day
R	Game played in rain
S	Game played in snow
U	Major upset
0:00	Time remaining in games decided in the final minutes; In case of ties, time followed by team scoring last
C	Capacity crowd

†Unanimous selection on official teams

SCORING VALUES

Seasons	Touch-down	Field Goal	Point After	Safety
1887-1897	4 points	5 points	2 points	2 points
1898-1903	5 points	5 points	1 point	2 points
1904-1908	5 points	4 points	1 point	2 points
1909-1911	5 points	3 points	1 point	2 points
1912-1957	6 points	3 points	1 point	2 points
1958 to date	6 points	3 points	1 point for kick	2 points
			2 points for run	
			or pass	

1887
Coach: None
Captain: Henry Luhn
N.23	L	Michigan	0-8	H
		(0-1-0)		

1888
Coach: None
Captain: Edward C. Prudhomme
Apr.20	L	Michigan	6-24	H
Apr.21	L	Michigan	4-10	H
D.6	W	Harvard School (Chi.)	20-0	H
		(1-2-0)	30-34	

1889
Coach: None
Captain: Edward C. Prudhomme
N.14	W	Northwestern	9-0	A
		(1-0-0)		

1890-1891 — No team

1892
Coach: None
Captain: Patrick H. Coady
O.19	W	South Bend H.S.	56-0	H
N.24TH	T	Hillsdale	10-10	H
		(1-0-1)	66-10	

1893
Coach: None
Captain: Frank M. Keough
O.25	W	Kalamazoo	34-0	H
N.11	W	Albion	8-6	H
N.23	W	DeLaSalle (S)	28-0	H
N.30TH	W	Hillsdale (S)	22-10	H
J.1'94	L	Chicago	0-8	A
		(4-1-0)	92-24	

1894

Coach: James L. Morison
Captain: Frank M. Keough

O.13	W	Hillsdale	14-0	H
O.20	T	Albion	6-6	H
N.15	W	Wabash	30-0	H
N.22	W	Rush Medical	18-6	H
N.29TH	L	Albion	12-19	H
		(3-1-1)	80-31	

1895

Coach: H. G. Hadden
Captain: Daniel V. Casey

O.19	W	Northwestern Law	20-0	H
N.7	W	Illinois Cycling Club	18-2	H
N.22	L	Indpls. Artillery (S)	0-18	H
N.28TH	W	Chicago Phys. & Surg.	32-0	H
		(3-1-0)	70-20	

1896

Coach: Frank E. Hering
Captain: Frank E. Hering

O.8	L	Chicago Phys. & Surg.	0-4	H
O.14	L	Chicago	0-18	H
O.27	W	S.B. Commercial A.C.	46-0	H
O.31	W	Albion	24-0	H
N.14	L	Purdue	22-28	H
N.20	W	Highland Views	82-0	H
N.26TH	W	Beloit (R)	8-0	H
		(4-3-0)	182-50	

1897

Coach: Frank E. Hering
Captain: John I. Mullen

O.13	T	Rush Medical	0-0	H
O.23	W	DePauw	4-0	H
O.28	W	Chicago Dental Surg.	62-0	H
N.6	L	Chicago	5-34	A
N.13	W	St. Viator	60-0	H
N.25TH	W	Michigan State (R)	34-6	H
		(4-1-1)	165-40	

1898

Coach: Frank E. Hering
Captain: John I. Mullen

O.8	W	Illinois	5-0	A
O.15	W	Michigan State	53-0	H
O.23	L	Michigan	0-23	A
O.29	W	DePauw	32-0	H
N.11	L	Indiana	5-11	H
N.19	W	Albion	60-0	A
		(4-2-0)	155-34	

1899

Coach: James McWeeney
Captain: John I. Mullen

S.27	W	Englewood H.S.	29-5	H
S.30	W	Michigan State	40-0	H
O.4	L	Chicago	6-23	A
O.14	W	Lake Forest	38-0	H
O.18	L	Michigan	0-12	A
O.23	W	Indiana	17-0	H
O.27	W	Northwestern (R)	12-0	H
N.4	W	Rush Medical	17-0	H
N.18	T	Purdue	10-10	A
N.30TH	L	Chicago Phys. & Surg.	0-5	H
		(6-3-1)	169-55	

1900

Coach: Pat O'Dea
Captain: John F. Farley

S.29	W	Goshen	55-0	H
O.6	W	Englewood H.S.	68-0	H
O.13	W	S.B. Howard Park	64-0	H
O.20	W	Cincinnati	58-0	H
O.25	L	Indiana	0-6	A
N.3	T	Beloit	6-6	H
N.10	L	Wisconsin	0-54	A
N.17	L	Michigan	0-7	A
N.24	W	Rush Medical (R)	5-0	H
N.29TH	W	Chicago Phys. & Surg.	5-0	H
		(6-3-1)	261-73	

1901

Coach: Pat O'Dea
Captain: Albert C. Fortin

S.28	T	South Bend A.C.	0-0	H
O.5	W	Ohio Medical U.	6-0	A
O.12	L	Northwestern (R)	0-2	A
O.19	W	Chicago Medical Col.	32-0	H
O.26	W	Beloit	5-0	A
N.2	W	Lake Forest	16-0	H
N.9	W	Purdue	12-6	H
N.16	W	Indiana (R)	18-5	H
N.23	W	Chicago Phys. & Surg.	34-0	H
N.28TH	W	South Bend A.C.	22-6	H
		(8-1-1)	145-19	

1902

Coach: James F. Faragher
Captain: Louis J. Salmon

S.27	W	Michigan State	33-0	H
O.11	W	Lake Forest	28-0	H
O.18	L	Michigan	0-23	N
O.25	W	Indiana	11-5	A
N.1	W	Ohio Medical U.	6-5	A
N.8	L	Knox	5-12	A
N.15	W	American Medical	92-0	H

N.22	W	DePauw	22-0	H	
N.27TH	T	Purdue	6-6	A	
		(6-2-1)	203-51		

N—at Toledo

1903

Coach: James F. Faragher
Captain: Louis J. Salmon

O.3	W	Michigan State	12-0	H
O.10	W	Lake Forest	28-0	H
O.17	W	DePauw (R)	56-0	H
O.24	W	American Medical	52-0	H
O.29	W	Chicago Phys. & Surg.	46-0	H
N.7	W	Missouri Osteopaths	28-0	H
N.14	T	Northwestern	0-0	A
N.21	W	Ohio Medical U.	35-0	A
N.26TH	W	Wabash	35-0	A
		(8-0-1)	292-0	

1904

Coach: Louis J. Salmon
Captain: Frank J. Shaughnessy

O.1	W	Wabash	12-4	H
O.8	W	American Medical	44-0	H
O.15	L	Wisconsin	0-58	N
O.22	W	Ohio Medical U.	17-5	A
O.27	W	Toledo A.A.	6-0	H
N.5	L	Kansas	5-24	A
N.19	W	DePauw	10-0	H
N.24TH	L	Purdue	0-36	A
		(5-3-0)	94-127	

N—at Milwaukee

1905

Coach: Henry J. McGlew
Captain: Patrick A. Beacom

S.30	W	N. Division H.S. (Chi.)	44-0	H
O.7	W	Michigan State	28-0	H
O.14	L	Wisconsin	0-21	N
O.21	L	Wabash	0-5	H
O.28	W	*American Medical	142-0	H
N.4	W	DePauw	71-0	H
N.11	L	Indiana	5-22	A
N.18	W	Bennett Med. Col. Chi.	22-0	H
N.24	L	Purdue	0-32	A
		(5-4-0)	312-80	

N—at Milwaukee
*After a 25-minute first half, with Notre Dame leading, 121-0, the second half was shortened to only 8 minutes to permit the "Doctors" time to eat before catching a train to Chicago. Notre Dame scored 27 touchdowns, but missed 20 extra points.

1906

Coach: Thomas A. Barry
Captain: Robert L. Bracken

O.6	W	Franklin	26-0	H
O.13	W	Hillsdale	17-0	H
O.20	W	Chi. Phys. & Surg.	28-0	H
O.27	W	Michigan State	5-0	H
N.3	W	Purdue	2-0	A
N.10	L	Indiana	0-12	N
N.24	W	Beloit (R)	29-0	H
		(6-1-0)	107-12	

N—at Indianapolis

1907

Coach: Thomas A. Barry
Captain: Dominic L. Callicrate

O.12	W	Chi. Phys. & Surg. (R)	32-0	H
O.19	W	Franklin	23-0	H
O.26	W	Olivet	22-4	H
N.2	T	Indiana	0-0	H
N.9	W	Knox	22-4	H
N.23	W	Purdue	17-0	H
N.28TH	W	St. Vincent's (Chi.)	21-12	A
		(6-0-1)	137-20	

1908

Coach: Victor M. Place
Captain: M. Harry Miller

O.3	W	Hillsdale	39-0	H
O.10	W	Franklin	64-0	H
O.17	L	Michigan	6-12	A
O.24	W	Chicago Phys. & Surg.	88-0	H
O.29	W	Ohio Northern	58-4	H
N.7	W	Indiana	11-0	N
N.13	W	Wabash	8-4	A
N.18	W	St. Viator	46-0	H
N.26TH	W	Marquette	6-0	A
		(8-1-0)	326-20	

N—at Indianapolis

1909*

Coach: Frank C. Longman
Captain: Howard Edwards

O.9	W	Olivet	58-0	H
O.16	W	Rose Poly	60-11	H
O.23	W	Michigan State	17-0	H
O.30	W	Pittsburgh	6-0	A
N.6	W	Michigan (U)	11-3	A
N.13	W	Miami (Ohio)	46-0	H
N.20	W	Wabash	38-0	H
N.25TH	T	Marquette	0-0	A
		(7-0-1)	236-14	

*"The Notre Dame Victory March" was introduced this season.

1910
Coach: Frank C. Longman
Captain: Ralph Dimmick

O.8	W	Olivet	48-0	H
O.22	W	Butchel (Akron)	51-0	H
N.5	L	Michigan State	0-17	A
N.12	W	Rose Poly	41-3	A
N.19	*W	Ohio Northern	47-0	H
N.24TH	T	Marquette	5-5	A
		(4-1-1)	192-25	

*Notre Dame's 100th victory

1911
Coach: John L. Marks
Captain: Luke L. Kelly

O.7	W	Ohio Northern	32-6	H
O.14	W	St. Viator	43-0	H
O.21	W	Butler (R)	27-0	H
O.28	W	Loyola (Chi.)	80-0	H
N.4	T	Pittsburgh	0-0	A
N.11	W	St. Bonaventure	34-0	H
N.20	W	Wabash	6-3	A
N.30TH	T	Marquette	0-0	A
		(6-0-2)	222-9	

1912
Coach: John L. Marks
Captain: Charles E. (Gus) Dorais

O.5	W	St. Viator	116-7	H
O.12	W	Adrian	74-7	H
O.19	W	Morris Harvey	39-0	H
O.26	W	Wabash	41-6	H
N.2	W	Pittsburgh (S)	3-0	A
N.9	W	St. Louis	47-7	A
N.28TH	W	Marquette	69-0	N
		(7-0-0)	389-27	

N—at Chicago

1913
Coach: Jesse C. Harper
Captain: Knute K. Rockne

O.4	W	Ohio Northern	87-0	H
O.18	W	South Dakota	20-7	H
O.25	W	Alma	62-0	H
N.1	W	Army (U)	35-13	A
N.7	W	Penn State (R)	14-7	A
N.22	W	Christian Bros. (St.L.)	20-7	A
N.27TH	W	Texas	30-7	A
		(7-0-0)	268-41	

Gus Dorais (QB)	INS (1)	
Ray Eichenlaub (FB)	C (2)	

1914
Coach: Jesse C. Harper
Captain: Keith K. Jones

O.3	W	Alma	56-0	H
O.10	W	Rose Poly	103-0	H
O.17	L	Yale	0-28	A
O.24	W	South Dakota	33-0	N1
O.31	W	Haskell	20-7	H
N.7	L	Army	7-20	A
N.14	W	Carlisle	48-6	N2
N.26TH	W	Syracuse	20-0	A
		(6-2-0)	287-61	

N1—at Sioux Falls; N2—at Chicago

1915
Coach: Jesse C. Harper
Captain: Freeman C. Fitzgerald

O.2	W	Alma	32-0	H
O.9	W	Haskell	34-0	H
O.23	L	Nebraska	19-20	A
O.30	W	South Dakota	6-0	H
N.6	W	Army	7-0	A
N.13	W	Creighton	41-0	A
N.25TH	W	Texas	36-7	A
N.27	W	Rice	55-2	A
		(7-1-0)	230-29	

1916
Coach: Jesse C. Harper
Captain: Stan Cofall

S.30	W	Case Tech	48-0	H
O.7	W	Western Reserve	48-0	A
O.14	W	Haskell	26-0	H
O.28	W	Wabash	60-0	H
N.4	L	Army	10-30	A
N.11	W	South Dakota	21-0	N
N.18	W	Michigan State	14-0	A
N.25	W	Alma	46-0	H
N.30TH	W	Nebraska	20-0	A
		(8-1-0)	293-30	

N—at Sioux Falls

Stan Cofall (HB)	INS (1)	
Charlie Bachman (G)	C (2)	

1917
Coach: Jesse C. Harper
Captain: James Phelan

O.6	W	Kalamazoo	55-0	H
O.13	T	Wisconsin	0-0	A
O.20	L	Nebraska	0-7	A
O.27	W	South Dakota (R)	40-0	H
N.3	W	Army (U)	7-2	A
N.10	W	Morningside	13-0	A

N.17   W   Michigan State   23-0   H
N.24   W   Wash. & Jefferson   3-0   A

N.17	W	Michigan State	23-0	H
N.24	W	Wash. & Jefferson	3-0	A
		(6-1-1)	141-9	

Frank Rydzewski (C)   INS, NEA (1); C (2)

1918
Coach: Knute K. Rockne
Captain: Leonard Bahan

S.28	W	Case Tech	26-6	A
N.2	W	Wabash	67-7	A
N.9	T	Great Lakes	7-7	H
N.16	L	Mich. State (U) (R)	7-13	A
N.23	W	Purdue	26-6	A
N.28TH	T	Nebraska (S)	0-0	A
		(3-1-2)	133-39	

1919
Coach: Knute K. Rockne
Captain: Leonard Bahan

O.4	W	Kalamazoo	14-0	H	5,000
O.11	W	Mount Union	60-7	H	4,000
O.18	W	Nebraska	14-9	A	10,000
O.25	W	Western St. Nor.	53-0	H	2,500
N.1	W	Indiana (R)	16-3	N	5,000
N.8	W	Army	12-9	A	8,000
N.15	W	Michigan State	13-0	H	5,000
N.22	W	Purdue	33-13	A	7,000
N.27TH	W	Morningside (S)	14-6	A	10,000
		(9-0-0)	229-47		56,500

N—at Indianapolis

1920
Coach: Knute K. Rockne
Captain: Frank Coughlin

O.2	W	Kalamazoo	39-0	H	5,000
O.9	W	Western St. Nor.	42-0	H	3,500
O.16	W	Nebraska	16-7	A	9,000
O.23	W	Valparaiso	28-3	A	8,000
O.30	W	Army	27-17	A	10,000
N.6	W	Purdue (HC)	28-0	H	12,000
N.13	W	Indiana	13-10	N	14,000
N.20	W	*Northwestern	33-7	A	c20,000
N.25TH	W	Michigan State	25-0	A	8,000
		(9-0-0)	251-44		89,500

N—at Indianapolis
*George Gipp's last game. He contracted a strep throat and died from complications of the disease on December 14 at the age of 25.

George Gipp (HB)   C, INS (1); NEA (1)
Roger Kiley (E)   INS (1)

1921
Coach: Knute K. Rockne
Captain: Edward N. Anderson

S.24	W	Kalamazoo	56-0	H	8,000
O.1	W	DePauw	57-10	H	8,000
O.8	L	Iowa (U)	7-10	A	7,500

O.15	W	Purdue	33-0	A	7,500
O.22	W	Nebraska (HC)	7-0	H	14,000
O.29	W	Indiana	28-7	N1	10,000
N.5	W	Army	28-0	A	7,000
N.8	W	Rutgers	48-0	N2	12,000
N.12	W	Haskell	42-7	H	5,000
N.19	W	Marquette	21-7	A	11,000
N.24TH	W	Michigan State	48-0	H	15,000
		(10-1-0)	375-41		105,000

N1—at Indianapolis; N2—at Polo Grounds, New York City, on Election Day

Roger Kiley (E)   INS (1); NEA (1); C (2)
Eddie Anderson (E)   FBW (1); INS (2)
Hunk Anderson (G)   INS (1)
Johnny Mohardt (HB)   C (2)
Paul Castner (HB)   INS (2)

1922
Coach: Knute K. Rockne
Captain: Glen Carberry

S.30	W	Kalamazoo	46-0	H	5,000
O.7	W	St. Louis	26-0	H	7,000
O.14	W	Purdue	20-0	A	9,000
O.21	W	DePauw	34-7	A	5,000
O.28	W	Georgia Tech	13-3	A	20,000
N.4	W	Indiana (HC)	27-0	H	c22,000
N.11	T	Army	0-0	A	15,000
N.18	W	Butler	31-3	A	12,000
N.25	W	Carnegie Tech (S)	19-0	A	30,000
N.30TH	L	Nebraska	6-14	A	16,000
		(8-1-1)	222-27		141,000

Ed DeGree (G)   INS (1)

1923
Coach: Knute K. Rockne
Captain: Harvey Brown

S.29	W	Kalamazoo	74-0	H	10,000
O.6	W	Lombard	14-0	H	8,000
O.13	W	Army	13-0	N	c30,000
O.20	W	Princeton	25-2	A	30,000
O.27	W	Georgia Tech	35-7	H	20,000
N.3	W	Purdue (HC)	34-7	H	20,000
N.10	L	Nebraska (U)	7-14	A	30,000
N.17	W	Butler	34-7	H	10,000
N.24	W	Carnegie Tech	26-0	A	30,000
N.29TH	W	St. Louis (R)	13-0	A	9,000
		(9-1-0)	275-37		197,000

N—at Ebbets Field, Brooklyn

Don Miller (HB)   INS (1)
Elmer Layden (FB)   INS (2)
Harvey Brown (G)   C (2)

1924
Coach: Knute K. Rockne
Captain: Adam Walsh

O.4	W	Lombard	40-0	H	8,000
O.11	W	Wabash	34-0	H	10,000
O.18	W	Army	13-7	N1	c55,000

O.25	W	Princeton	12-0	A	40,000
N.1	*W	Georgia Tech (HC)	34-3	H	c22,000
N.8	W	Wisconsin	38-3	A	28,425
N.15	W	Nebraska	34-6	H	c22,000
N.22	W	Northwestern	13-6	N2	45,000
N.29	W	Carnegie Tech	40-19	A	35,000
		(9-0-0)	258-44		265,425

ROSE BOWL

Jan.1	W	Stanford	27-10	N3	c53,000

N1—at Polo Grounds; N2—at Soldier Field; N3—at Pasadena, Calif.
*Notre Dame's 200th victory

Harry Stuhldreher (QB)	C, AA, INS, NEA, LIB (1)
Jim Crowley (HB)	AA, INS, NEA, FBW (1); C (2)
Elmer Layden (FB)	AA, INS, LIB (1)
Adam Walsh (C)	INS, NEA (2)

1925
Coach: Knute K. Rockne
Captain: Clem Crowe

S.26	W	Baylor (R)	41-0	H	13,000
O.3	W	Lombard	69-0	H	10,000
O.10	W	Beloit	19-3	H	10,000
O.17	L	Army	0-27	YS	c65,000
O.24	W	Minnesota	19-7	A	c49,000
O.31	W	Georgia Tech (R)	13-0	A	12,000
N.7	T	Penn State (R)	0-0	A	c20,000
N.14	W	Carnegie Tech (HC)	26-0	H	c27,000
N.21	W	Northwestern	13-10	H	c27,000
N.26TH	L	Nebraska (U)	0-17	A	c45,000
		(7-2-1)	200-64		278,000

1926
Coach: Knute K. Rockne
Co-Captains: Eugene Edwards and
  Thomas Hearden

O.2	W	Beloit	77-0	H	8,000
O.9	W	Minnesota	20-7	A	c48,648
O.16	W	Penn State (R)	28-0	H	18,000
O.23	W	Northwestern	6-0	A	c41,000
O.30	W	Georgia Tech (R)	12-0	H	11,000
N.6	W	Indiana	26-0	H	20,000
N.13	W	Army	7-0	YS	c63,029
N.20	W	Drake (HC) (S)	21-0	H	20,000
N.27	L	Carnegie Tech (U)	0-19	A	c45,000
D.4	W	So. Calif. (2:00)	13-12	A	c74,378
		(9-1-0)	210-38		349,055

	AP	UP	NEA	INS	COL	AA
Art Boeringer, C	1	2	1	1	1	1
Christy Flanagan, HB						2

1927
Coach: Knute K. Rockne
Captain: John P. Smith

O.1	W	Coe (R)	28-7	H	10,000
O.8	W	Detroit	20-0	A	c28,000
O.15	W	Navy	19-6	N1	45,101
O.22	W	Indiana	19-6	A	16,000

O.29	W	Georgia Tech	26-7	H	17,000
N.5	T	Minn. (S) (1:00-M)	7-7	H	25,000
N.12	L	Army	0-18	YS	c65,678
N.19	W	Drake	32-0	A	8,412
N.26	W	So. California	7-6	N2	*c120,000
		(7-1-1)	158-57		335,191

*Paid attendance: 99,573
N1—at Baltimore; N2—at Soldier Field

	AP	UP	NEA	INS	COL	AA	NA
Christy Flanagan, HB	1	1					
John Smith, G	1	1	1	1	1	1	2
John Polisky, T							2

1928
Coach: Knute K. Rockne
Captain: Frederick Miller

S.29	W	Loyola (N.O.)	12-6	A	15,000
O.6	L	Wisconsin	6-22	A	29,885
O.13	W	Navy	7-0	N1	*c120,000
O.20	L	Georgia Tech	0-13	A	c35,000
O.27	W	Drake	32-6	H	12,000
N.3	W	Penn State (R)	9-0	N2	30,000
N.10	W	Army (U) (2:30)	12-6	YS	c78,188
N.17	L	Carnegie Tech (R)	7-27	H†	c27,000
D.1	L	So. California	14-27	A	c72,632
		(5-4-0)	99-107		419,705

*Paid attendance: 103,081
†First defeat at home since 1905
N1—at Soldier Field; N2—at Philadelphia

	INS
Fred Miller, T	1

1929†
Coach: Knute K. Rockne
Captain: John Law

O.5	W	Indiana	14-0	A	16,111
O.12	W	Navy	14-7	N1	c64,681
O.19	W	Wisconsin	19-0	N2	90,000
O.26	W	Carnegie Tech	7-0	A	c66,000
N.2	W	Georgia Tech	26-6	A	22,000
N.9	W	Drake	19-7	N2	50,000
N.16	W	So. California	13-12	N2	*c112,912
N.23	W	Northwestern	26-6	A	c50,000
N.30	W	Army	7-0	YS	c79,408
		(9-0-0)	145-38		551,112

†No home games; Notre Dame Stadium was under construction
*Paid attendance: 99,351
N1—at Baltimore; N2—at Soldier Field

	AP	UP	NEA	INS	COL	AA	NA
†Frank Carideo, QB	1	1	1	1	1	1	1
Jack Cannon, G	1	1	1	1	1	1	
Ted Twomey, T	2		2				

1930
Coach: Knute K. Rockne
Captain: Thomas Conley

O.4	W	S.M.U. (4:00)	20-14	H	14,751
O.11	W	Navy†	26-2	H	40,593
O.18	W	Carnegie Tech	21-6	H	30,009
O.25	W	Pittsburgh	35-19	A	c66,586

N.1	W	Indiana	27-0	H	11,113	
N.8	W	Pennsylvania	60-20	A	c75,657	
N.15	W	Drake	28-7	H	10,106	
N.22	W	Northwestern	14-0	A	c44,648	
N.29	W	Army (R-S) (3:30)	7-6	N1	*c103,310	
D.6	W	So. California (U)	27-0	A	c73,967	
		(10-0-0)	265-74		470,740	

†Dedication of Notre Dame Stadium
*Paid attendance: 103,310
N1—at Soldier Field

	AP	UP	NEA	INS	COL	AA	NA
†Frank Carideo, QB	1	1	1	1	1	1	1
Marchy Schwartz, HB	1	1	1	1			1
Marty Brill, HB				2		1	2
Joe Savoldi, FB	2						
Bert Metzger, G	1	1					2
Tom Conley, E	2	2	2				
Al Culver, T			2				

1931†

Coach: Heartley W. (Hunk) Anderson
Captain: Thomas Yarr

O.3	W	Indiana	25-0	A	12,098
O.10	T	Northwestern (R)	0-0	N1	65,000
O.17	W	Drake	63-0	H	23,835
O.24	W	Pittsburgh	25-12	H	37,394
O.31	W	Carnegie Tech	19-0	A	42,271
N.7	W	Pennsylvania	49-0	H	39,173
N.14	W	Navy	20-0	N2	56,861
N.21	L	So. Calif. (U)(1:00)	14-16	H	*50,731
N.28	L	Army (U)	0-12	YS	c78,559
		(6-2-1)	215-40		404,922

*First capacity crowd in Notre Dame Stadium
N1—at Soldier Field; N2—at Baltimore
†Coach Knute K. Rockne, 43, and seven other persons were killed in a plane crash near Bazaar, Kansas, on March 31, 1931.

	AP	UP	NEA	INS	COL	AA	NA	LIB
†Marchy Schwartz, HB	1	1	1	1	1	1	1	1
Joe Kurth, T	2	1	1	2			1	1
Tommy Yarr, C	1	2		1		1	2	2
Nordy Hoffman, G	1		2	2			2	1

1932

Coach: Heartley W. (Hunk) Anderson
Captain: Paul A. Host

O.8	W	Haskell	73-0	H	8,369
O.15	W	Drake	62-0	H	6,663
O.22	W	Carnegie Tech	42-0	H	16,015
O.29	L	Pittsburgh (U)	0-12	A	55,616
N.5	W	Kansas	24-6	A	18,062
N.12	W	Northwestern	21-0	H	31,853
N.19	W	Navy	12-0	N	61,122
N.26	W	Army	21-0	YS	c78,115
D.10	L	So. California	0-13	A	93,924
		(7-2-0)	255-31		369,739

N—at Cleveland

	AP	UP	NEA	INS	COL	AA	NA	LIB
†Joe Kurth, T	1	1	1	1	1	1	1	1
Ed Krause, T	2			2		2		
George Melin-kovich, FB	2	2	2			1		
Ed Kosky, E	2							

1933

Coach: Heartley W. (Hunk) Anderson
Co-captains: Hugh J. Devore and Thomas A. Gorman

O.7	T	Kansas	0-0	H	9,221
O.14	W	Indiana	12-2	A	15,152
O.21	L	Carnegie Tech (U)	0-7	A	45,890
O.28	L	Pittsburgh	0-14	H	16,627
N.4	L	Navy	0-7	N	34,579
N.11	L	Purdue	0-19	H	27,476
N.18	W	Northwestern	7-0	A	31,182
N.25	L	So. California	0-19	H	25,037
D.2	W	Army (U)	13-12	YS	c73,594
		(3-5-1)	32-80		278,758

N—at Baltimore

1934

Coach: Elmer F. Layden
Captain: Dominic M. Vairo

O.6	L	Texas	6-7	H	20,353
O.13	W	Purdue	18-7	H	34,263
O.20	W	Carnegie Tech (R)	13-0	H	11,242
O.27	W	Wisconsin	19-0	H	25,354
N.3	L	Pittsburgh	0-19	A	56,556
N.10	L	Navy (R)	6-10	N	54,571
N.17	W	Northwestern	20-7	A	38,413
N.24	W	Army (4:00)	12-6	YS	c78,757
D.8	W	So.California	14-0	A	45,568
		(6-3-0)	108-56		365,077

N—at Cleveland

	AP	UP	AA	NA
Jack Robinson, C		2	2	1	1

1935

Coach: Elmer F. Layden
Captain: *Joseph G. Sullivan

S.28	W	Kansas	28-7	H	11,102
O.5	W	Carnegie Tech	14-3	A	27,542
O.12	W	Wisconsin	27-0	H	19,863
O.19	W	Pittsburgh (3:00)	9-6	H	39,989
O.26	W	Navy	14-0	N	c57,810
N.2	W	Ohio St. (U)(0:32)	18-13	A	c81,018
N.9	L	Northwestern (R)(U)	7-14	H	34,430
N.16	T	Army (0:29-ND)	6-6	YS	c78,114
N.23	W	So. California	20-13	H	38,305
		(7-1-1)	143-62		388,173

*Died from complications of pneumonia, March, 1935
N—at Baltimore

	UP	AA	NA	LIB	SN
Bill Shakespeare, HB	2	1			2
Wayne Millner, E	1	1	1	2	1
Andy Pilney, HB					2

1936

Coach: Elmer F. Layden
Captain: *William R. Smith–
  John P. Lautar

O.3	W	Carnegie Tech	21-7	H	15,673
O.10	W	Washington (St. L.)	14-6	H	9,879
O.17	W	Wisconsin (R)	27-0	H	16,423
O.24	L	Pittsburgh	0-26	A	c66,622
O.31	W	Ohio State (R)	7-2	H	50,017
N.7	L	Navy (U)	0-3	N	51,126
N.14	W	Army	20-6	YS	c74,423
N.21	W	Northwestern (U)	26-6	H	52,131
D.5	T	So. California	13-13	A	71,201
		(6-2-1)	128-69		407,495

*Captain-elect. Smith resigned his captaincy because of illness and Lautar was elected Acting Captain.
N—at Baltimore

	UP
John Lautar, G	1

AP

1. Minnesota
2. L.S.U.
3. Pittsburgh
4. Alabama
5. Washington
6. Santa Clara
7. Northwestern
8. NOTRE DAME
9. Nebraska
10. Pennsylvania

1937

Coach: Elmer F. Layden
Captain: Joseph B. Zwers

O.2	W	Drake	21-0	H	14,955
O.9	T	Illinois	0-0	A	42,253
O.16	L	Carnegie Tech (U)	7-9	A	30,418
O.23	W	Navy (S) (2:00)	9-7	H	45,000
O.30	W	Minnesota (U)	7-6	A	c63,237
N.6	L	Pittsburgh	6-21	H	c54,309
N.13	W	Army (R)	7-0	YS	c76,359
N.20	W	Northwestern	7-0	A	42,573
N.27	W	So. California (1:45)	13-6	H	28,920
		(6-2-1)	77-49		398,024

	AP	UP	NEA	AA	LIB	NW
Chuck Sweeney, E	1	1				1
Joe Beinor, T			1	1	1	

AP

1. Pittsburgh
2. California
3. Fordham
4. Alabama
5. Minnesota
6. Villanova
7. Dartmouth
8. L.S.U.
9. NOTRE DAME
10. Santa Clara

1938

Coach: Elmer F. Layden
Captain: James J. McGoldrick

O.1	W	Kansas	52-0	H	25,615
O.8	W	Georgia Tech	14-6	A	26,533
O.15	W	Illinois	14-6	H	29,142
O.22	W	Carnegie Tech	7-0	H	25,934
O.29	W	Army	19-7	YS	c76,338
N.5	W	Navy (R)	15-0	N	58,271
N.12	*W	Minnesota	19-0	H	c55,245
N.19	W	Northwestern	9-7	A	c46,343
D.3	L	So. California (U)	0-13	A	c97,146
		(8-1-0)	149-39		440,572

N—at Baltimore
*Notre Dame's 300th victory

	AP	UP	NEA	INS	COL	AA	SN	LIB	NW
†Joe Beinor, T	1	1	1	1		1	1	1	1
Earl Brown, E	2					1		1	
Jim McGoldrick, G		2							

AP

1. T.C.U.
2. Tennessee
3. Duke
4. Oklahoma
5. NOTRE DAME
6. Carnegie Tech
7. U.S.C.
8. Pittsburgh
9. Holy Cross
10. Minnesota

1939

Coach: Elmer F. Layden
Captain: John F. Kelly

S.30	W	Purdue	3-0	H	31,341
O.7	W	Georgia Tech	17-14	H	17,322
O.14	W	S.M.U.	20-19	H	29,730
O.21	W	Navy	14-7	N	c78,257
O.28	W	Carnegie Tech (S)	7-6	A	c61,420
N.4	W	Army	14-0	YS	c75,632
N.11	L	Iowa (U)	6-7	A	c42,380
N.18	W	Northwestern (3:30)	7-0	H	49,204
N.25	L	So. California	12-20	H	c54,799
		(7-2-0)	100-73		440,085

N—at Cleveland

	AP	UP	NEA	INS	AA	SN	NW
Bud Kerr, E	1	2	1	2	1	1	2
Milt Piepul, FB		2					

AP

1. Texas A&M
2. Tennessee
3. U.S.C.
4. Cornell
5. Tulane
6. Missouri
7. U.C.L.A.
8. Duke
9. Iowa
10. Duquesne

13. NOTRE DAME

1940

Coach: Elmer F. Layden
Captain: Milt Piepul

O.5	W	Col. of Pacific	25-7	H	22,670
O.12	W	Georgia Tech	26-20	H	32,492
O.19	W	Carnegie Tech	61-0	H	29,515
O.26	W	Illinois	26-0	A	c68,578
N.2	W	Army (R)	7-0	YS	c75,474
N.9	W	Navy (4:00)	13-7	N	c61,579
N.16	L	Iowa (5:00) (U)	0-7	H	45,960
N.23	L	Northwestern	0-20	A	c46,273
D.7	W	So. California	10-6	A	85,808
		(7-2-0)	168-67		468,349

N—at Baltimore

	SN
Milt Piepul, FB	2

AP
1. Minnesota
2. Stanford
3. Michigan
4. Tennessee
5. Boston College
6. Texas A&M
7. Northwestern
8. Nebraska
9. Mississippi State
10. Washington

1941

Coach: Frank Leahy
Captain: Paul B. Lillis

S.27	W	Arizona	38-7	H	19,567
O.4	W	Indiana (R)	19-6	H	34,713
O.11	W	Georgia Tech	20-0	A	c28,986
O.18	W	Carnegie Tech (R)	16-0	A	17,208
O.25	W	Illinois	49-14	H	34,896
N.1	T	Army (R)	0-0	YS	c75,226
N.8	W	Navy	20-13	N	c62,074
N.15	W	Northwestern	7-6	A	c46,211
N.22	W	So. California	20-18	H	c54,967
		(8-0-1)	189-64		373,848

N—at Baltimore

	UP	NEA	INS	COL	AA	LIB	NW
Bob Dove, E	1	1	1		1		1
Bernie Crimmins, G	2	2	2	1	1		

AP
1. Minnesota
2. Duke
3. NOTRE DAME
4. Texas
5. Michigan
6. Fordham
7. Missouri
8. Duquesne
9. Texas A&M
10. Navy

1942

Coach: Frank Leahy
Captain: George E. Murphy

S.26	T	Wisconsin	7-7	A	22,243
O.3	L	Georgia Tech (U)	6-13	H	20,545
O.10	W	Stanford	27-0	H	22,374
O.17	W	Iowa Pre-Flight (U)	28-0	H	26,800
O.24	W	Illinois	21-14	A	43,476
O.31	W	Navy (R)	9-0	N1	66,699
N.7	W	Army	13-0	YS	c74,946
N.14	L	Michigan	20-32	H	c54,379
N.21	W	Northwestern	27-20	H	26,098
N.28	W	So. California	13-0	A	94,519
D.5	T	Great Lakes (S)	13-13	N2	19,225
		(7-2-2)	184-99		472,304

N1—at Cleveland; N2—at Soldier Field

	AA	SN	LIB	NW	L	UP	NEA
Angelo Bertelli, QB		2	1	1	1		
Bob Dove, E	1	1	1	1	2	1	1
Harry Wright, G		2					

AP
1. Ohio State
2. Georgia
3. Wisconsin
4. Tulsa
5. Georgia Tech
6. NOTRE DAME
7. Tennessee
8. Boston College
9. Michigan
10. Alabama

1943

Coach: Frank Leahy
Captain: Patrick J. Filley

S.25	W	Pittsburgh	41-0	A	43,437
O.2	W	Georgia Tech	55-13	H	26,497
O.9	W	Michigan	35-12	A	c86,408
O.16	W	Wisconsin	50-0	A	16,235
O.23	W	Illinois (R)	47-0	H	24,676
O.30	W	Navy	33-6	N	c77,900
N.6	W	Army	26-0	YS	c75,121
N.13	W	Northwestern	25-6	A	c49,124
N.20	W	Iowa Pre-Flight	14-13	H	39,446
N.27	L	Great Lakes (U)	14-19	A	c23,000
		(0:33)			
		(9-1-0)	340-69		461,844

N—at Cleveland

	AP	UP	INS	COL	AA	SN	L
Angelo Bertelli, QB	2	1	1	1	1	1	1
Creighton Miller, HB	1	1	1	1	1	1	
John Yonakor, E			1	1		1	1
Jim White, T	1	1	1		1	1	2
Pat Filley, G	2	1		1		1	
Herb Coleman, C		2					

AP
1. NOTRE DAME
2. Iowa Pre-Flight
3. Michigan

Heisman Trophy—
Angelo Bertelli

4. Navy
5. Purdue
6. Great Lakes
7. Duke
8. Del Monte P
9. Northwestern
10. March Field

1944
Coach: Edward C. McKeever
Captain: Patrick J. Filley

S.30	W	Pittsburgh	58-0	A	46,069
O.7	W	Tulane	26-0	H	32,909
O.14	W	Dartmouth (R)	64-0	N1	c38,167
O.21	W	Wisconsin	28-13	H	36,086
O.28	W	Illinois	13-7	A	57,122
N.4	L	Navy	13-32	N2	c60,938
N.11	L	Army	0-59	YS	c75,142
N.18	W	Northwestern	21-0	H	39,701
N.25	W	Georgia Tech	21-0	A	28,662
D.2	W	Great Lakes	28-7	H	36,900
		(8-2-0)	272-118		451,696

N1—at Fenway Park, Boston; N2—at Baltimore

	UP	SN	L
Bob Kelly, HB		2	2
Pat Filley, G	2	2	

AP
1. Army
2. Ohio State
3. Randolph Field
4. Navy
5. Bainbridge
6. Iowa Pre-Flight
7. U.S.C.
8. Michigan
9. NOTRE DAME
10. 4th AAF

1945
Coach: Hugh J. Devore
Captain: Frank J. Dancewicz

S.29	W	Illinois	7-0	H	41,569
O.6	W	Georgia Tech	40-7	A	30,157
O.13	W	Dartmouth	34-0	H	34,645
O.20	W	Pittsburgh	39-9	A	c57,542
O.27	W	Iowa	56-0	H	42,841
N.3	T	Navy	6-6	N	c82,020
N.10	L	Army	0-48	YS	c74,621
N.17	W	Northwestern	34-7	A	c46,294
N.24	W	Tulane	32-6	A	51,368
D.1	L	Great Lakes	7-39	A	c23,000
		(7-2-1)	255-122		484,057

N—at Cleveland

	AP	UP	INS	SN	L	FC	FW
John Mastrangelo, G	2	2	1	2			2
Frank Dancewicz, QB	2	2		2	2	2	2

AP
1. Army
2. Alabama
3. Navy
4. Indiana
5. Oklahoma State
6. Michigan
7. St. Mary's
8. Pennsylvania
9. NOTRE DAME
10. Texas

1946
Coach: Frank Leahy
New Captain Each Game

S.28	W	Illinois	26-6	A	c75,119
O.5	W	Pittsburgh	33-0	H	50,350
O.12	W	Purdue	49-6	H	c55,452
O.26	W	Iowa	41-6	A	52,311
N.2	W	Navy	28-0	N	c63,909
N.9	T	Army	0-0	YS	c74,121
N.16	W	Northwestern (R)	27-0	H	c56,000
N.23	W	Tulane	41-0	H	65,841
N.30	W	So. California	26-6	H	c55,298
		(8-0-1)	271-24		548,401

N—at Baltimore

	AP	UP	NEA	INS	COL	AA	SN	L	FC
†John Lujack, QB	1	1	1	1	1	1	1	1	1
George Connor, T	1	1	1	1	1	1	1	2	1
John Mastrangelo, G	2	2		1	1		1		
George Strohmeyer, C		2		1			1	1	2

AP
1. NOTRE DAME
2. Army   Outland Trophy—
3. Georgia   George Connor
4. U.C.L.A.
5. Illinois
6. Michigan
7. Tennessee
8. L.S.U.
9. North Carolina
10. Rice

1947
Coach: Frank Leahy
Captain: George Connor

O.4	W	Pittsburgh	40-6	A	c64,333
O.11	W	Purdue	22-7	A	42,000
O.18	W	Nebraska	31-0	H	c56,000
O.25	W	Iowa	21-0	H	c56,000
N.1	W	Navy	27-0	N	c84,070
N.8	W	Army	27-7	H	c59,171
N.15	W	Northwestern (R)	26-19	A	c48,000
N.22	W	Tulane	59-6	H	c57,000
D.6	W	So. California	38-7	A	c104,953
		(9-0-0)	291-52		571,527

N—at Cleveland

	AP	UP	NEA	INS	COL	AA	SN	L	FC
†John Lujack, QB	1	1	1	1	1	1	1	1	1
George Connor, T	1	2			1	1	1		1
Bill Fischer, G	1	1	1					1	1
Ziggy Czarobski, T	2		1		1			2	
Leon Hart, E									1

AP

•1. NOTRE DAME
2. Michigan
3. S.M.U.
4. Penn State
5. Texas
6. Alabama
7. Pennsylvania
8. U.S.C.
9. North Carolina
10. Georgia Tech

Heisman Trophy—
John Lujack

•Post-season poll voted
Michigan nation's top
team.

1948

Coach: Frank Leahy
Captain: William Fischer

S.25	W	Purdue	28-27	H	c59,343
O.2	W	Pittsburgh	40-0	A	c64,000
O.9	W	Michigan State	26-7	H	c58,126
O.16	W	Nebraska	44-13	A	c38,000
O.23	W	Iowa	27-12	A	c53,000
O.30	W	Navy	41-7	N	c63,314
N.6	W	Indiana (R)	42-6	A	c34,000
N.13	W	Northwestern	12-7	H	c59,305
N.27	W	Washington	46-0	H	50,609
D.4	T	So. Calif. (0:35-ND)	14-14	A	c100,571
		(9-0-1)	320-93		580,268

N—at Baltimore

	AP	UP	NEA	INS	COL	AA	SN	L
Bill Fischer, G	1	1	1				1	1
Leon Hart, E	1		1			1	1	1
Emil Sitko, FB	2	2					1	1
Marty Wendell, G					1			2

AP

1. Michigan
2. NOTRE DAME
3. North Carolina
4. California
5. Oklahoma
6. Army
7. Northwestern
8. Georgia
9. Oregon
10. S.M.U.

Outland Trophy—
Bill Fischer

1949

Coach: Frank Leahy
Co-Captains: Leon J. Hart and
  James E. Martin

S.24	W	Indiana	49-6	H	53,844
O.1	W	Washington	27-7	A	c41,500
O.8	W	Purdue	35-12	A	c52,000
O.15	W	Tulane	46-7	H	c58,196
O.29	W	Navy	40-0	N	c62,000
N.5	W	Michigan State	34-21	A	c51,277
N.12	W	North Carolina	42-6	YS	c67,000
N.19	W	Iowa	28-7	H	c56,790
N.26	W	So. California	32-0	H	c57,214
D.3	W	S.M.U.	27-20	A	75,457
		(10-0-0)	360-86		575,278

N—at Baltimore

	AP	UP	NEA	INS	COL	AA	SN	L
†Emil Sitko, FB	1	1	1	1	1	1	1	1
†Leon Hart, E	1	1	1	1	1	1	1	1
Bob Williams, QB	2	1				1	1	1
Jim Martin, T	1	2	1	1			2	2

AP

1. NOTRE DAME
2. Oklahoma
3. California
4. Army
5. Rice
6. Ohio State
7. Michigan
8. Minnesota
9. L.S.U.
10. College Pacific

Heisman Trophy—
Leon Hart

Maxwell Trophy—
Leon Hart

1950

Coach: Frank Leahy
Captain: Jerome P. Groom

S.30	W	No. Carolina (2:40)	14-7	H	c56,430
O.7	L	Purdue (U) (R)	14-28	H	c56,746
O.14	W	Tulane	13-9	A	73,159
O.21	L	Indiana (U)	7-20	A	c34,000
O.28	L	Michigan State	33-36	H	c57,866
N.4	W	Navy (R-S)	19-10	N	71,074
N.11	W	Pittsburgh	18-7	H	c56,966
N.18	T	Iowa	14-14	A	c52,863
D.2	L	So. California	7-9	A	70,177
		(4-4-1)	139-140		529,281

N—at Cleveland

	AP	UP	NEA	SN	L
Bob Williams, QB	1	1		1	1
Jerry Groom, C	2	1	1	1	

AP

1. Oklahoma
2. Army
3. Texas
4. Tennessee
5. California
6. Princeton
7. Kentucky
8. Michigan State
9. Michigan
10. Clemson

UP

1. Oklahoma
2. Texas
3. Tennessee
4. California
5. Army
6. Michigan
7. Kentucky
8. Princeton
9. Michigan State
10. Ohio State

1951

Coach: Frank Leahy
Captain: Jim Mutscheller

S.29	W	Indiana	48-6	H	55,790

O.5	W	Detroit (Nt)	40-6	N1	52,331
O.13	L	S.M.U. (U)	20-27	H	c58,240
O.20	W	Pittsburgh	33-0	A	c60,127
O.27	W	Purdue	30-9	H	c57,890
N.3	W	Navy	19-0	N2	44,237
N.10	L	Michigan State	0-35	A	c51,296
N.17	*W	North Carolina	12-7	A	c44,500
N.24	T	Iowa (0:55-ND)	20-20	H	40,685
D.1	W	So. California (R)	19-12	A	55,783
		(7-2-1)	241-122		520,879

N1—at Briggs Stadium, Detroit; N2—at Baltimore
*Notre Dame's 400th victory

	AP	UP	SN
Bob Toneff, T	1	2	2
Jim Mutscheller		2	

AP	UP
1. Tennessee	1. Tennessee
2. Michigan State	2. Michigan State
3. Maryland	3. Illinois
4. Illinois	4. Maryland
5. Georgia Tech	5. Georgia Tech
6. Princeton	6. Princeton
7. Stanford	7. Stanford
8. Wisconsin	8. Wisconsin
9. Baylor	9. Baylor
10. Oklahoma	10. T.C.U.

1952

Coach: Frank Leahy
Captain: James F. Alessandrini

S.27	T	Pennsylvania	7-7	A	c74,518
O.4	W	Texas (U)	14-3	A	c67,666
O.11	L	Pittsburgh (U)	19-22	H	45,507
O.18	W	Purdue	26-14	A	49,000
O.25	W	North Carolina	34-14	H	54,338
N.1	W	Navy	17-6	N	61,927
N.8	W	Oklahoma (U)	27-21	H	c57,446
N.15	L	Michigan State	3-21	H	c52,472
N.22	W	Iowa	27-0	A	46,600
N.29	W	So. California (U)	9-0	H	c58,394
		(7-2-1)	183-108		567,868

N—at Cleveland

	AP	UP	NEA	INS	COL	AA	SN	L
†John Lattner, HB	1	1	1	1	1	1	1	1
Bob O'Neil, DE			2					

AP	UP
1. Michigan State	1. Michigan State
2. Georgia Tech	2. Georgia Tech
3. NOTRE DAME	3. NOTRE DAME
4. Oklahoma	4. Oklahoma
5. U.S.C.	5. U.S.C.
6. U.C.L.A.	6. U.C.L.A.
7. Mississippi	7. Mississippi
8. Tennessee	8. Tennessee
9. Alabama	9. Alabama
10. Texas	10. Wisconsin

Maxwell Trophy—John Lattner
Academic All-America—Joe Heap

1953

Coach: Frank Leahy
Captain: Donald Penza

S.26	W	Oklahoma	28-21	A	c59,500
O.3	W	Purdue	37-7	A	49,135
O.17	W	Pittsburgh	23-14	H	c57,998
O.24	W	Georgia Tech	27-14	H	c58,254
O.31	W	Navy	38-7	H	c58,154
N.7	W	Pennsylvania	28-20	A	c74,711
N.14	W	North Carolina	34-14	A	c43,000
N.21	T	Iowa (0:06-ND)	14-14	H	c56,478
N.28	W	So. California	48-14	H	97,952
D.5	W	S.M.U.	40-14	H	55,522
		(9-0-1)	317-139		610,704

	AP	UP	NEA	INS	COL	AA	SN	L
†John Lattner, HB	1	1	1	1	1	1	1	1
Art Hunter, T	2	1	2	1		1	1	
Don Penza, E		2					2	

AP	UP
1. Maryland	1. Maryland
2. NOTRE DAME	2. NOTRE DAME
3. Michigan State	3. Michigan State
4. Oklahoma	4. U.C.L.A.
5. U.C.L.A.	5. Oklahoma
6. Rice	6. Rice
7. Illinois	7. Illinois
8. Georgia Tech	8. Texas
9. Iowa	9. Georgia Tech
10. West Virginia	10. Iowa

Heisman Trophy—John Lattner
Maxwell Trophy—John Lattner
Academic All-America—Joe Heap

1954

Coach: Terry Brennan
Co-Captains: Paul A. Matz and
  Daniel J. Shannon

S.25	W	Texas	21-0	H	c57,594
O.2	L	Purdue (U)	14-27	H	c58,250
O.9	W	Pittsburgh	33-0	A	c60,114
O.16	W	Michigan State (R)	20-19	H	c57,238
O.30	W	Navy	6-0	N	c60,000
N.6	W	Pennsylvania	42-7	A	61,189
N.13	W	North Carolina	42-13	H	55,410
N.20	W	Iowa	34-18	A	c56,576
N.27	W	So. Calif. (R) (5:57)	23-17	H	c56,438
D.4	W	S.M.U.	26-14	A	c75,501
		(9-1-0)	261-115		598,310

N—at Baltimore

	AP	UP	NEA	INS	COL	AA	SN	L
†Ralph Guglielmi, QB	1	1	1	1	1	1	1	1
Frank Varrichione, T	2		2			1		
Dan Shannon, E							2	

AP	UP
1. Ohio State	1. U.C.L.A.
2. U.C.L.A.	2. Ohio State
3. Oklahoma	3. Oklahoma
4. NOTRE DAME	4. NOTRE DAME

5. Navy		5. Navy		
6. Mississippi		6. Mississippi		
7. Army		7. Army		
8. Maryland		8. Arkansas		
9. Wisconsin		9. Miami (Florida)		
10. Arkansas		10. Wisconsin		

Academic All-America—Joe Heap

1955

Coach: Terry Brennan
Captain: Raymond E. Lemek

S.24	W	S.M.U.	17-0	H	c56,454
O.1	W	Indiana	19-0	H	c56,494
O.7	W	Miami (Fla.) (Nt)	14-0	A	c75,685
O.15	L	Michigan State	7-21	A	c52,007
O.22	W	Purdue	22-7	A	c55,000
O.29	W	Navy (R)	21-7	H	c59,475
N.5	W	Pennsylvania	46-14	A	45,226
N.12	W	North Carolina	27-7	A	38,000
N.19	W	Iowa (2:15)	17-14	H	c59,955
N.26	L	So. California (U)	20-42	A	94,892
		(8-2-0)	210-112		593,188

	AP	UP	NEA	INS	COL	AA	SN	L
Paul Hornung, HB		1	1				1	1
Don Schaefer, FB	2			1	1		2	1
Pat Bisceglia, G	1						2	

AP	UP
1. Oklahoma	1. Oklahoma
2. Michigan State	2. Michigan State
3. Maryland	3. Maryland
4. U.C.L.A.	4. U.C.L.A.
5. T.C.U.	5. Ohio State
6. Ohio State	6. T.C.U.
7. Georgia Tech	7. Georgia Tech
8. NOTRE DAME	8. Auburn
9. Mississippi	9. NOTRE DAME
10. Auburn	10. Mississippi

Academic All-America—Don Schaefer

1956

Coach: Terry Brennan
Captain: James A. Morse

S.22	L	S.M.U.(U)(Nt)(1:50)	13-19	A	61,000
O.6	W	Indiana	20-6	H	c58,372
O.13	L	Purdue	14-28	H	c58,778
O.20	L	Michigan State	14-47	H	c59,378
O.27	L	Oklahoma	0-40	H	c60,128
N.3	L	Navy (R)	7-33	N	57,773
N.10	L	Pittsburgh	13-26	A	c58,697
N.17	W	No. Carolina (1:16)	21-14	H	c56,793
N.24	L	Iowa	8-48	A	c56,632
D.1	L	So. California	20-28	A	64,538
		(2-8-0)	130-289		592,089

N—at Baltimore

	AP	UP	NEA	SN	L
Paul Hornung, QB	2	1	2	1	1

AP	UP
1. Oklahoma	1. Oklahoma
2. Tennessee	2. Tennessee
3. Iowa	3. Iowa
4. Georgia Tech	4. Georgia Tech
5. Texas A&M	5. Texas A&M
6. Miami (Florida)	6. Miami (Florida)
7. Michigan	7. Michigan
8. Syracuse	8. Syracuse
9. Michigan State	9. Minnesota
10. Oregon State	10. Michigan State

Heisman Trophy—Paul Hornung

1957

Coach: Terry Brennan
Co-Captains: Richard Prendergast and
   Edward A. Sullivan

S.28	W	Purdue	12-0	A	52,108
O.5	W	Indiana	26-0	H	54,026
O.12	W	Army	23-21	N	95,000
O.26	W	Pittsburgh	13-7	H	c58,775
N.2	L	Navy (R)	6-20	H	c58,922
N.9	L	Michigan State	6-34	A	c75,391
N.16	W	Oklahoma (U) (3:50)	7-0	A	c63,170
N.23	L	Iowa	13-21	H	c58,734
N.30	W	So. California (S)	40-12	H	54,793
D.7	W	S.M.U.	54-21	A	51,000
		(7-3-0)	200-136		621,919

N—at Philadelphia

	AP	UP	INS	SN
Al Ecuyer, G	2	1	1	1

AP	UP
1. Auburn	1. Ohio State
2. Ohio State	2. Auburn
3. Michigan State	3. Michigan State
4. Oklahoma	4. Oklahoma
5. Navy	5. Iowa
6. Iowa	6. Navy
7. Mississippi	7. Rice
8. Rice	8. Mississippi
9. Texas A&M	9. NOTRE DAME
10. NOTRE DAME	10. Texas A&M

1958

Coach: Terry Brennan
Co-Captains: Allen J. Ecuyer and
   Charles F. Puntillo

S.27	W	Indiana	18-0	H	49,347
O.4	W	S.M.U.	14-6	A	61,500
O.11	L	Army	2-14	H	c60,564
O.18	W	Duke	9-7	H	c59,068
O.25	L	Purdue (R)	22-29	H	c59,563
N.1	W	Navy	40-20	N	c57,773
N.8	L	Pittsburgh (0:11)	26-29	A	55,330
N.15	W	North Carolina	34-24	H	c56,839
N.22	L	Iowa	21-31	A	c58,230
N.29	W	So. California	20-13	A	66,903
		(6-4-0)	206-173		585,117

N—at Baltimore

	AP	UPI	NEA	FC	SN	L
Nick Pietrosante, FB				2	1	2	1
Al Ecuyer, G		1				1
Monty Stickles, E	2	2				1

AP	UP
1. L.S.U.	1. L.S.U.
2. Iowa	2. Iowa
3. Army	3. Army
4. Auburn	4. Auburn
5. Oklahoma	5. Oklahoma
6. Air Force	6. Wisconsin
7. Wisconsin	7. Ohio State
8. Ohio State	8. Air Force
9. Syracuse	9. T.C.U.
10. T.C.U.	10. Syracuse
17. NOTRE DAME	14. NOTRE DAME

Academic All-America—Bob Wetoska

1959

Coach: Joseph L. Kuharich
Captain: Kenneth M. Adamson

S.26	W	North Carolina (R)	28-8	H	56,746
O.3	L	Purdue	7-28	A	c50,362
O.10	W	California	28-6	A	68,500
O.17	L	Michigan State	0-19	A	73,480
O.24	L	Northwestern (R)	24-30	H	c59,078
O.31	W	Navy (0:32)	25-22	H	c58,652
N.7	L	Georgia Tech (4:27)	10-14	H	c58,575
N.14	L	Pittsburgh (R)	13-28	A	52,337
N.21	W	Iowa (3:25)	20-19	A	c58,500
N.28	W	So. California (U)	16-6	H	48,684
	(5-5-0)		171-180		584,914

	AP	UPI	SN
Monty Stickles, E	2	1	1

AP	UP
1. Syracuse	1. Syracuse
2. Mississippi	2. Mississippi
3. L.S.U.	3. L.S.U.
4. Texas	4. Texas
5. Georgia	5. Georgia
6. Wisconsin	6. Wisconsin
7. T.C.U.	7. Washington
8. Washington	8. T.C.U.
9. Arkansas	9. Arkansas
10. Alabama	10. Penn State
17. NOTRE DAME	

From 1960 through 1963 Notre Dame failed to finish in the top 20 of the AP and UP polls.

1960

Coach: Joseph L. Kuharich
Captain: Myron Pottios

S.24	W	California	21-7	H	49,286
O.1	L	Purdue	19-51	H	c59,235
O.8	L	North Carolina (R)	7-12	A	41,000
O.15	L	Michigan State	0-21	H	c59,133
O.22	L	Northwestern	6-7	A	c55,682
O.29	L	Navy (R)	7-14	N	63,000
N.5	L	Pittsburgh	13-20	H	55,696
N.12	L	Miami (Fla.)(Nt)	21-28	A	58,062
N.19	L	Iowa	0-28	A	45,000
N.26	W	So. Cal. (U)(R)	17-0	H	54,146
	(2-8-0)		111-188		540,240

N—at Philadelphia

		T
Myron Pottios, G		1

1961

Coach: Joseph L. Kuharich
Co-Captains: Norbert W. Roy and
 Nicholas A. Buoniconti

S.30	W	Oklahoma	19-6	H	55,198
O.7	W	Purdue	22-20	A	c51,295
O.14	W	So. California	30-0	H	50,427
O.21	L	Michigan State	7-17	A	c76,132
O.28	L	Northwestern	10-12	H	c59,075
N.4	L	Navy	10-13	H	c59,075
N.11	W	Pittsburgh	26-20	A	50,527
N.18	W	Syracuse (0:00)	17-15	H	49,246
N.25	L	Iowa	21-42	A	c58,000
D.2	L	Duke	13-37	A	35,000
	(5-5-0)		175-182		543,975

	UPI	FC	SN	FN
Nick Buoniconti, G	2	2	2	1

1962

Coach: Joseph L. Kuharich
Captain: Mike Lind

S.29	W	Oklahoma	13-7	A	c60,500
O.6	L	Purdue	6-24	H	*c61,296
O.13	L	Wisconsin	8-17	A	c61,098
O.20	L	Michigan State (R)	7-31	H	c60,116
O.27	L	Northwestern	6-35	A	c55,752
N.3	W	Navy (R)	20-12	N	35,000
N.10	W	Pittsburgh	43-22	H	52,215
N.17	W	North Carolina	21-7	H	35,553
N.24	W	Iowa	35-12	H	42,653
D.1	L	So. California	0-25	A	81,676
	(5-5-0)		159-192		545,859

N—at Philadelphia
*Notre Dame Stadium record

	FN
Jim Kelly, E	1

1963

Coach: Hugh J. Devore
Captain: Joseph Robert Lehmann

S.28	L	Wisconsin (1:07)	9-14	H	56,806
O.5	L	Purdue	6-7	A	c51,723
O.12	W	So. Cal. (U)(6:28)	17-14	H	c59,135
O.19	W	U.C.L.A.	27-12	H	42,948
O.26	L	Stanford (U)	14-24	A	55,000
N.2	L	Navy	14-35	H	c59,362
N.9	L	Pittsburgh	7-27	H	41,306
N.16	L	Michigan State	7-12	A	70,128

N.23	..	Iowa*	... A	....
N.28	L	Syracuse (3:28)	7-14 YS	56,972
		(2-7-0)	108-159	493,380

*Game cancelled because of the death of President Kennedy

	AP	UPI	FC	FN
Jim Kelly, E		1	1	1
Bob Lehmann, G	2			

Academic All-America—Bob Lehmann

1964

Coach: Ara Parseghian
Captain: James S. Carroll

S.26	W	Wisconsin (R)	31-7	A	c64,398
O.3	W	Purdue	34-15	H	c59,611
O.10	W	Air Force	34-7	A	c44,384
O.17	W	U.C.L.A.	24-0	H	58,335
O.24	W	Stanford	28-6	H	56,721
O.31	W	Navy	40-0	N	66,752
N.7	W	Pittsburgh	17-15	A	56,628
N.14	W	Michigan State	34-7	H	c59,265
N.21	W	Iowa	28-0	H	c59,135
N.28	L	So. Calif. (U)(1:33)	17-20	A	83,840
		(9-1-0)	287-77		609,069

N—at Philadelphia

	AP	UPI	NEA	FC	SN	L	T	CP	FN
John Huarte, QB	1	1		2				1	1
Jack Snow, E	2	1	1	1	1	1	1	1	1
Jim Carroll, LB		2			1		1		1
Tony Carey, DB			2						

AP	UP
1. Alabama	1. Alabama
2. Arkansas	2. Arkansas
3. NOTRE DAME	3. NOTRE DAME
4. Michigan	4. Michigan
5. Texas	5. Texas
6. Nebraska	6. Nebraska
7. L.S.U.	7. L.S.U.
8. Oregon State	8. Oregon State
9. Ohio State	9. Ohio State
10. U.S.C.	10. U.S.C

Heisman Trophy—John Huarte

1965

Coach: Ara Parseghian
Captain: Philip F. Sheridan

S.18	W	California	48-6	A	53,000
S.25	L	Purdue	21-25	A	c61,291
O.2	W	Northwestern	38-7	H	c59,273
O.9	W	Army (Nt)	17-0	N	c61,000
O.23	W	So. California (R)	28-7	H	c59,235
O.30	W	Navy	29-3	H	c59,206
N.6	W	Pittsburgh	69-13	A	c57,169
N.13	W	North Carolina	17-0	H	c59,216
N.20	L	Michigan State	3-12	H	c59,291
N.27	T	Miami (Fla.)(Nt)	0-0	A	68,077
		(7-2-1)	270-73		596,758

N—at Shea Stadium, New York

	AP	UPI	NEA	FC	SN	L	FN
Dick Arrington, G	1	1	1	1		1	1
Nick Rassas, DB	1	1	1		1	1	1
Tom Regner, G			2				
Jim Lynch, LB			2				

AP	UP
1. Alabama	1. Michigan State
2. Michigan State	2. Arkansas
3. Arkansas	3. Nebraska
4. U.C.L.A.	4. Alabama
5. Nebraska	5. U.C.L.A.
6. Missouri	6. Missouri
7. Tennessee	7. Tennessee
8. L.S.U.	8. NOTRE DAME
9. NOTRE DAME	9. U.S.C.
10. U.S.C.	10. Texas Tech

1966

Coach: Ara Parseghian
Captain: James R. Lynch

S.24	W	Purdue	26-14	H	c59,075
O.1	W	Northwestern	35-7	A	c55,356
O.8	W	Army	35-0	H	c59,075
O.15	W	North Carolina	32-0	H	c59,075
O.22	W	Oklahoma	38-0	A	c63,439
O.29	W	Navy	31-7	N	70,101
N.5	W	Pittsburgh	40-0	H	c59,075
N.12	W	Duke	64-0	H	c59,075
N.19	T	Michigan State	10-10	A	c80,011
N.26	W	So. California	51-0	A	88,520
		(9-0-1)	362-38		652,802

N—at Philadelphia

	AP	UPI	NEA	FC	SN	L	T	CP	FN
†Nick Eddy, HB	1	1	1	1	2	1		1	1
†Jim Lynch, LB	1	1	1	1	1	1	1	1	1
Tom Regner, G	1	1	1	1	1		1	1	1
Alan Page, DE	2	2	1		1	1	1	1	1
Pete Duranko, DT	1			1	2				
Kevin Hardy, DT	2	2			1		1		1
Jim Seymour, E	2	2							1
Paul Seiler, T				2					
George Goeddeke, C	2								
Tom Schoen, DB	2								
Larry Conjar, FB									1

AP	UP
1. NOTRE DAME	1. NOTRE DAME
2. Michigan State	2. Michigan State
3. Alabama	3. Alabama
4. Georgia	4. Georgia
5. U.C.L.A.	5. U.C.L.A.
6. Nebraska	6. Purdue
7. Purdue	7. Nebraska
8. Georgia Tech	8. Georgia Tech
9. Miami (Florida)	9. S.M.U.
10. S.M.U.	10. Miami (Florida)

Academic All-America—Jim Lynch
Tom Regner

Maxwell Trophy—Jim Lynch

1967

Coach: Ara Parseghian
Captain: Robert P. (Rocky) Bleier

S.23	W	California	41-8	H	c59,075
S.30	L	Purdue	21-28	A	c62,316
O.7	W	Iowa	56-6	H	c59,075
O.14	L	So. California	7-24	H	c59,075
O.21	W	Illinois	47-7	A	c71,227
O.28	W	Michigan State	24-12	H	c59,075
N.4	W	Navy	43-14	H	c59,075
N.11	W	Pittsburgh	38-0	A	54,075
N.18	W	Georgia Tech	36-3	A	c60,024
N.24	W	Miami (Fla.)(Nt)	24-22	A	c77,265
	(8-2-0)		337-124		620,282

	AP	UPI	FC	SN	L	T	CP
Tom Schoen, DB	1	1	1	1	1	1	1
Kevin Hardy, DE	1	1		1		1	2
Jim Seymour, E			1				1
Mike McGill, LB					2		1
John Pergine, LB			2				
Dick Swatland, G							2
Jim Smithberger, DB				2			

AP	UP
1. U.S.C.	1. U.S.C.
2. Tennessee	2. Tennessee
3. Oklahoma	3. Oklahoma
4. Indiana	4. NOTRE DAME
5. NOTRE DAME	5. Wyoming
6. Wyoming	6. Indiana
7. Oregon State	7. Alabama
8. Alabama	8. Oregon State
9. Purdue	9. Purdue
10. Penn State	10. U.C.L.A.

Academic All-America—Jim Smithberger

1968

Coach: Ara Parseghian
Co-captains: George J. Kunz and
Robert L. Olson

S.21	W	Oklahoma	45-12	H	c59,075
S.28	L	Purdue	22-37	H	c59,075
O.5	W	Iowa	51-28	A	58,046
O.12	W	Northwestern	27-7	H	c59,075
O.19	W	Illinois	58-8	H	c59,075
O.26	L	Michigan State	17-21	A	c77,339
N.2	W	Navy	45-14	N	63,738
N.9	W	Pittsburgh	56-7	H	c59,075
N.16	W	Georgia Tech	34-6	H	c59,075
N.30	T	So. California	21-21	A	82,659
	(7-2-1)		376-170		636,229

N—at Philadelphia

	AP	UPI	NEA	FC	SN	L	T	CP	FN	WCF
George Kunz, T	2	1	1	1	1	1	1	1	1	1
Terry Hanratty, QB	1	1	2	1	1	1	1	1	1	1
Jim Seymour, E	2	1		1	1		2			1

AP	UP
1. Ohio State	1. Ohio State
2. Penn State	2. Southern Cal
3. Texas	3. Penn State

4. So. California	4. Georgia
5. NOTRE DAME	5. Texas
6. Arkansas	6. Kansas
7. Kansas	7. Tennessee
8. Georgia	8. NOTRE DAME
9. Missouri	9. Arkansas
10. Purdue	10. Oklahoma

Academic All-America—George Kunz

1969

Coach: Ara Parseghian
Co-captains: Robert L. Olson and
Michael Oriard

S.20	W	Northwestern	35-10	H	c59,075
S.27	L	Purdue	14-28	A	c68,179
O.4	W	Michigan State	42-28	H	c59,075
O.11	W	Army	45-0	N1	c63,786
O.18	T	Southern California	14-14	H	c59,075
O.25	W	Tulane (Nt)	37-0	A	40,250
N.1	W	Navy	47-0	H	c59,075
N.8	W	Pittsburgh (R)	49-7	A	44,084
N.15	W	Georgia Tech (Nt)	38-20	A	41,104
N.22	W	Air Force	13-6	H	c59,075
	(8-1-1)		334-113		552,778

	COTTON BOWL				
J.1	L	Texas (1:08)	17-21	N2	73,000

N1—at Yankee Stadium, New York
N2—at Dallas, Texas

	AP	UPI	NEA	FC	SN	L	T	CP	FN	WCF
†Mike McCoy, DT	1	1	1	1	1	1	1	1	1	1
Jim Reilly, T			2		1	2				
Larry DiNardo, G	1						2		1	
Bob Olson, LB	2						2			
Mike Oriard, C					2					

AP	UP
1. Texas	1. Texas
2. Penn State	2. Penn State
3. U.S.C.	3. Arkansas
4. Ohio State	4. U.S.C.
5. NOTRE DAME	5. Ohio State
6. Missouri	6. Missouri
7. Arkansas	7. L.S.U.
8. Mississippi	8. Michigan
9. Michigan	9. NOTRE DAME
10. L.S.U.	10. U.C.L.A.

Academic All-America—Jim Reilly

1970

Coach: Ara Parseghian
Co-captains: Larry DiNardo and
Tim Kelly

S.19	W	Northwestern	35-14	A	50,049
S.26	W	Purdue	48-0	H	c59,075
O.3	W	Michigan State	29-0	A	c76,103
O.10	W	Army	51-10	H	c59,075
O.17	W	Missouri	24-7	A	c64,200
O.31	W	Navy	56-7	N1	45,226
N.7	W	Pittsburgh	46-14	H	c59,075

N.14 W Georgia Tech (6:28) 10-7 H c59,075
N.21 W Louisiana State 3-0 H c59,075
    (2:54)
N.28 L Southern Cal(R)(U) 28-38 A 64,694
    (9-1-0) 330-97 595,647

COTTON BOWL
J.1 W Texas 24-11 N2 c73,000
N1—at Philadelphia
N2—at Dallas, Texas

	AP	UPI	NEA	FC	SN	L	CP	FN	WCF
Larry DiNardo, G	1	1	2	1	1	1	1	1	1
Tom Gatewood, E	1	1	1	2	1	1		1	
Clarence Ellis, DB	1	1							
Joe Theismann, QB	1	2	2					2	1

AP	UP
1. Nebraska	1. Texas
2. NOTRE DAME	2. Ohio State
3. Texas	3. Nebraska
4. Tennessee	4. Tennessee
5. Ohio State	5. NOTRE DAME
6. Arizona State	6. L.S.U.
7. L.S.U.	7. Michigan
8. Stanford	8. Arizona State
9. Michigan	9. Auburn
10. Auburn	10. Stanford

Academic All-America—Tom Gatewood
Larry DiNardo

1971

Coach: Ara Parseghian
Co-captains: Walter Patulski and
  Thomas Gatewood

S.18 W Northwestern 50-7 H c59,075
S.25 W Purdue (2:58) (R) 8-7 A c69,765
O.2 W Michigan State 14-2 H c59,075
O.9 W Miami (Fla.)(Nt) 17-0 A 66,089
O.16 W North Carolina 16-0 H c59,075
O.23 L So. California (U) 14-28 H c59,075
O.30 W Navy 21-0 H c59,075
N.6 W Pittsburgh 56-7 A 55,528
N.13 W Tulane 21-7 H c59,075
N.20 L Louisiana State (Nt) 8-28 A c66,986
    (8-2-0) 225-86 612,718

	AP	UPI	NEA	FC	SN	L	T	FN	WCF
†Walt Patulski, DE	1	1	1	1	1	1	1	1	1
Clarence Ellis, DB	1	1	1		1		1	1	1
Tom Gatewood, E	2				1				
Mike Kadish, DT					1				

AP	UP
1. Nebraska	1. Nebraska
2. Oklahoma	2. Alabama
3. Colorado	3. Oklahoma
4. Alabama	4. Michigan
5. Penn State	5. Auburn
6. Michigan	6. Arizona State
7. Georgia	7. Colorado
8. Arizona State	8. Georgia
9. Tennessee	9. Tennessee
10. Stanford	10. L.S.U.
13. NOTRE DAME	15. NOTRE DAME

Academic All-America—Tom Gatewood
Greg Marx

1972

Coach: Ara Parseghian
Co-Captains: John Dampeer and
  Greg Marx

S.23 W Northwestern 37-0 A c55,155
S.30 W Purdue 35-14 H c59,075
O.7 W Michigan State 16-0 A c77,828
O.14 W Pittsburgh 42-16 H c59,075
O.21 L Missouri (U)(R) 26-30 H c59,075
O.28 W T.C.U. 21-0 H c59,075
N.4 W Navy 42-23 N1 43,089
N.11 W Air Force 21-7 A c48,671
N.18 W Miami (Fla.) 20-17 H c59,075
D.2 L Southern Cal 23-45 A 75,243
    (8-2-0) 283-152 595,361

ORANGE BOWL
J.1 L Nebraska (Nt) 6-40 N2 c80,010
N1—at Philadelphia; N2—at Miami

	AP	UPI	NEA	FC	SN	FW	T	FN	WCF
†Greg Marx, DT	1	1		1	1	1	1	1	1

AP	UP
1. Southern Cal	1. Southern Cal
2. Oklahoma	2. Oklahoma
3. Texas	3. Ohio State
4. Nebraska	4. Alabama
5. Auburn	5. Texas
6. Michigan	6. Michigan
7. Alabama	7. Auburn
8. Tennessee	8. Penn State
9. Ohio State	9. Nebraska
10. Penn State	10. L.S.U.
14. NOTRE DAME	12. NOTRE DAME

Vince Lombardi Trophy—Walt Patulski
Academic All-America—Greg Marx
Mike Creaney

1973

Coach: Ara Parseghian
Tri-Captains: Dave Casper, Frank
  Pomarico (Off.) and Mike Townsend (Def.)

S.22 W Northwestern 44-0 H c59,075
S.29 W Purdue 20-7 H c69,391
O.6 W Michigan State 14-10 H c59,075
O.13 W Rice (Nt) 28-0 A 50,321
O.20 W Army 62-3 A c42,503
O.27 W Southern Cal (R) 23-14 H c59,075
N.3 W Navy 44-7 H c59,075
N.10 W Pittsburgh (S) 31-10 A c56,593
N.22TH W Air Force 48-15 H 57,236
D.1 W Miami (Fla.)(Nt) 44-0 A 42,968
    (10-0-0) 358-66 555,312

D.31 W Alabama 24-23 c85,161
(4:26)(Nt)

	AP	UPI	NEA	FC	SN	FW	T	FN	WCF
Dave Casper, TE	2	1	1	1		1			1
Mike Townsend, DB	1	1	1			1	1	1	1

AP
1. NOTRE DAME
2. Ohio State
3. Oklahoma
4. Alabama
5. Penn State
6. Michigan
7. Nebraska
8. Southern Cal
9. Arizona State
10. Houston

UP
1. Alabama
2. Oklahoma
3. Ohio State
4. NOTRE DAME
5. Penn State
6. Michigan
7. Southern Cal
8. Texas
9. UCLA
10. Arizona State

Academic All-America—Dave Casper
Bob Thomas
Gary Potempa

1974

Coach: Ara Parseghian
Co-Captains: Tom Clements and
Greg Collins

S.9	W	Georgia Tech	31-7	A	45,228
S.21	W	Northwestern	49-3	A	c55,000
S.28	L	Purdue (U)(R)	20-31	H	c59,075
O.5	W	Michigan State	19-14	A	c77,431
O.12	W	Rice (3:08)	10-3	H	c59,075
O.19	W	Army (S)	48-0	H	c59,075
O.26	W	Miami (Fla.)	38-7	H	c59,075
N.2	W	Navy	14-6	N1	48,634
N.16	W	Pitt (R)(2:49)	14-10	H	c59,075
N.23	W	Air Force (R)	38-0	H	c59,075
N.30	L	Southern Cal	24-55	A	83,522
		(9-2-0)	305-136		664,265

ORANGE BOWL

J.1 W Alabama (U) 13-11 N2 71,801

N1—at Philadelphia; N2—at Miami

	AP	UPI	NEA	FC	SN	FW	T	FN	WCF
Pete Demmerle, SE	1	1	1	1					1
Mike Fanning, DT	2		1		1		1		1
Gerry DiNardo, G		1		1			1		
Tom Clements, QB						1	2		
Greg Collins, LB	2						2		
Steve Niehaus, DT							1		

AP
1. Oklahoma
2. Southern Cal
3. Michigan
4. Ohio State
5. Alabama
6. NOTRE DAME
7. Penn State
8. Auburn

UP
1. Southern Cal
2. Alabama
3. Ohio State
4. NOTRE DAME
5. Michigan
6. Auburn
7. Penn State
8. Nebraska

9. Nebraska
10. Miami (O.)

9. N. C. State
10. Miami (O.)

Academic All-America—Pete Demmerle
Reggie Barnett

1975

Coach: Dan Devine
Co-captains: Ed Bauer and Jim Stock

S.15	W	Boston College	17-3	A	c61,501
S.20	W	Purdue	17-0	A	c69,795
S.27	W	Northwestern	31-7	H	c59,075
O.4	L	Michigan State	3-10	H	c59,075
O.11	W	North Carolina	21-14	A	c49,500
O.18	W	Air Force	31-30	A	43,204
O.25	L	Southern Cal	17-24	H	c59,075
N.1	W	Navy	31-10	H	c59,075
N.8	W	Georgia Tech	24-3	H	c59,075
N.15	L	Pittsburgh	20-34	A	c56,480
N.22	W	Miami (Fla.)	32-9	A	24,944
		(8-3-0)	244-144		600,799

	AP	UPI	NEA	FC	SN	FW	T	FN	WCF
†Steve Niehaus	1	1		1	1	1	1	1	1
Ken MacAfee		1							

Notre Dame's All-Time Leaders

(Includes Regular-Season Games Only)

Total Offense Yards

Career:	Plays	Yards	Avg.
Joe Theismann, 1968-70	807*	5432*	6.7
Terry Hanratty, 1966-68	731	4738	6.5
Tom Clements, 1972-74	760	4664	6.1
George Gipp, 1917-20	556	4110	7.4*
Ralph Guglielmi, 1951-54	644	3285	5.1
Paul Hornung, 1954-56	442	2747	6.2

Season:			
Joe Theismann, 1970	391*	2813*	7.2
John Huarte, 1964	242	2069	8.5
Tom Clements, 1974	310	1918	6.2
Joe Theismann, 1969	308	1909	6.2
Terry Hanratty, 1968	253	1745	6.9
Terry Hanratty, 1967	281	1622	5.8

Rushing Yards

Career:	Carries	Yards	Avg.	TD
George Gipp, 1917-20	369	2341*	6.3	16
Emil Sitko, 1946-49	362	2226	6.1	25
Neil Worden, 1951-53	476*	2039	4.3	29
Marchy Schwartz, 1929-31	335	1945	5.8	16
Don Miller, 1922-24	283	1933	6.8*	17
Jim Crowley, 1922-24	294	1841	6.3	15
Christy Flanagan, 1925-27	285	1822	6.4	15

Season:				
Marchy Schwartz, 1930	124	927*	7.5	9
Creighton Miller, 1943	151	911	6.0	10
Neil Worden, 1953	145	859	5.9	11
Wayne Bullock, 1974	203*	885	4.2	12
George Gipp, 1920	102	827	8.1*	8
John Mohardt, 1921	136	781	5.7	11

Passes Completed

Career:	Att.	Comp.	Int.	Pct.	Yards	TD
Terry Hanratty, 1966-68	550*	304*	34	.553	4152	27
Joe Theismann, 1968-70	509	290	35*	.570*	4411*	31*
Tom Clements, 1972-74	490	265	29	.541	3594	24
Ralph Guglielmi, 1951-54	436	209	24	.479	3117	18
Bob Williams, 1948-50	374	190	24	.508	2519	26
Angelo Bertelli, 1941-43	318	167	30	.525	2578	28

Season:	Att.	Comp.	Int.	Pct.	Yards	TD
Joe Theismann, 1970	268	155*	14	.578	2429*	16†
Tom Clements, 1974	215	122	11	.567	1549	8
Terry Hanratty, 1968	197	116	9	.589	1466	10
John Huarte, 1964	205	114	11	.556	2062	16†

Terry Hanratty, 1967	206	110	15	.534	1439	9
Joe Theismann, 1969	192	108	16†	.563	1531	13

Passes Caught

Career:	Ct.	Yards	TD
Tom Gatewood, 1969-71	157*	2283*	19*
Jim Seymour, 1966-68	138	2113	16
Bob Gladieux, 1966-68	72	947	6
Joe Heap, 1951-54	71	1166	7
Jack Snow, 1962-64	70	1242	9
Pete Demmerle, 1974	69	1071	11
Season:			
Tom Gatewood, 1970	77*	1123*	7
Jack Snow, 1964	60	1114	9*
Jim Seymour, 1968	53	736	4
Jim Seymour, 1966	48	862	8
Tom Gatewood, 1969	47	743	8

Interceptions

Career:	No.	Yards
Tom MacDonald, 1961-63	15*	167
Ralph Stepaniak, 1969-71	13	179
Clarence Ellis, 1969-71	13	157
Johnny Lattner, 1951-53	13	128
Mike Townsend, 1971-73	13	86
Angelo Bertelli, 1941-43	12	60
Tom Schoen, 1965-67	11	226*
Tony Carey, 1963-65	11	130
Season:		
Mike Townsend, 1972	10*	39
Tom MacDonald, 1962	9	81
Tony Carey, 1964	8	121
Angelo Bertelli, 1942	8	41

Punt Return Average
(Min. 1.5 Returns Per Game)

Career:	No.	Yards	Avg.
Nick Rassas, 1963-65	39	612	15.7*
Bill Gay, 1947-50	46	580	12.6
Andy Puplis, 1935-37	47	527	11.2
Frank Carideo, 1928-30	92*	947*	10.3
Tom Schoen, 1965-67	71	700	9.9
Season:			
Nick Rassas, 1965	24	459	19.1*
Andy Puplis, 1937	21	281	13.4
Bill Gay, 1949	19	254	13.4
Frank Dancewicz, 1945	18	240	13.3
Steve Juzwik, 1941	22	280	12.7

Kickoff Return Average

Career:	No.	Yards	Avg.
(Min. 0.5 Rets. P.G.)			
Paul Castner, 1920-22	21	767*	36.5*
Nick Eddy, 1964-66	14	404	28.9
Paul Hornung, 1954-56	23	663	28.8
Jim Crotty, 1957-59	16	424	26.5
Ron Bliey, 1962-63	18	440	24.4
Gary Diminick, 1971-73	30*	711	23.7
Season: (Min. 6 Returns)			
Paul Castner, 1922	11	490	44.5
Johnny Lattner, 1953	8	331	41.4
Paul Hornung, 1956	16	496*	31.0
Christy Flanagan, 1926	6	183	30.5
Chet Wynne, 1921	9	258	28.7

Scoring

Career:	TD	XPt.	FG	Pts.
Louis (Red) Salmon, 1900-03	36*	60	2	250*§
Stan Cofall, 1914-16	30	60	2	246
Gus Dorais, 1910-13	12¶	96	11	198
Ray Eichenlaub, 1911-14	30‡	0	0	176
Neil Worden, 1951-53	29	0	0	174
Season:				
Louis (Red) Salmon, 1903	15	30	0	105*
Bob Gladieux, 1968	14	0	0	84
Bob Kelly, 1944	14	0	0	84
Stan Cofall, 1916	12	12	0	84

Kick-Scoring

Career:	XPt.	FG	Pts.
Scott Hempel, 1968-70	122*	14	164*
Bob Thomas, 1971-73	98	21*	161
Gus Dorais, 1910-13	96	11	129
Joe Azzaro, 1964, 66-67	79	13	118
Bob Thomas, 1971-72	55	12	91
Ken Ivan, 1963-65	54	12	90
Season:			
Bob Thomas, 1973	43	9*	70*
Joe Azzaro, 1967	37	8	61
Scott Hempel, 1968	45*	5	60
Scott Hempel, 1969	41	5	56
Bob Thomas, 1972	34	7	55
Ken Ivan, 1965	27	7	48

Punting Average

Career:	No.	Yards	Avg.
Bill Shakespeare, 1933-35	91	3705	40.7*
Brian Doherty, 1971-73	134*	5333*	39.8
Paul Castner, 1920-22	84	3329	39.6
Dan McGinn, 1963-65	94	3684	39.2
Harry Stevenson, 1937-39	92	3529	38.4
George Gipp, 1917-20	96	3670	38.2

———

*Notre Dame record.
†Notre Dame record shared.
§Salmon's TD and FG were worth 5 points each.
¶Three of Dorais' touchdowns were worth 5 points each.
‡Four of Eichenlaub's touchdowns were worth 5 points each.

General Team Records

Won-Lost Record — Home and Away

	Won	Lost	Tied	Pct.
Home	309	56	12	.840
Away	193	78	19	.697
Neutral Sites	69	19	7	.763
Totals	571	153	38	.789

Consecutive Wins
21	(1946-48)
20	(1919-20)
20	(1929-31)

Consecutive Games Without Defeat
39	(2 ties)	(1946-50)
27	(3 ties)	(1910-14)
26	(1 tie)	(1929-31)

Consecutive Losses
8 (1960)

Consecutive Wins at Home
39 (From Nov. 9, 1907, vs. Knox through Nov. 17, 1917, vs. Michigan State)

Consecutive Games Undefeated at Home
93 (Including 3 ties; from Oct. 28, 1905, vs. American Medical through Oct. 27, 1928, vs. Drake. Carnegie Tech ended streak with a 27-7 victory on Nov. 17, 1928)

Consecutive Games Scoring
73 (From Sept. 24, 1966; intact start of 1976 season)

Consecutive Shutouts
9 (1903)

Consecutive Games Shut Out by Opponents
4 (1933)

Consecutive Capacity Crowds at Notre Dame Stadium
48 (From Nov. 14, 1964, vs. Michigan State. Ended vs. Air Force, Nov. 22, 1973)

Points Scored, Half and Quarter*
Half
1st: 121—American Medical, 1905; MR: 49—Pittsburgh, 1968
2nd: 74—St. Viator, 1912; MR: 39—Pittsburgh, 1944
Quarter
1st: 35—Kalamazoo, 1921; MR: 32—Tulane, 1947
2nd: 35—Indiana, 1951
3rd: 42—St. Viator, 1912; MR: 27—Illinois, 1968; SMU, 1952
4th: 32—St. Viator, 1912; MR: 28—Illinois, 1941

*Game was divided into quarters in 1910

Highlights
of All-Time
Record

Under Knute Rockne (1918-1930)
Notre Dame won 105, lost 12, tied 5—.898

Under Heartley (Hunk) Anderson (1931-33)
Notre Dame won 16, lost 9, tied 2—.640

Under Elmer Layden (1934-1940)
Notre Dame won 47, lost 13, tied 3—.783

Under Edward McKeever (1944)
Notre Dame won 8, lost 2—.800

Under Frank Leahy (1941-43; 1946-53)
Notre Dame won 87, lost 11, tied 9—.888

Under Terry Brennan (1954-58)
Notre Dame won 32, lost 18—.640

Under Joe Kuharich (1959-1962)
Notre Dame won 17, lost 23—.425

Under Hugh Devore (1945; 1963)
Notre Dame won 9, lost 9, tied 1—.500

Under Ara Parseghian (1964-1974)
Notre Dame won 95, lost 17, tied 4—.848

Biggest score for Notre Dame
1905—Notre Dame 142, American Medical 0

Biggest score under Rockne
1926—Notre Dame 77, Beloit 0

Biggest score under Anderson
1932—Notre Dame 73, Haskell 0

Biggest score under Layden
1940—Notre Dame 61, Carnegie Tech 0

Biggest score under McKeever
1944—Notre Dame 64, Dartmouth 0

Biggest score under Leahy
1947—Notre Dame 59, Tulane 6

Biggest score under Brennan
1957—Notre Dame 54, Southern Methodist 21

Biggest score under Kuharich
1961—Notre Dame 30, Southern California 0

Biggest score under Devore
1945—Notre Dame 56, Iowa 0

Biggest score under Parseghian
1965—Notre Dame 69, Pittsburgh 13

Worst defeat of all time
1944—Notre Dame 0, Army 59

Worst defeat under Rockne
1925—Notre Dame 0, Army 27

Worst defeat under Anderson
1933—Notre Dame 0, Purdue 19
1933—Notre Dame 0, Southern Cal. 19

Worst defeat under Layden
1936—Notre Dame 0, Pittsburgh 26

Worst defeat under McKeever
1944—Notre Dame 0, Army 59

Worst defeat under Leahy
1951—Notre Dame 0, Michigan State 35

Worst defeat under Brennan
1956—Notre Dame 0, Oklahoma 40
1956—Notre Dame 8, Iowa 48

Worst defeat under Kuharich
1960—Notre Dame 19, Purdue 51

Worst defeat under Devore
1945—Notre Dame 0, Army 48

Worst defeat under Parseghian
1972—Notre Dame 6, Nebraska 40

Most points scored by Notre Dame at home: 142
(Oct. 28, 1905—ND 142, American Medical 0)

Most points scored by Notre Dame away from home: 69
(Nov. 6, 1965—ND 69, Pittsburgh 13)

Most points scored against Notre Dame at home: 51
(Oct. 1, 1960—Purdue 51, ND 19)

Most points scored against Notre Dame away: 59
(Nov. 11, 1944—Army 59, ND 0, in New York)

Worst defeat for Notre Dame at home
Oklahoma 40, ND 0 (Oct. 27, 1956)

Worst defeat for Notre Dame away
Army 59, ND 0 (Nov. 11, 1944)

Head Football Coaches

Year	Coach	Won	Lost	Tied	
1887-88-89-92-93	No head coaches	7	4	1	.636
1894	J. L. Morison	3	1	1	.750
1895	H. G. Hadden	3	1	0	.750
1896-98	Frank E. Hering	12	6	1	.667
1899	James McWeeney	6	3	1	.667
1900-01	Patrick O'Dea	14	4	2	.778
1902-03	James Faragher	14	2	2	.875
1904	Louis Salmon	5	3	0	.625
1905	Henry J. McGlew	5	4	0	.556
1906-07	Thomas Barry	12	1	1	.923
1908	Victor M. Place	8	1	0	.889
1909-10	Frank C. Longman	11	1	2	.917
1911-12	L. H. Marks	13	0	2	1.000
1913-17	Jesse C. Harper	34	5	1	.872
1918-30	Knute Rockne	105	12	5	.897
1931-33	Heartley (Hunk) Anderson	16	9	2	.640
1934-40	Elmer Layden	47	13	3	.783
1941-43, 46-53	Frank Leahy	87	11	9	.888
1944	Edward McKeever	8	2	0	.800
1945; 1963	Hugh Devore	9	9	1	.500
1954-58	Terry Brennan	32	18	0	.640
1959-62	Joseph Kuharich	17	23	0	.425
1964-74	Ara Parseghian	95	17	4	.848
1975	Dan Devine	8	3	0	.727
		571	153	38	.789

Notre Dame All-Time Individual Records

(Includes Regular Season Games Only)

Total Offense

(Rushing and Passing Combined)

Plays
Game: 75—Terry Hanratty vs. Purdue, 1967
(420 yards)
71—Joe Theismann vs. Southern Cal, 1970
(512 yards)
Season: 391—Joe Theismann, 1970 (2813 yards)
310—Tom Clements, 1974 (1918 yards)
308—Joe Theismann, 1969 (1909 yards)
Career: 807—Joe Theismann, 1968-70 (5432 yards)
760—Tom Clements, 1972-74 (4664 yards)
731—Terry Hanratty, 1966-68 (4738 yards)

Plays Per Game
Season: 39.1—Joe Theismann, 1970 (391 in 10)
Career: 28.1—Terry Hanratty, 1966-68 (731 in 26)

Yards Gained
Game: 512—Joe Theismann vs. Southern Cal, 1970
(526 passing, minus 14 rushing)
420—Terry Hanratty vs. Purdue, 1967 (366
passing, 54 rushing)
Season: 2813—Joe Theismann, 1970 (384 rushing,
2429 passing)
2069—John Huarte, 1964 (7 rushing, 2062
passing)
Career: 5432—Joe Theismann, 1968-70 (1021 rushing, 4411 passing)
4738—Terry Hanratty, 1966-68 (586 rushing,
4738 passing)

Yards Per Game
Season: 281.3—Joe Theismann, 1970 (2813 in 10)
249.3—Terry Hanratty, 1968 (1745 in 7)
Career: 187.3—Joe Theismann, 1968-70 (5432 in 29)
182.2—Terry Hanratty, 1966-68 (4738 in 26)

Yards Per Play
Game: (Min. 20 plays) 13.7—John Huarte vs. Navy,
1964 (20 for 273)
Season: (Min. 1000 yards) 9.37—George Gipp,1920
(164 for 1536)
8.55—John Huarte, 1964
(242 for 2069)
Career: (Min. 2000 yards) 7.46—John Huarte,
1962-64
(306 for 2283)
7.39—George Gipp,
1917-20
(556 for 4110)

Points Responsible For
(Points Scored and Passed For)
Game: 35—Art Smith vs. Loyola, Chicago, 1911 (7
TDs, 5 points each)
Season: 126—John Mohardt, 1921 (scored 12 TDs,
passed for 9)

124—Joe Theismann, 1970 (scored 26 points, passed for 98)

Career: 280—Joe Theismann, 1968-70 (scored 92 points, passed for 31 TDs and one 2-point conversion)

264—Terry Hanratty, 1966-68 (scored 98 points, passed for 27 TDs and two 2-point conversions)

Points Responsible For Per Game
Season: 12.4—Joe Theismann, 1970 (124 in 10)
11.8—John Huarte, 1964 (118 in 10)
Career: 10.2—Terry Hanratty, 1966-68 (264 in 26)
9.7—Joe Theismann, 1968-70 (280 in 29)

Rushing

Carries
Game: 36—Wayne Bullock vs. Michigan State, 1974 (127 yards)
29—Denny Allan vs. Michigan State, 1969 (102 yards)
29—Creighton Miller vs. Northwestern, 1942 (151 yards)
Season: 203—Wayne Bullock, 1974 (855 yards)
181—Neil Worden, 1951 (676 yards)
Also holds per-game record at 18.1
162—Wayne Bullock, 1973 (752 yards)
Career: 476—Neil Worden, 1951-53 (2039 yards)
Also holds per-game record at 15.9 (476 in 30)
392—Wayne Bullock, 1972-74 (1730 yards)
369—George Gipp, 1917-20 (2341 yards)

Consecutive Carries by Same Player
Game: 8—Larry Conjar vs. Army, 1965
8—Neil Worden vs. Oklahoma, 1952

Yards Gained
Game: 186—Emil Sitko vs. Michigan State, 1948 (24 carries)
185—Marchy Schwartz vs. Carnegie Tech, 1931 (19 carries)
Season: 927—Marchy Schwartz, 1930 (124 carries)
911—Creighton Miller, 1943 (151 carries)
Career: 2341—George Gipp, 1917-20 (369 carries)
2226—Emil Sitko, 1946-49 (362 carries)

Yards Gained Per Game
Season: 103.4—George Gipp, 1920 (827 in 8)
95.4—Don Miller, 1924 (763 in 8)
Career: 86.7—George Gipp, 1917-20 (2341 in 27)
74.3—Don Miller, 1922-24 (1933 in 26)

Average Per Carry
Game: (Min. 10 carries) 17.1—John Petitbon vs. Michigan State, 1950 (10 for 171)
(Min. 5 carries) 24.4—Coy McGee vs. Southern Cal, 1946 (6 for 146)
Season: (Min. 100 carries) 8.1—George Gipp, 1920 (102 for 827)
7.5—Marchy Schwartz, 1930 (124 for 927)
Career: (Min. 150 carries) 6.8—Don Miller, 1922-24 (283 for 1933)
6.4—Christy Flanagan, 1926-28 (285 for 1822)

Touchdowns Scored by Rushing
Game: 7—Art Smith vs. Loyola, Chicago, 1911
6—Bill Downs vs. DePauw, 1905
Season: 16—Bill Downs, 1905
(Per Game) 1.7—Ray Eichenlaub, 1913 (12 in 7)
Career: 36—Louis (Red) Salmon, 1900-03
30—Stan Cofall, 1914-16
Also holds per-game record at 1.2 (30 in 25)
29—Neil Worden, 1951-53

Longest Rush
92—Bob Livingstone vs. Southern Cal, 1947 (TD)

Passing

Attempts
Game: 63—Terry Hanratty vs. Purdue, 1967 (completed 29)
58—Joe Theismann vs. Southern Cal, 1970 (completed 33)
Season: 268—Joe Theismann, 1970 (completed 155)
215—Tom Clements, 1974 (completed 122)
210—Bob Williams, 1950 (completed 99)
Career: 550—Terry Hanratty, 1966-68 (completed 304)
509—Joe Theismann, 1968-70 (completed 290)

Attempts Per Game
Season: 28.1—Terry Hanratty, 1968 (197 in 7)
Career: 21.2—Terry Hanratty, 1966-68 (550 in 26)

Completions
Game: 33—Joe Theismann vs. Southern Cal, 1970 (attempted 58)
29—Terry Hanratty vs. Purdue, 1967 (attempted 63)
Season: 155—Joe Theismann, 1970 (attempted 268)

122—Tom Clements, 1974 (attempted 215)
116—Terry Hanratty, 1968 (attempted 197)
Career: 304—Terry Hanratty, 1966-68 (attempted 550)
290—Joe Theismann, 1968-70 (attempted 509)

Completions Per Game
Season: 16.6—Terry Hanratty, 1968 (116 in 7)
Career: 11.7—Terry Hanratty, 1966-68 (304 in 26)

Consecutive Passes Completed
Game: 10—Angelo Bertelli vs. Stanford, 1942

Consecutive Games Completing a Pass
Career: 34—Ralph Guglielmi; last 4 games of 1951, all 10 of 1952, 1953, 1954

Percent Completed
Game: (Min. 10 comp.) 81.3%—Bob Williams vs. Michigan State, 1949 (13 of 16)
78.9%—Cliff Brown vs. Tulane, 1971 (15 of 19)
Season: (Min. 100 atts.) 58.9%—Terry Hanratty, 1968 (116 of 197)
57.8%—Joe Theismann, 1970 (155 of 268)
Career: (Min. 150 atts.) 57.0%—Joe Theismann, 1968-70 (290 of 509)
55.3%—Terry Hanratty, 1966-68 (304 of 550)

Passes Had Intercepted
Game: 7—Frank Dancewicz vs. Army, 1944
Season: 16—Joe Theismann, 1969; Angelo Bertelli, 1942; John Niemiec, 1928 (also holds per-game record at 1.8, 16 in 9)
Career: 35—Joe Theismann, 1968-70
(Per Game) 1.3—Terry Hanratty, 1966-68 (34 in 26)

Lowest Percentage Had Intercepted
Season: (Min. 100 atts.) 3.5%—Ralph Guglielmi, 1953 (4 of 113)
4.6%—Terry Hanratty, 1968 (9 of 197)
Career: (Min. 150 atts.) 4.3%—John Huarte, 1962-64 (11 of 255)
5.5%—Ralph Guglielmi, 1951-54 (24 of 436)

Attempts Without Interception
Game: 31—Frank Dancewicz vs. Navy, 1944

Consecutive Attempts Without Interception
Career: 91—John Huarte, all of 1962 and 1963 and first two games of 1964

Yards Gained
Game: 526—Joe Theismann vs. Southern Cal, 1970
366—Terry Hanratty vs. Purdue, 1967
Season: 2429—Joe Theismann, 1970
2062—John Huarte, 1964
Career: 4411—Joe Theismann, 1968-70
4152—Terry Hanratty, 1966-68

Yards Per Game
Season: 242.9—Joe Theismann, 1970 (2429 in 10)
209.4—Terry Hanratty, 1968 (1466 in 7)
Career: 159.7—Terry Hanratty, 1966-68 (4152 in 26)
152.1—Joe Theismann, 1968-70 (4411 in 29)

Yards Per Attempt
Game: (Min. 20 atts.) 12.8—George Izo vs. Pittsburgh, 1958 (26 for 332)
Season: (Min. 100 atts.) 10.1—John Huarte, 1964 (205 for 2062)
9.4—Joe Theismann, 1970 (268 for 2529)
Career: (Min. 150 atts.) 9.2—John Huarte, 1962-64 (255 for 2343)
8.7—Joe Theismann, 1968-70 (509 for 4411)

Yards Per Completion
Game: (Min. 10 comp.) 27.4 John Huarte vs. Navy, 1964 (10 for 274)
Season: (Min. 50 comp.) 18.1—John Huarte, 1964 (114 for 2062)
17.8—George Izo, 1958 (60 for 1067)
Career: (Min. 75 comp.) 17.3—George Izo, 1957-59 (121 for 2095)
17.0—John Huarte, 1962-64 (138 for 2343)

Touchdown Passes
Game: 4—Daryle Lamonica vs. Pittsburgh, 1962
4—Angelo Bertelli vs. Stanford, 1942
Season: 16—Joe Theismann, 1970; John Huarte, 1964; Bob Williams, 1949
Career: 31—Joe Theismann, 1968-70
28—Angelo Bertelli, 1941-43

Touchdown Passes Per Game

Season: 1.7—Angelo Bertelli, 1943 (10 in 6)
Career: 1.08—Angelo Bertelli, 1941-43 (28 in 26)
           1.07—Joe Theismann, 1968-70 (31 in 29)

Longest Pass Play

91—John Huarte to Nick Eddy vs. Pittsburgh, 1964 (TD)

Receiving

Passes Caught

Game: 13—Jim Seymour vs. Purdue, 1966 (276 yards, 3 TD)
           12—Tom Gatewood vs. Purdue, 1970 (192 yards, 3 TD)
Season: 77—Tom Gatewood, 1970 (1123 yards)
           60—Jack Snow, 1964 (1114 yards)
Career: 157—Tom Gatewood, 1969-71 (2283 yards)
           138—Jim Seymour, 1966-68 (2113 yards)

Catches Per Game

Season: 7.7—Tom Gatewood, 1970 (77 in 10)
           6.9—Jim Seymour, 1966 (48 in 7)
Career: 5.3—Jim Seymour, 1966-68 (138 in 26)
           5.2—Tom Gatewood, 1969-71 (157 in 30)

Yards Gained

Game: 276—Jim Seymour vs. Purdue, 1966 (caught 13, 3 TD)
         217—Jack Snow vs. Wisconsin, 1964 (caught 9, 2 TD)
Season: 1123—Tom Gatewood, 1970 (caught 77)
        1114—Jack Snow, 1964 (caught 60)
Career: 2283—Tom Gatewood, 1969-71 (caught 157)
        2113—Jim Seymour, 1966-68 (caught 138)

Yards Per Game

Season: 123.1—Jim Seymour, 1966 (862 in 7)
        112.3—Tom Gatewood, 1970 (1123 in 10)
Career: 81.3—Jim Seymour, 1966-68 (2113 in 26)
        76.1—Tom Gatewood, 1969-71 (2283 in 30)

Yards Per Catch

Game: (Min. 5) 41.6—Jim Morse vs. Southern Cal, 1955 (5 for 208)
                 24.9—Larry Parker vs. Southern Cal, 1970 (7 for 174)
Season: (Min. 20) 22.1—Jim Morse, 1956 (20 for 442)
         (Min. 30) 18.6—Jack Snow, 1964 (60 for 1114)
Career: (Min. 40) 21.2—Jim Morse, 1954-56 (52 for 1102)
                 17.7—Jack Snow, 1962-64 (70 for 1242)

Touchdown Passes

Game: 3—Tom Gatewood vs. Purdue, 1970; Jim Seymour vs. Purdue, 1966; Jim Kelly vs. Pittsburgh, 1962; Jim Mutscheller vs. Michigan State, 1950; Bill Barrett vs. North Carolina, 1949; Eddie Anderson vs. Northwestern, 1920
Season: 9—Jack Snow, 1964
Career: 19—Tom Gatewood, 1969-71
           16—Jim Seymour, 1966-68

Touchdown Passes Per Game

Season: 1.1—Jim Seymour, 1966 (8 in 7)
Career: 0.6—Tom Gatewood, 1969-71 (19 in 30)

Punting

Punts

Game: 15—Marchy Schwartz vs. Army, 1931 (509 yards)
Season: 67—Fred Evans, 1941 (2557 yards)
           64—Johnny Lattner, 1952 (2345 yards)
Career: 134—Brian Doherty, 1971-73 (5333 yards)
           122—Bob Williams, 1948-50 (4606 yards)
           119—Johnny Lattner, 1951-53 (4200 yards)

Punts Per Game

Season: 7.4—Fred Evans, 1941 (67 in 9)
Career: 5.5—Fred Evans, 1940-42 (105 in 19)

Average Per Punt

Game: (Min. 5) 48.7 —Joe O'Neill vs. Pittsburgh 1936 (7 for 341)
        (Min. 10) 44.8 —Paul Castner vs. Purdue, 1921 (12 for 537)
Season: (Min. 30) 42.7 —Brian Doherty, 1973 (39 for 1664)
                40.02—Bill Shakespeare, 1935 (45 for 1801)
                40.00—Bill Shakespeare, 1934 (41 for 1638)
Career: (Min. 50) 40.7 —Bill Shakespeare, 1933-35 (91 for 3705)
                39.6 —Paul Castner, 1920-22 (84 for 3329)
        (Min. 100) 39.8 —Brian Doherty, 1971-73 (134 for 5333)

Longest Punt

86—Bill Shakespeare vs. Pittsburgh, 1935

Interceptions

Interceptions Made
Game: 3—By 11 players. Last: Mike Townsend vs. Air Force, 1972

Season: 10—Mike Townsend, 1972 (39 yards) Also holds per-game record at 1.0 (10 in 10)
9—Tom MacDonald, 1962 (81 yards)

Career: 15—Tom MacDonald, 1961-63 (167 yards) Also holds per-game record at 0.6 (15 in 24)

Interceptions by a Linebacker
Season: 5—John Pergine, 1966 (72 yards)

Career: 9—John Pergine, 1965-67 (91 yards)

Yards Gained
Game: 96—Jack Elder vs. Army, 1929 (1 interception)

Season: 197—Nick Rassas, 1965 (6 interceptions) Also holds per-game record at 19.7
151—Frank Carideo, 1929 (5 interceptions)

Career: 226—Tom Schoen, 1965-67 (11 interceptions)
220—Nick Rassas, 1963-65 (7 interceptions). Also holds per-game record at 10.5 (220 in 21)

Average Per Return
Game: (Min. 2) 42.5—Steve Juzwik vs. Army, 1940 (2 for 85)

Season: (Min. 4) 32.8—Nick Rassas, 1965 (6 for 197)
30.2—Frank Carideo, 1929 (5 for 151)

Career: (Min. 6) 31.4—Nick Rassas, 1963-65 (7 for 220)
21.2—Paul Hornung, 1954-56 (10 for 212)

Touchdowns
Game: 1—By many players. Last: Randy Harrison vs. Navy, 1974

Season: 2—Tom Schoen, 1966; Randy Harrison, 1974

Career: 3—Tom Schoen, 1965-67

Longest Interception Return
96—Jack Elder vs. Army, 1929 (TD)

Punt Returns

Punt Returns
Game: 9—Tom Schoen vs. Pittsburgh, 1967 (167 yards)

Season: 42—Tom Schoen, 1967 (447 yards) Also holds per-game record at 4.7
40—Gene Edwards, 1925 (173 yards)

Career: 92—Frank Carideo, 1928-30 (947 yards) Also holds per-game record at 3.3 (92 in 28)
88—Harry Stuhldreher, 1922-24 (701 yards)

Yards Gained
Game: 167—Tom Schoen vs. Pittsburgh, 1967 (9 returns)
157—Chet Grant vs. Case Tech, 1916 (3 returns)

Season: 459—Nick Rassas, 1965 (24 returns)
447—Tom Schoen, 1967 (42 returns) Also holds per-game record at 49.7 (447 in 9)

Career: 947—Frank Carideo, 1928-30 (92 returns) Also holds per-game record at 33.8 (947 in 28)
701—Harry Stuhldreher, 1922-24 (88 returns)

Average Per Return
Game: (Min. 3) 52.3—Chet Grant vs. Case Tech, 1916 (3 for 157)
(Min. 5) 22.0—Frank Carideo vs. Georgia Tech, 1929 (5 for 110)

Season: (Min. 1.5 rets. per game)
19.1—Nick Rassas, 1965 (24 for 459)
13.4—Andy Puplis, 1937 (21 for 281)

Career: (Min. 1.5 rets. per game)
15.7—Nick Rassas, 1963-65 (39 for 612)
12.6—Bill Gay, 1948-50 (46 for 580)

Touchdowns
Game: 2—Vince McNally vs. Beloit, 1926

Season: 3—Nick Rassas, 1965

Career: 3—Nick Rassas, 1963-65

Longest Punt Return
95—Chet Grant vs. Case Tech, 1916 (TD)
95—Harry (Red) Miller vs. Olivet, 1909 (did not score, 110-yard field)

Kickoff Returns

Kickoff Returns
Game: 8—George Gipp vs. Army, 1920 (157 yards)
6—Mark McLane vs. Southern Cal, 1974 (95 yards)

6—Jack Landry vs. Michigan State, 1951 (112 yards)

Season: 16—Bill Wolski, 1963 (379 yards)
Also holds per-game record at 1.8 (16 in 9)
16—Paul Hornung, 1956 (496 yards)

Career: 30—Gary Diminick, 1971-73 (711 yards)
24—Bill Wolski, 1963-65 (559 yards)
24—Bob Scarpitto, 1958-60 (493 yards)
(Per Game) 1.1—Ron Bliey, 1962-63 (18 in 16 games)

Yards Gained
Game: 253—Paul Castner vs. Kalamazoo, 1922 (4 returns)
174—Willie Maher vs. Kalamazoo, 1923 (4 returns)

Season: 496—Paul Hornung, 1956 (16 returns)
(Per Game) 70.0—Paul Castner, 1922 (490 in 7)
490—Paul Castner, 1922 (11 returns)

Career: 767—Paul Castner, 1920-22 (21 returns)
Also holds per-game record at 29.5 (767 in 26)
711—Gary Diminick, 1971-73 (30 returns)
663—Paul Hornung, 1954-56 (23 returns)

Average Per Return
Game: (Min. 2) 74.0—Johnny Lattner vs. Penn, 1953 (2 for 148)
Season: (Min. 0.5 rets. per game) 48.3—Nick Eddy, 1966 (4 for 193)
Career: (Min. 12) 36.5—Paul Castner, 1920-22 (21 for 767)
28.9—Nick Eddy, 1964-66 (14 for 404)

Touchdowns
Game: 2—Paul Castner vs. Kalamazoo, 1922
Season: 2—Nick Eddy, 1966; Johnny Lattner, 1953; Willie Maher, 1923; Paul Castner, 1922
Career: Same as season record

Longest Kickoff Return
105—Alfred Bergman vs. Loyola, Chicago, 1911 (did not score, 110 yard field)
100—Joe Savoldi vs. SMU, 1930 (TD)

Total Kick Returns

(Combined Punt and Kickoff Returns)

Kick Returns
Game: 10—George Gipp vs. Army, 1920 (2 punts, 8 kickoffs; 207 yards)
9—Tom Schoen vs. Pittsburgh, 1967 (9 punts; 167 yards)

Season: 43—Gene Edwards, 1925 (40 punts, 3 kickoffs; 213 yards)
42—Tom Schoen, 1967 (42 punts; 447 yards). Also holds per-game record at 4.7 (42 in 9)

Career: 96—Frank Carideo, 1928-30 (92 punts, 4 kickoffs; 1006 yards). Also holds per-game record at 3.4 (96 in 28)
91—Harry Stuhldreher, 1922-24 (88 punts, 3 kickoffs; 724 yards)

Yards Gained
Game: 254—Willie Maher vs. Kalamazoo, 1923 (80 on punts, 174 on kickoffs)
253—Paul Castner vs. Kalamazoo, 1922 (253 on kickoffs)

Season: 559—Paul Hornung, 1956 (63 on punts, 496 on kickoffs). Also holds per-game record at 55.9
541—Nick Rassas, 1965 (459 on punts, 82 on kickoffs)

Career: 1006—Frank Carideo, 1928-30 (947 on punts, 59 on kickoffs). Also holds per-game record at 35.9 (1006 in 28)
797—Nick Rassas, 1963-65 (612 on punts, 185 on kickoffs)

Average Per Return
Game: (Min. 5) 22.7—Angelo Dabiero vs. Pittsburgh, 1960 (6 for 136)
22.0—Frank Carideo vs. Georgia Tech, 1929 (5 for 110)

Season: (Min. 1.5 rets. per game) 28.0—Paul Hornung, 1956 (20 for 559)
23.3—Bill Gay, 1948 (15 for 349)

Career: (Min. 1.5 rets. per game) 17.7—George Gipp, 1917-20 (38 for 671)
17.0—Nick Rassas, 1963-65 (47 for 797)

Touchdowns Scored
Game: 2—Vince McNally vs. Beloit (punt returns)
2—Paul Castner vs. Kalamazoo, 1922 (kickoff returns)
Season: 3—Nick Rassas, 1965 (punt returns)
Career: 3—Nick Rassas, 1963-65 (punt returns)

All-Purpose Running

(Yardage gained from rushing, receiving and all runbacks)

Yards Gained
Game: 361—Willie Maher vs. Kalamazoo, 1923 (107 rushing, 80 punt returns, 174 kickoff returns)
367—George Gipp vs. Army, 1920 (150 rushing, 50 punt returns, 157 kick-off returns)
Season: 1512—Bob Gladieux, 1968 (717 rushing, 442 receiving, 91 punt returns, 262 kickoff returns)
Also holds per-game record at 151.2
1387—Creighton Miller, 1943
Career: 3116—Johnny Lattner, 1951-53 (1724 rushing, 581 receiving, 128 interceptions, 307 punt returns, 376 kickoff returns)
3064—George Gipp, 1917-20

Yards Per Game
Career: 113.5—George Gipp, 1917-20 (3064 in 27; 2341 rushing, 52 interceptions, 217 punt returns, 454 kickoffs)
103.9—Johnny Lattner, 1951-53 (3116 in 30)

Total Yardage Gained

(Yardage gained from rushing, passing, receiving and all runbacks)

Yards Gained
Game: 519—Joe Theismann vs. Southern Cal, 1970 (526 passing, 7 receiving, minus 14 rushing)
420—Terry Hanratty vs. Purdue, 1967
Season: 2820—Joe Theismann, 1970 (2429 passing, 384 rushing, 7 receiving). Also holds per-game record at 282.0
2080—John Huarte, 1964
Career: 5551—Joe Theismann, 1968-70 (4411 passing, 1021 rushing, 20 receiving, 99 punt returns). Also holds per-game record at 191.4 (5551 in 29)
4833—George Gipp, 1917-20

Scoring

Points Scored
Game: 35—Art Smith vs. Loyola, Chicago, 1911 (7 TD, 5 points each)
30—Bill Wolski vs. Pittsburgh, 1965 (5 TD); Willie Maher vs. Kalamazoo, 1923 (5 TD); Bill Downs vs. DePauw, 1905 (6 TD, 5 points each)
Season: 105—Louis (Red) Salmon, 1903 (15 TD, 5 points each, 30 PAT)
84—Bob Gladieux, 1968; Bob Kelly, 1944; Stan Cofall, 1916
Career: 250—Louis (Red) Salmon, 1900-03 (36 TD, 5 points each, 60 PAT, 2 FG, 5 points each)

Points Per Game
Season: 11.7—Louis (Red) Salmon, 1903 (105 in 9)
11.1—Alvin Berger, 1912 (78 in 7)
Career: 10.3—Stan Cofall, 1914-16 (246 in 24)
7.1—Gus Dorais, 1910-13 (198 in 28)

Touchdowns
Game: 7—Art Smith vs. Loyola, Chicago, 1911
6—Bill Downs vs. DePauw, 1905
Season: 16—Bill Downs, 1905
Also holds per-game record at 1.8 (16 in 9)
15—Louis (Red) Salmon, 1903
Career: 36—Louis (Red) Salmon, 1900-03
30—Stan Cofall, 1914-16; Ray Eichenlaub, 1911-14
(Per Game) 1.3—Stan Cofall, 1914-16 (30 in 24)

First Notre Dame Touchdown
Harry Jewett vs. Michigan, April 20, 1888 (5-yard run)

2-Point Attempts
Game: 3—Joe Theismann vs. Pittsburgh, 1970; Terry Hanratty vs. Pittsburgh, 1966; John Huarte vs. Wisconsin and Michigan State, 1964
Season: 9—John Huarte, 1964
6—Terry Hanratty, 1966
Career: 10—John Huarte, 1962-68
8—Terry Hanratty, 1966-68

2-Point Attempts Scored
Season: 2—Bob Minnix, 1971; Bill Wolski, 1965

Successful 2-Point Passes
Season: 2—John Huarte, 1964 (attempted 9)

Kick-Scoring

Field Goals Made
Game: 3—Bob Thomas vs. Southern Cal, 1973 (3 attempts); Michigan State and Northwestern, 1972 (3 attempts) and North Carolina, 1971 (3 attempts); Gus Dorais vs. Texas, 1913 (7 attempts)

Season: 9—Bob Thomas, 1973 (18 attempts)
8—Joe Azzaro, 1967 (10 attempts)
7—Dave Reeve, 1974; Bob Thomas, 1972; Ken Ivan, 1965

Career: 21—Bob Thomas, 1971-73 (35 attempts)
14—Scott Hempel, 1968-70 (21 attempts)
13—Joe Azzaro, 1964, 66-67 (18 attempts)

Field Goals Attempted
Game: 7—Gus Dorais vs. Texas, 1913 (made 3)
4—Paul Castner vs. Purdue and Nebraska, 1921

Season: 18—Bob Thomas, 1971-73 (made 9)
14—Paul Castner, 1921 (made 4)

Career: 35—Bob Thomas, 1971-73 (made 21)
28—Paul Castner, 1920-22 (made 6)

Longest Field Goal Made
49—Joe Perkowski vs. Southern Cal, 1961

First Notre Dame Field Goal
Mike Daly vs. Chicago, 1897 (35 yards)

Points After Touchdown Made
Game: 9—By four players. Last: Ken Ivan vs. Pittsburgh, 1965 (10 attempts)

Season: 45—Scott Hempel, 1968 (50 attempts)
Also holds per-game record at 4.5
43—Bob Thomas, 1973 (45 attempts)

Career: 122—Scott Hempel, 1968-70 (132 attempts)
Also holds per-game record at 4.4 (122 in 28)
98—Bob Thomas, 1971-73 (101 attempts)

Points After Touchdown Attempted
Game: 12—Frank Winters vs. Englewood H.S., 1900 (made 9)
10—Ken Ivan vs. Pittsburgh, 1965 (made 9)

Season: 52—Steve Oracko, 1949 (made 38)
51—Scott Hempel, 1968 (made 45)

Career: 132—Scott Hempel, 1968-70 (made 122)
105—Gus Dorais, 1910-13 (made 96)

Percent Made
Season: (Min. 20 made)
100%—Bob Thomas, 1972 (34 of 34)
95.6%—Bob Thomas, 1973 (43 of 45)
95.5%—Bob Thomas, 1971 (21 of 22)

Career: (Min. 50 made)
97.0%—Bob Thomas, 1971-73 (98 of 101)
92.4%—Scott Hempel, 1968-70 (122 of 132)

Consecutive PAT Made
62—Bob Thomas, from Nov. 6, 1971 vs. Pittsburgh to Oct. 20, 1973 vs. Army (missed 6th attempt)
30—Scott Hempel, from Nov. 16, 1968 vs. Georgia Tech to Oct. 25, 1969 vs. Tulane

Points Scored by Kicking (PAT and FG)
Game: 13—Bob Thomas vs. Northwestern, 1972 (4 PAT, 3 FG)
12—Bob Thomas vs. Air Force, 1973 (6 PAT, 2 FG)
12—Scott Hempel vs. Purdue, 1970 (6 PAT, 2 FG)
12—Gus Dorais vs. Texas, 1913 (3 PAT, 3 FG)

Season: 70—Bob Thomas, 1973 (43 PAT, 9 FG) Also holds per-game record at 7.0
61—Joe Azzaro, 1967 (37 PAT, 8 FG)

Career: 164—Scott Hempel, 1968-70 (122 PAT, 14 FG). Also holds per-game record at 5.9 (164 in 28)
161—Bob Thomas, 1971-73 (98 PAT, 21 FG)

Defensive Records

Tackles Made (Since 1956)
Season: 144—Greg Collins, 1974; 142—Bob Olson, 1969

Career: 369—Bob Olson, 1967-69; 295—Greg Collins, 1972-74

Tackles For Minus Yardage (Since 1967)
Season: 19—Jim Stock, 1974 (120 yards)
17—Walt Patulski, 1970 (112 yards)

Career: 40—Walt Patulski, 1969-71 (264 yards)
30—Jim Stock, 1972-74 (186 yards)

Passes Broken Up (Since 1956)
Season: 13—Clarence Ellis, 1969; 11—Tom Schoen, 1967; Luther Bradley, 1973

Career: 32—Clarence Ellis, 1969-71; 19—Tom O'Leary, 1965-67

Opponent Fumbles Recovered (Since 1952)
Season: 5—Jim Musuraca, 1971; Don Penza, 1953; Dave Flood, 1952

Career: 7—Jim Stock, 1972-74
6—Jim Musuraca, 1970-72; Bob Scholtz, 1957-59

Notre Dame Pacesetters

Scoring

	(†)	TD	XPts	FG	Pts
1918	George Gipp	6	7	0	43
1919	George Gipp	7	4	1	49
1920	George Gipp	8	16	0	64
1921	John Mohardt	12	0	0	72
1922	Paul Castner	8	10	2	64
1923	Don Miller	10	0	0	60
	Red Maher	10	0	0	60
1924	Jim Crowley	9	17	0	71
1925	Christy Flanagan	7	3	0	45
1926	Bucky Dahman	6	5	0	41
1927	John Niemiec	4	7	0	31
1928	Jack Chevigny	3	0	0	18
1929	Jack Elder	7	0	0	42
1930	Marchy Schwartz	9	0	0	54
1931	Marchy Schwartz	5	0	0	30
1932	George Melinkovich	8	0	0	48
1933	Nick Lukats	2	0	0	12
1934	George Melinkovich	6	0	0	36
1935	Bill Shakespeare	4	0	0	24
1936	Bob Wilke	6	0	0	36
1937	Andy Puplis	3	6	0	24
1938	Benny Sheridan	4	0	0	24
	Earl Brown	4	0	0	24
1939	Milt Piepul	6	0	0	36
1940	Steve Juzwik	7	1	0	43
1941	Fred Evans	11	1	0	67
1942	Corwin Clatt	5	0	0	30
	Creighton Miller	5	0	0	30
1943	Creighton Miller	13	0	0	78
1944	Bob Kelly	13	6	0	84
1945	Elmer Angsman	7	0	0	42
1946	Terry Brennan	6	0	0	36
	Jim Mello	6	0	0	36
1947	Terry Brennan	11	0	0	66
1948	Emil Sitko	9	0	0	54
1949	Emil Sitko	9	0	0	54
	Billy Barrett	9	0	0	54
1950	Jim Mutscheller	7	0	0	42
1951	Neil Worden	8	0	0	48
1952	Neil Worden	10	0	0	60
1953	Neil Worden	11	0	0	66
1954	Joe Heap	8	0	0	48
1955	Paul Hornung	6	5	2	47
1956	Paul Hornung	7	14	0	56
1957	Monty Stickles	3	11	1	32
1958	Monty Stickles	7	15	1	60
1959	Bob Scarpitto	8	0	0	48
1960	Bob Scarpitto	5	0	0	30
1961	Joe Perkowski	0	16	5	31
1962	Joe Farrell, Jim Kelly and Daryle Lamonica, 4 TDs and 24 points each.				
1963	Frank Budka	4	0	0	24
1964	Bill Wolski	11	0	0	66
1965	Bill Wolski	8	4	0	52
1966	Nick Eddy	10	0	0	60

†Scoring Records: TD — 16, Bill Downs, 1905; Pts. — 105, Red Salmon, 1903.

*Notre Dame record.

Rushing

		Rushes	Yards
1918	George Gipp	98	541
1919	George Gipp	106	729
1920	George Gipp	102	827
1921	John Mohardt	136	781
1922	Jim Crowley	75	566
1923	Don Miller	89	698
1924	Don Miller	107	763
1925	Christy Flanagan	99	556
1926	Christy Flanagan	68	535
1927	Christy Flanagan	118	731
1928	Jack Chevigny	120	539
1929	Joe Savoldi	112	597
1930	Marchy Schwartz	124	927*
1931	Marchy Schwartz	146	692
1932	George Melinkovich	88	503
1933	Nick Lukats	107	339
1934	George Melinkovich	73	324
1935	Bill Shakespeare	104	374
1936	Bob Wilke	132	434
1937	Bunny McCormick	91	347
1938	Bob Saggau	60	353
1939	Milt Piepul	82	414
1940	Steve Juzwik	71	407
1941	Fred Evans	141	490
1942	Corwin Clatt	138	698
1943	Creighton Miller	151	911
1944	Bob Kelly	136	681
1945	Elmer Angsman	87	616
1946	Emil Sitko	53	346
1947	Emil Sitko	60	426
1948	Emil Sitko	129	742
1949	Emil Sitko	120	712
1950	Jack Landry	109	491
1951	Neil Worden	181*	676
1952	John Lattner	148	732
1953	Neil Worden	145	859
1954	Don Schaefer	141	766
1955	Don Schaefer	145	638
1956	Paul Hornung	94	420
1957	Nick Pietrosante	90	449
1958	Nick Pietrosante	117	549
1959	Gerry Gray	50	256

1960	Angelo Dabiero	80	325
1961	Angelo Dabiero	92	637
1962	Don Hogan	90	454
1963	Joe Kantor	88	330
1964	Bill Wolski	136	657
1965	Nick Eddy	115	582
1966	Nick Eddy	78	553
1967	Jeff Zimmerman	133	591
1968	Bob Gladieux	152	713
1969	Denny Allan	148	612
1970	Ed Gulyas	118	534
1971	Bob Minnix	78	337
1972	Eric Penick	124	726
1973	Wayne Bullock	162	752
1974	Wayne Bullock	203	855
1975	Jerome Heavens	129	756

*Notre Dame record.

Passing

		Att	Comp	Yards	TDP
1918	George Gipp	45	19	293	1
1919	George Gipp	72	41	727	3
1920	George Gipp	62	30	709	3
1921	John Mohardt	98	53	995	9
1922	Jim Crowley	21	10	154	1
1923	Jim Crowley	36	13	154	1
1924	Harry Stuhldreher	33	25	471	4
1925	Harry O'Boyle	21	7	107	0
1926	Christy Flanagan	29	12	207	0
1927	John Niemiec	33	14	187	0
1928	John Niemiec	108	37	456	3
1929	Jack Elder	25	8	187	1
1930	Marchy Schwartz	56	17	319	3
1931	Marchy Schwartz	51	9	174	3
1932	Nick Lukats	28	13	252	2
1933	Nick Lukats	67	21	329	0
1934	Bill Shakespeare	29	9	230	2
1935	Bill Shakespeare	66	19	267	3
1936	Bob Wilke	52	19	365	2
1937	Jack McCarthy	53	16	225	3
1938	Bob Saggau	28	8	179	3
1939	Harry Stevenson	50	14	236	1
1940	Bob Saggau	60	21	483	4
1941	Angelo Bertelli	123	70	1027	8
1942	Angelo Bertelli	159	72	1039	10
1943	Johnny Lujack	71	34	525	4
1944	Frank Dancewicz	153	68	989	9
1945	Frank Dancewicz	90	30	489	5
1946	Johnny Lujack	100	49	778	6
1947	Johnny Lujack	109	61	791	9
1948	Frank Tripucka	91	53	660	11
1949	Bob Williams	147	83	1374	16*
1950	Bob Williams	210	99	1035	10
1951	John Mazur	110	48	645	5
1952	Ralph Guglielmi	143	62	725	4
1953	Ralph Guglielmi	113	52	792	8
1954	Ralph Guglielmi	127	68	1162	6

Year	Player				
1955	Paul Hornung	103	46	743	9
1956	Paul Hornung	111	59	917	3
1957	Bob Williams	106	53	565	3
1958	George Izo	118	60	1067	9
1959	George Izo	95	44	661	6
1960	George Haffner	108	30	548	3
1961	Frank Budka	95	40	636	3
1962	Daryle Lamonica	128	64	821	6
1963	Frank Budka	40	21	239	4
1964	John Huarte	205	114	2062	16*
1965	Bill Zloch	88	36	558	3
1966	Terry Hanratty	147	78	1247	8
1967	Terry Hanratty	206	110	1439	9
1968	Terry Hanratty	197	116	1466	10
1969	Joe Theismann	192	108	1531	13
1970	Joe Theismann	268*	155*	2429*	16*
1971	Cliff Brown	111	56	669	4
1972	Tom Clements	162	83	1163	8
1973	Tom Clements	113	60	882	8
1974	Tom Clements	215	122	1549	8
1975	Rick Slager	139	66	686	2

*Notre Dame record.

Receiving

Year	Player	Caught	Yards	TD
1918	Bernie Kirk	7	102	1
1919	Bernie Kirk	21	372	2
1920	Eddie Anderson	17	293	3
1921	Eddie Anderson	26	394	2
1922	Don Miller	6	144	1
1923	Don Miller	9	149	1
1924	Don Miller	16	297	2
1925	Gene Edwards	4	28	0
1926	Ike Voedisch	6	95	0
1927	John Colrick	11	126	1
1928	John Colrick	18	199	2
1929	John Colrick	4	90	0
1930	Ed Kosky	4	76	1
1931	Paul Host	6	48	2
1932	George Melinkovich	7	106	1
1933	Steve Banas	6	59	0
1934	Dom Vairo	4	135	2
1935	Wally Fromhart	11	174	1
1936	Joe O'Neill	8	140	1
1937	Andy Puplis	5	86	1
1938	Earl Brown	6	192	4
1939	Bud Kerr	6	129	0
1940	Bob Hargrave	9	98	1
1941	Steve Juzwik	18	307	2
1942	Bob Livingstone	17	272	3
1943	John Yonakor	15	323	4
1944	Bob Kelly	18	283	5
1945	Bob Skoglund	9	100	1
1946	Terry Brennan	10	154	2
1947	Terry Brennan	16	181	4
1948	Leon Hart	16	231	4
1949	Leon Hart	19	257	5

Year	Player	Caught	Yards	TD
1950	Jim Mutscheller	35	426	7
1951	Jim Mutscheller	20	305	2
1952	Joe Heap	29	437	2
1953	Joe Heap	22	335	5
1954	Joe Heap	18	369	0
1955	Jim Morse	17	424	3
1956	Jim Morse	20	442	1
1957	Dick Lynch	13	128	0
1958	Monty Stickles	20	328	7
1959	Bob Scarpitto	15	297	4
1960	Les Traver	14	225	0
1961	Les Traver	17	349	2
1962	Jim Kelly	41	523	4
1963	Jim Kelly	18	264	2
1964	Jack Snow	60	1114	9*
1965	Nick Eddy	13	233	2
1966	Jim Seymour	48	862	8
1967	Jim Seymour	37	515	4
1968	Jim Seymour	53	736	4
1969	Tom Gatewood	47	743	8
1970	Tom Gatewood	77*	1123*	8
1971	Tom Gatewood	33	417	4
1972	Willie Townsend	25	369	4
1973	Pete Demmerle	26	404	5
1974	Pete Demmerle	43	667	6
1975	Ken MacAfee	26	333	5

*Notre Dame record.
(Season totals exclusive of bowl games)

Notre Dame Bowl Game Records

Scoring Summaries

1925 Rose Bowl — Notre Dame 27, Stanford 10

Notre Dame		0	13	7	7 —27
Stanford		3	0	7	0 —10

Attendance: 53,000

Team	Score S-ND	Qtr.	*Time Left	Play
Stanford	3-0	1	8:00	Cuddeback 27 FG
ND	3-6	2	13:30	Layden 3 run (Crowley kick failed)
ND	3-13	2	8:00	Layden 78 interception (Crowley kick)
ND	3-20	3	5:00	Hunsinger 20 fumble return (Crowley kick)
Stanford	10-20	3	1:00	Shipkey 7 pass from Walker (Cuddeback kick)
ND	10-27	4	0:30	Layden 70 interception (Crowley kick)

*Time approximate

1970 Cotton Bowl — Texas 21, Notre Dame 17

Notre Dame		3	7	0	7 — 17
Texas		0	7	0	14 — 21

Attendance: 73,000 — Weather: Fair, 48 degrees

Team	Score ND-T	Qtr.	Time Left	Play
ND	3-0	1	8:41	Hempel 26 FG
ND	10-0	2	14:40	Gatewood 54 pass from Theismann (Hempel kick)
Texas	10-7	2	11:12	Bertelsen 1 run (Feller kick)
Texas	10-14	4	10:05	Koy 3 run (Feller kick)
ND	17-14	4	6:52	Yoder 24 pass from Theismann (Hempel kick)
Texas	17-21	4	1:08	Dale 1 run (Feller kick)

1971 Cotton Bowl — Notre Dame 24, Texas, 11

Notre Dame		14	10	0	0 — 24
Texas		3	8	0	0 — 11

Attendance: 73,000 — Weather: Fair, 52 degrees

Team	Score T-ND	Qtr.	Time Left	Play
Texas	3-0	1	11:28	Feller 23 FG
ND	3-7	1	7:58	Gatewood 26 pass from Theismann (Hempel kick)
ND	3-14	1	5:11	Theismann 3 run (Hempel kick)

Team	Score	Qtr.	Time Left	Play
ND	3-21	2	13:28	Theismann 15 run (Hempel kick)
Texas	11-21	2	1:52	Bertelsen 2 run (Lester pass from Phillips)
ND	11-24	2	0:24	Hempel 36 FG

1973 Orange Bowl — Nebraska 40, Notre Dame 6

Nebraska	7	13	20	0	— 40
Notre Dame	0	0	0	6	— 6

Attendance: 80,010 — Weather: Fair, 74 degrees

Team	Score N-ND	Qtr.	Time Left	Play
Neb	7-0	1	11:19	Rodgers 8 run (Sanger kick)
Neb	14-0	2	14:21	Dixon 1 run (Sanger kick)
Neb	20-0	2	12:20	Anderson 52 pass from Rodgers (Sanger kick failed)
Neb	26-0	3	11:17	Rodgers 4 run (Humm pass failed)
Neb	33-0	3	7:33	Rodgers 5 run (Sanger kick)
Neb	40-0	3	6:00	Rodgers 50 pass from Humm (Sanger kick)
ND	40-6	4	13:51	Demmerle 5 pass from Clements (Clements pass failed)

1974 Sugar Bowl — Notre Dame 24, Alabama 23

Notre Dame	6	8	7	3	— 24
Alabama	0	10	7	6	— 23

Attendance: 85,161 — Weather: Fair, 55 degrees

Team	Score ND-A	Qtr.	Time Left	Play
ND	6-0	1	3:19	Bullock 6 run (kick failed, bad center snap)
Ala	6-7	2	7:30	Billingsley 6 run (Davis kick)
ND	14-7	2	7:17	Hunter 93 kickoff return (Demmerle pass from Clements)
Ala	14-10	2	0:39	Davis 39 FG
Ala	14-17	3	11:02	Jackson 5 run (Davis kick)
ND	21-17	3	2:30	Penick 12 run (Thomas kick)
Ala	21-23	4	9:33	Todd 25 pass from Stock (Davis kick failed)
ND	24-23	4	4:26	Thomas 19 FG

1975 Orange Bowl — Notre Dame 13, Alabama 11

Notre Dame	7	6	0	0	— 13
Alabama	0	3	0	8	— 11

Attendance: 71,801 — Weather: Fair, 70 degrees

Team	Score ND-A	Qtr.	Time Left	Play
ND	7-0	1	6:41	Bullock 4 run (Reeve kick)
ND	13-0	2	8:29	McLane 9 run (Reeve kick failed)
Ala	13-3	2	1:45	Ridgeway 21 FG
Ala	13-11	4	3:13	Schamun 48 pass from Todd (Pugh pass from Todd)

Individual Records

Total Offense

Plays

Game:	38	Joe Theismann, 1970 (279 yards)
	34	Joe Theismann, 1971 (198 yards)
Career:	73	Tom Clements, 1973-74-75 (369 yards)
	72	Joe Theismann, 1970-71 (477 yards)

Yards Gained

Game:	279	Joe Theismann, 1970 (38 plays)
	243	Tom Clements, 1974 (27 plays)
Career:	477	Joe Theismann, 1970-71 (72 plays)
	369	Tom Clements, 1973-74-75 (73 plays)

Rushing

Carries

Game:	24	Wayne Bullock, 1975 (83 yards)
	19	Wayne Bullock, 1974 (79 yards)
Career:	43	Wayne Bullock, 1974-75 (162 yards)
	32	Tom Clements, 1973-74-75 (78 yards)

Yards Gained

Game:	83	Wayne Bullock, 1975 (24 carries)
	79	Wayne Bullock, 1974 (19 carries)
Career:	162	Wayne Bullock, 1974-75 (43 carries)
	91	Eric Penick, 1973-74-75 (23 carries)

Passing

Attempts

Game:	27	Joe Theismann, 1970 (completed 17)
	22	Tom Clements, 1973 (completed 9)
Career:	43	Joe Theismann, 1970-71 (completed 26)
	41	Tom Clements, 1973-74-75 (completed 20)

Completions

Game:	17	Joe Theismann, 1970 (attempted 27)
	9	Tom Clements, 1973 (attempted 22)
	9	Joe Theismann, 1971 (attempted 16)
Career:	26	Joe Theismann, 1970-71 (attempted 43)
	20	Tom Clements, 1973-74-75 (attempted 41)

Yards Gained

Game: 231   Joe Theismann, 1970
        176   Joe Theismann, 1971
Career: 407   Joe Theismann, 1970-71
        291   Tom Clements, 1973-74-75

Touchdown Passes

Game: 2   Joe Theismann, 1970
Career: 3   Joe Theismann, 1970-71

Receiving

Catches

Game: 6   Tom Gatewood, 1970 (112 yards)
Career: 8   Tom Gatewood, 1970-71 (155 yards)
         6   Pete Demmerle, 1973-74-75 (76 yards)

Yards Gained

Game: 112   Tom Gatewood, 1970 (6 catches)
         75   Dave Casper, 1975 (3 catches)
Career: 155   Tom Gatewood, 1970-71 (8 catches)
         76   Pete Demmerle, 1973-74-75 (6 catches)

Touchdown Passes

Career: 2   Tom Gatewood, 1970-71

Scoring

Points

Game: 18   Elmer Layden, 1925
        12   Joe Theismann, 1971
Career: 18   Elmer Layden, 1925

Touchdowns

Game: 18   Elmer Layden, 1925
         2   Joe Theismann, 1971
Career: 3   Elmer Layden, 1925

Longest Plays

Yards

Rush . . . . 27 . . . . .Jim Crowley, 1925
Pass . . . . 60*   Joe Theismann to Jim Yoder, 1971
Interception . . . . 78* . . . . .Elmer Layden, 1925
Punt . . . . 74 . . . . .Jim Yoder, 1971
Kickoff Return . 93* . . . . .Al Hunter, 1974
Field Goal . . . . . 36 . . . . .Scott Hempel, 1971
Fumble Return . 20* . . . . .Ed Hunsinger, 1925
*TD.

All Time
Notre Dame
Teams

Not only was the task of selecting one all-time team too formidable; it was also decided that football had changed enough in three quarters of a century to warrant some sort of modern-old timers distinction. The selections are based on the usual blend of observation, research, interviews, questionnaires, and prejudice. The chronological break occurs just prior to the arrival of Frank Leahy. Since our lineups do not recognize defensive specialists, Jim Lynch, a two time All-American linebacker, becomes a center. It's likely that he would have performed with the same distinction at that position.

Frank Carideo (28-30)	**QB**	Johnny Lujack (43,46,47)
George Gipp (17-20)	**HB**	Johnny Lattner (51-53)
Don Miller (22-24)	**HB**	Paul Hornung (54-56)
Marchmont Schwartz (29-31)	**FB**	Emil Sitko (46-49)
Eddie Anderson (18-21)	**E**	Leon Hart (46-49)
Roger Kiley (19-21)	**E**	Jim Seymour (66-68)
Adam Walsh (22-24)	**C**	Jim Lynch (64-66)
Joe Kurth (30-32)	**T**	George Connor (46-47)
Ed Beinor (36-38)	**T**	Mike McCoy (67-69)
Jack Cannon (27-29)	**G**	Bill Fischer (45-48)
John Smith (25-27)	**G**	Larry DiNardo (68-70)

All-Time Roster

Following are the names of the Notre Dame players who appeared in at least one varsity game. Each year listed is the season the player participated in a game.

A

Achterhoff, Jay   1973-74
Adamonis, Stan   1937
Adams, John (Tree)   1942-43-44
Adamson, Ken   1957-58-59
Agnew, Ed   1930
Agnone, John   1945-46
Ahern, Bill   1960-61-62
Albert, Frank   1937-38-39
Alessandrini, Jack   1950-51-52
Alexander, Ben   1931-32
Alexander, Harry   1965-66
Allan, Denny   1968-69-70
Allen, Wayne   1962
Allison, Bill (Tex)   1916-17
Allocco, Frank   1972-73-74
Allocco, Rich   1974
Alvarado, Joe   1971-72-73
Ambrose, John   1919
Ames, Dick   1938
Anderson, Eddie   1918-19-20-21
Anderson, Heartley (Hunk)   1918-19-20-21
Andler, Ken   1974
Andreotti, Pete   1963-64-65
Andres, Bill   1917
Andrews, Frank (Bodie)   1916-17
Angsman, Elmer   1943-44-45
Anson, George   1894
Arboit, Ennio   1936-37
Arboit, Pete   1937-39
Archer, Art   1944
Archer, Clyde   1938
Arment, Bill   1974
Armstrong, Lennox   1911
Arndt, Russ   1922-23-24
Arrington, Dick   1963-64-65
Arrix, Bob   1952
Ashbaugh, Russell (Pete)   1941-42-46-47
Atamian, John   1962-63-64
Augustine, Charlie   1959-60
Azzaro, Joe   1964-65-66-67

B

Bach, Joe   1923-24
Bachman, Charlie   1914-15-16
Bagarus, Steve   1939-40
Bahan, Leonard (Pete)   1917-18-19
Bailie, Roy   1929-30
Bake, Tom   1974
Balliet, Calvin   1973-74
Banas, Steve   1931-32-33
Banicki, Fred   1949
Banks, Mike   1973-74
Barber, Bob   1938
Bardash, Virgil   1950-51-52
Barnard, Jack   1962
Barnett, Reggie   1972-73-74
Barrett, John   1893-94
Barrett, Billy   1949-50-51
Barry, George   1923
Barry, Norm   1917-18-19-20
Barry, Norm   1940-41
Barstow, Fred   1931-32-34
Bartlett, Jim   1949-50
Barz, Bill   1968-69-70
Bauer, Ed   1972-74
Baujan, Harry   1913-14-15-16
Beach, Joe   1933-34
Beacom, Pat   1903-04-05-06
Beams, Byron   1954-55
Bechtold, Joe   1938

Becker, Doug   1974
Becker, Harry   1933-34-35
Bednar, George   1961-62-63
Begley, Gerry   1947-48-49
Beh, Carleton   1914
Beinor, Ed   1936-37-38
Belden, Bill   1935
Belden, Bob   1966-67-68
Benda, Joe   1925-26-27
Benigni, George   1944
Bennett, Anson   1898
Bereolos, Hercules   1939-40-41
Berezney, Pete   1943-44-45
Berger, Alvin (Heine)   1911-12-13-14
Bergman, Alfred (Dutch)   1910-11-13-14
Bergman, Arthur (Dutch)   1915-16-19
Bergman, Joe (Dutch)   1921-22-23
Berkey, Ken   1916
Berta, Bill   1938
Berteling, John (Doc)   1906-07
Bertelli, Angelo   1941-42-43
Berve, Ben   1906
Beschen, Dick   1958
Best, Art   1972-73-74
Biagi, Frank   1938-39
Bianco, Don   1951
Bigelow, Jim   1952-53-54
Bill, Bob   1959-60-61
Binkowski, Ben   1936-37-38
Binz, Frank   1908
Bisceglia, Pat   1953-54-55
Bitsko, Mickey   1961
Bleier, Bob (Rocky)   1965-66-67
Bliey, Ron   1962-63
Boeringer, Art (Bud)   1925-26
Boji, Byron   1949-50-51
Boland, Joe   1924-25-26
Boland, Ray   1932
Bolger, Matt   1941
Bolger, Tom   1971-72-73
Bonar, Bud   1933-34
Bonder, Frank   1974
Bondi, Gus   1927-28-29
Bonvechio, Sandy   1963-64
Borer, Harold   1938
Borowski, Chuck   1936
Bosse, Joe   1954-55
Bossu, Augie   1936-37-38
Bossu, Frank   1968-69-70
Bossu, Steve   1974
Boulac, Brian   1960-61-62
Bouwens, Seraphine   1897
Boyle, Rich   1958
Bracken, Bob   1904-05-06
Bradley, Luther   1973
Brady, Jim   1927-28
Brancheau, Ray   1931-32-33
Brandy, Joe   1917-19-20
Brantley, Tony   1973-74
Bray, Jim   1926-27-28
Brennan, Ed   1894
Brennan, Jim   1944-46-47
Brennan, Joe   1909
Brennan, Terry   1945-46-47-48
Brennan, Terry   1967-68-69
Brennan, Tom   1938
Brenneman, Mark   1971-73-74
Brent, Francis   1901
Brew, Frank   1937-38
Briick, Herb   1970-71-72
Brill, Marty   1929-30
Brocke, Jim   1963
Brock, Tom   1940-41-42

Brogan, John 1905
Broscoe, Eddie 1936-38
Brosey, Cliff 1939-40
Brown, Bob 1895-96
Brown, Cliff 1971-72-73
Brown, Earl 1936-37-38
Brown, Earl 1892
Brown, Frank 1926
Brown, Harvey 1921-22-23
Brown, Ivan 1973
Brown, Roger 1946-47
Browner, Ross 1973
Bruno, Bill 1934-35-36
Brutz, Jim 1939-40-41
Brutz, Marty 1942-46
Bucci, Don 1951-52-53
Buches, Steve 1968-69-70
Buczkiewicz, Ed 1952
Budka, Frank 1961-62-63
Budynkiewicz, Ted 1947-48
Bulger, Jim 1970-71
Bullock, Wayne 1972-73-74
Buoniconti, Nick 1959-60-61
Burdick, Henry 1906-07-08
Burgener, Mike 1965-66-67
Burgmeier, Ted 1974
Burke, Ed 1960-61-62
Burke, Frank 1944
Burke, John 1907
Burke, Kevin 1956-58
Burnell, Max 1936-37-38
Burnell, Max 1959-60
Burnett, Al 1945
Burns, Bill 1962-63
Burns, Paul 1949-50-51
Bush, Hardy 1913-14
Bush, Jack 1949-50-51
Bush, Joe 1951-52-53
Bush, Roy 1945
Buth, Doug 1974
Butler, Frank 1930
Byrne, Bill (Illy) 1926
Byrne, John 1921
Byrne, Tom 1925-26-27

C

Cabral, Walter 1951-52-53-54
Caito, Leo 1960
Caldwell, George 1932-33-34
Callaghan, Leo 1954
Callicrate, Dom 1905-06-07
Cameron, Alexander 1921
Campbell, Stafford 1889
Canale, Frank 1931-32-34
Cannon, Jack 1927-28-29
Capers, Tony 1968
Caprara, Joe 1949-50
Carberry, Glen (Judge) 1920-21-22
Carey, Tom 1951-52-53-54
Carey, Tony 1964-65
Carideo, Frank 1928-29-30
Carideo, Fred 1933-34-35
Carmody, James 1930
Carney, Mike 1974
Carollo, Joe 1959-60-61
Carrabine, Gene 1951-52
Carrabine, Luke 1954
Carroll, Jim 1962-63-64
Carter, Don 1947
Carter, Tom 1949-50
Cartier, Dezera 1889
Cartier, George 1887

Casey, Dan 1894-95
Cash, Tony 1944
Casper, Dave 1971-72-73
Cassidy, Bill 1929
Cassidy, Thaddeus 1938-40
Castin, Jack 1960
Castner, Paul 1920-21-22
Cavalier, John 1936
Cavanaugh, Tom 1895-96
Cavanaugh, Vince 1930-31
Cerney, Bill 1922-23-24
Chandler, Bill 1944
Chanowicz, Stan 1935
Chauncey, Jim 1974
Chevigny, Jack 1926-27-28
Chidester, Abraham (Abe) 1893-94
Chlebeck, Andy 1940
Christensen, Ross 1974
Christman, Norb 1928-29-30-31
Church, Augie (Sonny) 1934-35
Church, Durant 1904
Cibula, George 1943
Ciechanowicz, Emil 1947-48
Cieszkowski, John 1969-70-71-72
Ciesielski, Dick 1956-58-59
Cifelli, Gus 1946-47-48-49
Clark, Bill 1959-60
Clark, Oswald 1945
Clasby, Ed 1944
Clatt, Corwin (Cornie) 1942-46-47
Clear, Eugene 1904
Clement, B. 1908
Clements, Bill 1960
Clements, Jack 1971
Clements, Tom 1972-73-74
Clifford, Jerry 1935-36-37
Clinnen, Walter 1908-10
Clippinger, Art 1910
Cloherty, John 1969-70-71
Coad, Dick 1904
Coady, Ed 1888-89
Coady, Pat 1892
Coady, Tom 1888-89
Cody, Francis (Lew) 1925
Cofall, Stan 1914-15-16
Colella, Phil 1945
Coleman, Charles 1901
Coleman, Herb 1942-43
Collins, Chuck 1922-23-24
Collins, Eddie 1926-27-28-29
Collins, Fred 1925-26-27-28
Collins, Greg 1972-73-74
Collins, Joe 1908-09-10
Collins, Leo 1966
Colosimo, Jim 1957-59
Colrick, John 1927-28-29
Conjar, Larry 1965-66
Conley, Tom 1928-29-30
Connell, Ward (Doc) 1922-23-24
Connor, George 1946-47
Connor, Joe 1935
Connor, John 1948-49
Connors, Ben 1918-19
Conway, Denny 1964-65
Cook, Bill 1912-13
Cook, Ed 1953-54
Cook, Harold 1922
Cooke, Larry 1954-55-56
Corbisiero, John 1944
Corby, Sidney 1894-96
Corgan, Mike 1937-38
Corry, Clarence 1894
Corson, Bob 1957
Costa, Don 1958

Costa, Paul 1961-63-64
Costello, Al 1932-33-34
Cotter, Bob 1969
Cotter, Dick 1948-49-50
Cotton, Forrest (Fod) 1920-21-22
Coughlin, Bernie 1922-24-25
Coughlin, Danny 1920-21
Coughlin, Frank 1916-19-20
Coutre, Larry 1946-47-48-49
Cowhig, Gerry 1942-46
Cowin, Jeff 1969
Coyne, Bob 1954
Crawley, Pat 1892
Creaney, Mike 1970-71-72
Creevey, John 1942-46
Creevey, Tom 1973
Creevy, Dick 1940-41-42
Creevy, Tom 1942
Crimmins, Bernie 1939-40-41
Criniti, Frank 1966-67-68
Cripe, Clarence 1907
Cronin, Art 1934-35-36
Cronin, Carl 1929-30-31
Cronin, Dick 1945
Crotty, Jim 1957-58-59
Crotty, Mike 1969-70-71
Crowe, Clem 1923-24-25
Crowe, Emmett 1936-37-38
Crowley, Charlie 1910-11-12
Crowley, Charlie 1918-19
Crowley, Jim 1922-23-24
Cullen, Jack 1960-61
Cullen, John 1892-93
Cullinan, Joe (Jepers) 1900-01-02-03
Cullins, Ron 1974
Culver, Al 1929-30-31
Curley, Bob 1943
Cusack, Joe 1887-88
Cusick, Frank 1942
Cyterski, Len 1951
Czarobski, Zygmont (Ziggy) 1942-43-46-47

D

Dabiero, Angelo 1959-60-61
Dahman, Ray (Bucky) 1925-26-27
Dailer, Jim 1944-47-48
Dainton, Bill 1965
Daly, Charles 1899
Daly, Mike 1896-97
Dampeer, John 1970-71-72
Danbom, Larry 1934-35-36
Dancewicz, Frank 1943-44-45
Daniels, Bert 1908
Darcy, John 1936
Daut, John 1949
Davila, Jenaro 1895
Davin, David 1954
Davlin, Mike 1944
Davis, Irwin 1933-34
Davis, Ray 1943
Davitt, Harold 1901
deArrietta, Jim 1968-69
DeBuono, Dick 1945
Dee, John 1944
DeFranco, Joe 1937-38-39
DeGree, Ed 1920-21-22
DeGree, Walter (Cy) 1916-17-19
Deinhart, Joe 1924
Demmerle, Pete 1972-73-74
Dempsey, John 1894
DeNardo, Ron 1957

Denchfield, Art   1927
Dennery, Vince   1962-63-64
DePola, Nick   1960
DePrimio, Dennis   1969-70-71
Desch, Gus   1921-22
Desmond, Bill   1902
Devine, Ed   1968
Devine, Tom   1971-72
Devore, Hugh   1931-32-33
Dew, Billy   1927-28
Dewan, Darryll   1970-71-72
DiCarlo, Mike   1961-62-63
Dickerson, Sydney   1889
Dickman, Dan   1967
Dickson, George   1949
Diebold, Clarence   1900
Diebold   1910
Diener, John   1906-07-08
Dillon, Dan   1903
Diminick, Gary   1971-72-73
Dimmick, Ralph   1908-09-10
DiNardo, Gerry   1972-73-74
DiNardo, Larry   1968-69-70
Dinkle, Nicholas   1892-93-94
Dionne, Louis   1908
Ditton, James   1907
Dixon, Sherwood   1916-17
Djubasak, Paul   1957
Doar, Jim   1901-02
Doarn, John   1926-27-28
Doherty, Brian   1971-72-73
Doherty, Kevin   1973-74
Doherty, Pat   1912
Dolan, Bill   1911-12
Dolan, Pat   1955-56-57
Dolan, Sam (Rosey)   1906-07-08-09
Donahue, John   1898
Donoghue, Dick   1927-28-29-30
Donohue, Pete   1967
Donovan, Bob (Smousherette)   1906
Donovan, Dick (Smoush)   1903-04-05
Donovan, Red   1918
Doody, Frank   1938-40
Dooley, Jim   1919-20-21
Dorais, Charles (Gus)   1910-11-12-13
Dorais, Joe   1915-16
Dove, Bob   1940-41-42
Downs, Bill   1905
Downs, Morris   1905
Doyle, Pat   1957-58-59
Doyle, Nick   1906
Draper, Bill   1903-04-05
Drennan, William   1922
Drew, Dave   1970-71-72
Dubenetzky, John   1974
DuBrul, Ernest   1892-93
Duffy, John   1907-08-09-10
Dugan, Bill   1907
Dugan, Mike   1957-58
Duggan, Eddie   1911-12-13-14
Duncan, Ernest   1899
Dunlay, Jim   1950-51
Dunn, Ed   1934-35
Dunphy, Ray   1912
Duranko, Pete   1963-64-65-66
Dushney, Ron   1966-67-68
Dwan, Alan   1906
Dwyer, Gene   1942
Dwyer, Pete   1908-09-10

E

Earley, Bill   1940-41-42
Earley, Fred   1943-45-46-47
Earley, Mike   1966
Eastman, Tom   1974
Eaton, Tom   1968-69-70
Eaton, Wilbur   1923-24
Ebli, Ray   1940-41
Eckman, Mike   1969
Ecuyer, Al   1956-57-58
Eddy, Nick   1964-65-66
Edmonds, Wayne   1953-54-55
Edwards, Gene (Red)   1924-25-26
Edwards, Howard (Cap)   1908-09
Eggeman, Fred   1906
Eggeman, Joe   1923
Eggeman, John   1897-98-99
Eggert, Herb   1924
Eichenlaub, Ray   1911-12-13-14
Elder, Jack   1927-28-29
Ellis, Clarence   1969-70-71
Ellis, Howard   1915
Elser, Don   1933-34-35
Elward, Allen (Mal)   1912-13-14-15
Ely, Gene   1936-37
Emanuel, Denny   1936-37
Emerick, Lou   1950
Endress, Frank   1944
Enright, Rex   1923-25
Epstein, Frank   1950
Espanan, Ray   1946-47-48-49
Etten, Nick   1962-63
Etter, Bill   1969-71-72
Eurick, Terry   1974
Evans, Fred (Dippy)   1940-41-42

F

Fagan, Bill   1897
Fallon, Jack   1944-45-46-48
Fanning, Mike   1972-73-74
Fansler, Mike   1902-03-04
Faragher, Jim   1900-01
Farley, John   1897-98-99-1900
Farrell, Joe   1962-63-64
Farrell, Tom   1923
Fay, Ed   1944-45
Fedorenko, Nick   1974
Feeney, Al   1910-11-12-13
Fehr, Frank   1887-88-89
Feigel, Chuck   1948-49-50
Feltes, Norm   1922
Fennessey, John   1897
Filley, Pat   1941-42-43-44
Fine, Tom   1973-74
Finegan, Charles (Sam)   1911-12-13-14
Finneran, Jack   1937-38-39
Fischer, Bill   1945-46-47-48
Fischer, Ray   1968
Fitzgerald, Art   1944
Fitzgerald, Dick   1953-54-55
Fitzgerald, Freeman (Fitz)   1912-13-14-15
Fitzgibbons, James   1889
Fitzpatrick, Bill   1926
Fitzpatrick, George   1916-19
Flanagan, Christy   1925-26-27
Flanagan, Jim   1943
Flanigan, John (Thunder)   1917
Flannigan, John   1892-93
Fleming, Charles   1898-99
Fleming, Steve   1889

G

Flinn, Neil   1922
Flood, Dave   1950-51-52
Flor, Ollie   1958-59
Flynn, Bill   1945-48-49-50
Flynn, Charles   1889
Flynn, Dave   1950
Flynn, Ed   1950
Flynn, Jack   1921-22
Flynn, John   1931-32
Fogel, John   1935-36-37
Foley, Joe   1931
Foley, Tom   1910
Ford, Bill   1960
Ford, Gerald   1943
Ford, Jim   1940
Fortin, Al   1898-99-00-01
Foster, Harvey   1936-37
Fox, Harry   1936
Fox, Roger   1966
Frampton, John   1947-48
Francis, Al   1955
Frantz, George   1915-16
Frasor, Dick   1951-52-53-54
Frawley, George   1942
Frederick, John   1925-26-27
Freebery, Joe   1967-68
Freeze, Chet   1907-08
Freistroffer, Tom   1970-71-72
Frericks, Tom   1974
Friske, Joe   1923
Fromhart, Wally   1933-34-35
Frost, Bob   1938
Fry, Willie   1973
Funk, Art   1902-03-04-05
Furlong, Nick   1902-03
Furlong, Nick   1967-68-69
Furlong, Tom   1967

G

Gaffney, John   1953-54
Galanis, John   1974
Galardo, Armando   1952-53
Galen, Albert   1895
Gallagher, Bill   1969-70-71
Gallagher, Frank   1936
Gallagher, John   1895
Gallagher, Tom   1938-39-40
Gambone, John   1973
Gander, Del   1949-50-51
Ganey, Mike   1943-44-45
Gardner, John   1968
Gargan, Joe   1912-13
Gargiulo, Frank   1959-60
Garner, Terry   1970-71-72
Garunde   1908
Garvey, Art (Hector)   1920-21
Gasparella, Joe   1944-45
Gasseling, Tom   1968-69-70
Gasser, John   1968-69
Gatewood, Tom   1969-70-71
Gaudreau, Bill   1951
Gaul, Frank   1945-47-48
Gaul, Frank   1933-34-35
Gay, Bill   1947-48-49-50
Gaydos, Bob   1955-56-57
Gebert, Al (Bud)   1928-29
Geniesse, Oswald   1924
George, Don   1953-54
Geremia, Frank   1956-57-58
Gildea, Hubert   1931-32
Gillen, Charles   1900-01-02
Gipp, George   1917-18-19-20

Girolami, Tony   1940
Glaab, John   1944-45
Gladieux, Bob   1966-67-68
Gleason, Joe (Red)   1935-36-37
Gleckler, Ed   1974
Glueckert, Charles   1922-23-24
Glynn, Ed (Cupid)   1909
Glynn, Ralph   1899-00
Gmitter, Don   1964-65-66
Goberville, Tom   1961-62-63
Goeddeke, George   1964-65-66
Goeke, John   1895
Gompers, Bill   1945-46-47
Goodman, Ron   1972-73-74
Gores, Tom   1969
Gorman, Tim   1965-66
Gorman, Tom (Kitty)   1931-32-33
Gottsacker, Harold   1936-37-38
Grable, Charles   1965
Grabner, Hank   1918
Grady, Bill   1914
Graney, Mike   1958
Grant, Chet   1916-20-21
Grau, Frank   1960-61
Gray, Gerry   1959-61-62
Greeney, Norm   1930-31-32
Grenda, Ed   1969
Griffith, Dan   1958-60
Groble, George   1954-55-56
Groom, Jerry   1948-49-50
Grothaus, Walt   1945-47-48-49
Gubanich, John   1938-39-40
Guglielmi, Ralph   1951-52-53-54
Gullickson, Tom   1974
Gulyas, Ed   1969-70-71
Gunderman, Reuben   1931
Gushurst, Fred (Gus)   1912-13
Gustafson, Phil   1969
Guthrie, Dave   1904
Guthrie, Tom   1944
Gutowski, Denny   1970-72

H

Hack, Jim   1934-36
Hadden   1895
Haffner, George   1959-60
Hagan, Lowell   1932-33
Hagerty, Bob   1966
Haggar, Joe   1970-72
Hagopian, Gary   1969
Hague, Harry   1907
Haley, Dave   1966-67
Hamby, Jim   1949-51
Hamilton, Don   1908-09
Hanley, Dan   1930-33-34
Hanley, Frank   1896-99
Hanlon, Bob   1943
Hanousek, Dick   1924-25
Hanratty, Terry   1966-67-68
Hardy, Kevin   1964-65-66-67
Hardy, Russell   1915
Hargrave, Bob   1939-40-41
Harmon, Joe   1922-23-24
Harrington, Vince   1922-23-24
Harris, Jim   1930-31-32
Harrison, Randy   1974
Harshman, Dan   1965-66-67
Hart, Leon   1946-47-48-49
Harchar, John   1973
Hartman, Pete   1972-73
Harvat, Paul   1911-12
Harvey, Tad   1937-38-39

Hayduk, George   1971-72-73
Hayes, Art   1898-99-00
Hayes, Dave   1917-19-20
Hayes, Jackie   1939-40
Healy, Pat   1959
Healy, Tom   1903-04-05
Heap, Joe   1951-52-53-54
Hearden, Tom   1924-25-26
Heath, Cliff   1938
Heaton, Mike   1965-66-67
Hebert, Carl   1955-57
Hecomovich, Tom   1959-60-61
Hedrick, Gene   1955-56
Heenan, Pat   1959
Hein, Jeff   1971-72-73
Helwig, John   1948-49-50
Heman, Dick   1945
Hempel, Scott   1968-69-70
Hendricks, Dick   1953-54
Heneghan, Curt   1966-67-68
Henley, James   1892
Henneghan, Bill   1960
Henning, Art   1906-07-08
Hepburn, Joseph   1887-88-89
Hering, Frank   1896
Herwit, Norm   1928
Hesse, Frank   1893-95-96
Heywood, Bill   1946
Hickey, Louis   1934-36
Hickman, Bill   1957
Hicks, Bill   1912
Higgins, Bill   1948-49-50
Higgins, Luke   1942
Higi, Joe   1921
Hill, Greg   1971-72-73
Hines, Mike   1941
Hoebing, Bob   1945
Hoerster, Ed   1960-61-62
Hofer, Bill   1936-37-38
Hoffman, Frank (Nordy)   1930-31
Hogan, Don   1939-40-41
Hogan, Don   1962
Hogan, John   1926
Hogan, Paul   1918
Hollendoner, Frank   1937-38
Holmes, George (Ducky)   1914-16
Holton, Barry   1917-20
Holtzapfel, Mike   1966-67-68
Hooten, Herman   1970-71
Hoppel, Leo   1936
Horan, Bill   1936
Horney, John   1964-65-66
Hornung, Paul   1954-55-56
Host, Paul   1930-31-32
Houck, George   1887
Houser, Max   1923-24
Howard, Al   1929-30
Huarte, John   1962-63-64
Huber, Bill   1942
Hudak, Ed   1947-48-49
Huff, Andy   1969-71-72
Hughes, Ernie   1974
Hughes, Tom   1954-55-56
Humbert, Jim   1969-70-71
Humenik, Dave   1961-62
Hunsinger, Ed   1922-23-24
Hunter, Al   1973
Hunter, Art   1951-52-53
Hurd, Bill   1967
Hurd, Dave   1957-58
Hurlbert, Jim   1926-27
Hurley, Bill   1926-27
Hutzell, Oscar   1906

I

Ivan, Ken   1963-64-65
Izo, George   1957-58-59

J

Jackson, Ernie   1968
James, Johnny   1922
Jaskwhich, Chuck   1930-31-32
Jeffers, Jack   1947-48
Jewett, Harry   1887-88
Jeziorski, Ron   1964-65-66
Jockisch, Bob   1967-68
Johnson, Frank (Rodney)   1945-47-48
Johnson, Murray   1950
Johnson, Pete   1974
Johnson, Ron   1968-70
Johnston, Frank   1949-50
Jonardi, Ray   1949-50
Jones, Bill   1926-27
Jones, Jerry   1915-16
Jones, Keith (Deak)   1911-12-13-14
Jones, Ray   1911
Joseph, Bob   1951-52
Joyce, Tom   1905
Just, Jim   1956-57-58
Juzwik, Steve   1939-40-41

K

Kadish, Mike   1969-70-71
Kafka, Mike   1974
Kane, Mickey   1920-21-22
Kantor, Joe   1961-63-64
Kapish, Bob   1949-50-51
Kapish, Gene   1953-54-55
Kaplan, Clarence   1929-30
Karr, Jim   1938
Kasper, Cy   1919-20
Kassis, Tom   1928-29-30
Katchik, Joe   1951
Keach, Leroy   1906
Kearns, John   1892
Keefe, Emmett   1912-13-14-15
Keefe, Frank   1926
Keefe, Larry   1924
Keefe, Walter   1904-06
Kegaly, John   1954
Kegler, Bill   1896-97
Kell, Paul   1936-37-38
Kelleher, Bill   1911-12-13-14
Kelleher, Dan   1974
Kelleher, John   1938-39
Keller, Dick   1953-54
Kelley, Ed   1895
Kelly, Al (Red)   1909
Kelly, Bob   1943-44
Kelly, Bob   1950-51
Kelly, Chuck   1974
Kelly, Gerald   1965-66
Kelly, Jim   1940
Kelly, Jim   1961-62-63
Kelly, Jim   1964-66
Kelly, Joe   1944
Kelly, Johnny   1936
Kelly, Johnny   1937-38-39
Kelly, Luke   1908-09-10-11
Kelly, Pete   1938-39-40
Kelly, Tim   1968-69-70
Kelly, Will   1916
Kenneally, Tommy   1927-28-29

Kennedy, Charles   1967-68-69
Kennedy, John   1908
Keough, Frank   1892-93-94
Kersjes, Frank   1930
Kerr, Bud   1937-38-39
Kienast, Phil   1961
Kiley, Roger (Rodge)   1919-20-21
Kiliany, Dennis   1967-68
Kineally, Kevin   1973
King, Hollis (Hoot)   1913-14-15
King, Tom   1916-17
Kiousis, Marty   1949
Kirby, Harry   1901-02
Kirby, Maurice   1893
Kirk, Bernie   1918-19
Kizer, Noble   1922-23-24
Klees, Vince   1973-74
Knott, Dan   1973
Koch, Bob   1938-39-40
Koch, Dave   1949
Kohanowich, Al   1951-52
Koken, Mike   1930-31-32
Kolasinski, Dan   1960
Kolski, Steve   1960-61-62
Kondrk, John   1970-71-72
Kondrla, Mike   1968
Konieczny, Rudy   1965-66
Kopczak, Frank   1934-35-36
Koreck, Bob   1959-60
Kornman, Russ   1972-73-74
Korth, Howard   1938-40
Kos, Gary   1968-69-70
Kosikowski, Frank   1946-47
Kosky, Ed   1930-31-32
Kostelnik, Tom   1962-63-64
Kovalcik, George (Jake)   1936-38
Kovatch, John   1939-40-41
Kowalski, George   1914
Kozak, George   1931
Krall, Rudy   1944
Krause, Ed (Moose)   1931-32-33
Krivik, Stan   1945
Krupa, Ed   1942-43
Kuchta, Frank   1956-57
Kucmicz, Mike   1965-66
Kudlacz, Stan   1941-42
Kuechenberg, Bob   1966-67-68
Kuffel, Ray   1943
Kuh, Dick   1948
Kuharich, Joe   1935-36-37
Kulbitski, Vic   1943
Kunz, George   1966-67-68
Kuppler, George   1898-99-00
Kurth, Joe   1930-31-32
Kurzynske, Jim   1945
Kutzavitch, Bill   1961

L

LaBorne, Frank   1931-32-33
LaFollette, Clarence   1923
Laiber, Joe   1939-40-41
Lally, Bob   1947-48-49
Lamantia, Pete   1966
Lambeau, Earl (Curly)   1918
Lambert, Steve   1968
Lamonica, Daryle   1960-61-62
Lanahan, John   1940-41-42
Landolfi, Chuck   1967-68
Landry, Jack   1948-49-50
Laney, Tom   1973-74
Lantry, Joe   1906
Larkin, Art (Bunny)   1912-13-14

Larkin, Ed   1938
Larson, Fred (Ojay)   1918-20-21
Larson, John   1911
Lasch, Bob   1953-54
Lathrop, Ralph (Zipper)   1911-12-13-14
Lattner, Johnny   1951-52-53
Lauck, Chick   1966-67-68
Lautar, John   1934-35-36
Lavin, John   1966-67-68
Law, John   1926-27-28-29
Lawrence, Don   1956-57-58
Lawson, Tom   1967-69
Layden, Elmer   1922-23-24
Layden, Mike   1933-34-35
Leahy, Bernie   1929-30-31
Leahy, Frank   1928-29
Leahy, James   1968
LeBlanc, Joe   1911
Lebrau, John   1944
LeCluyse, Len   1946-47
Leding, Mike   1931-32
Lee, Al   1938-40
Lee, Jack   1951-52-53-54
Lee, Jay   1911
Lehmann, Bob   1961-62-63
Lemek, Ray   1953-54-55
Lennon, Peter   1898
Leonard, Bill   1945-47
Leonard, Bob   1938-39-40
Leonard, Jim   1931-32-33
Leppig, George   1926-27-28
Lesko, Al   1945-48
Levicki, John   1934-35-36
Lewallen, Brian   1968-69
Lewis, Aubrey   1955-56-57
Lieb, Tom   1921-22
Liggio, Tom   1960-61
Likovich, John   1974
Lillis, Paul   1939-40-41
Lima, Chuck   1955-56-57
Limont, Mark   1944
Limont, Paul   1942-43-46
Lind, Mike   1960-61-62
Linehan, Ed   1892
Linehan, John   1960
Lins, George   1896-97-98-99-00-01
Listzwan, Tom   1928
Littig, Edward   1897
Lium, John   1966
Livergood, Bernie   1922-23-24
Livingstone, Bob   1942-46-47
Loboy, Alan   1963-64
Lockard, Frank (Abbie)   1917-18
Locke, Joe   1927-29
Lodish, Mike   1957-58-59
Logan, Les   1920-21-22
Lombardo, Camilo   1918
Loncaric, Lou   1954-55-56
Lonergan, Frank (Happy)   1901-02-03
Long, Harry   1963-64-65
Longhi, Ed   1936-37-38
Longo, Tom   1963-64-65
Loop, Paul   1958
Lopienski, Tom   1972-73-74
Loula, Jim   1960
Lower, Harold   1912
Lozzi, Dennis   1972-73
Luecke, Dan   1960
Luhn, Henry   1887
Lujack, Johnny   1943-46-47
Lukats, Nick   1930-32-33
Lyden, Mike   1943
Lynch, Dick   1955-56-57
Lynch, Ed   1907-08-09

Lynch, Jim   1964-65-66
Lynn, Brad   1937
Lyon, Francis   1896

M

MacAfee, Ken   1974
MacDonald, Tom   1961-62-63
Maciag, Dick   1970-72
Mack, Bill (Red)   1958-59-60
Maddock, Bob   1939-40-41
Madigan, Edward (Slip)   1916-17-19
Maggioli, Achille (Chick)   1943-44
Magevney, Hugh (Red)   1921
Maglicic, Ken   1962-63-64
Magnotta, Mike   1959-60
Mahaffey, Tom   1931-32
Mahalic, Drew   1972-73-74
Maher, Willie (Red)   1921-22-23
Mahoney, Dick   1930-31
Mahoney, Gene   1927
Mahoney, Jim   1948-49
Malone, Grover   1915-16-19
Malone, Mike   1968
Maloney, James   1887
Maloney, Jim   1908-09
Maloney, John   1938
Mangialardi, Fred   1951-52-53
Manzo, Lou   1953
Marchand, Gerry   1950
Marelli, Ray   1925-26
Mariani, John   1970-71-72
Marino, Nunzio   1944
Markowski, Joe   1953
Marquardt, Clarence   1938
Marr, John   1934-35-36
Marsico, Joe   1966
Martell, Gene   1953-54-55
Marshall, Walt   1935-36-37
Martin, Bill   1910
Martin, Bob   1952-53
Martin, Dave   1965-66-67
Martin, Jim   1946-47-48-49
Martin, Jim (Pepper)   1934-35-36
Martin, Mark   1968
Martin, Mike   1970
Martz, George   1944
Marx, Greg   1970-71-72
Maschmeier, Tom   1974
Massey, Bob   1930
Massey, Jim   1969
Masterson, Bernie   1938
Mastrangelo, John   1944-45-46
Mathews, Lee   1908-09-10
Mathews   1914
Mattera, Vince   1963-64
Mattes, Francis   1886
Matthews, Ed   1933
Matz, Paul   1951-52-53-54
Mavraides, Menil (Minnie)   1951-52-53
Maxwell, Joe   1960-61-62
Maxwell, Joe   1924-25-26
May, Paul   1965-66
Mayer, Frank   1925-26
Mayl, Gene   1921-22-23
Mazziotti, Tony   1933-34-35
Mazur, John   1949-50-51
McAdams, Vince (Bennie)   1926
McAvoy, Tom   1905
McBride, Bob   1941-42-43
McBride, Mike   1972-73
McCabe, Harold (Dinger)   1925-26
McCarthy, Bill   1951

McCarthy, Bill   1934-35-36
McCarthy, Frank   1927
McCarthy, Jack   1935-36-37
McCarthy, William   1895
McCarty, Pat   1936-37
McCormick, Nevin (Bunny)   1936-37
McCoy, Mike   1967-68-69
McDermott, Ed   1902-03
McDermott, Frank   1921
McDermott   1892
McDonald, Angus   1896-98-99
McDonald, Paul   1907-08
McDonnell, John   1954-55-56
McDonough, Joe   1938
McGannon, Bill   1938-39-40
McGee, Coy   1945-46-47-48
McGehee, Ralph   1946-47-48-49
McGill, Mike   1965-66-67
McGinley, John   1956-57
McGinn, Dan   1963-64-65
McGinnis, Jan   1910-11-12
McGinnis, John   1942
McGlew, Henry (Fuzzy)   1900-01-02-03
McGoldrick, Jim   1936-37-38
McGovern, George   1936
McGrath, Bob   1936
McGrath, Chester (Mugsy)   1910-11
McGrath, Frank   1923
McGrath, Jack   1926-27-28
McGraw, Pat   1970-71-72
McGuff, Al   1932
McGuire, Bob   1917
McGuire, Mike   1974
McGurk, Jim   1945-46
McHale, John   1940
McHale, John   1968-69-70
McHugh, Tom   1951-52-53
McInerny, Arnold   1915-16
McIntyre, John   1938-39
McKenna, Jim   1935
McKeon, Tom   1889
McKillip, Leo   1948-49-50
McKinley, Tom   1966-67-68
McKinney, Charles   1926-27
McLane, Mark   1974
McLaughlin, Dave   1941
McLaughlin, Pat   1974
McLaughlin, Tom   1911-12-13
McMahon, Joe   1934-35-36
McMahon, Johnny   1936-37-38
McManmon, Art   1929-30
McManmon, John   1924-25-26
McMullan, John   1923-24-25
McMullan, John   1953-54-55
McNally, Vince   1925-26
McNamara, Regis   1929-30-31
McNeill, Chuck   1941
McNerny, Larry   1903-04-05
McNichols, Austin   1946
McNulty, Mike   1898-99
McNulty, Paul   1922
McSorley, John   1926-27
Meagher, Jack   1916
Meagher, John   1888
Meeker, Bob   1963-64-65
Megin, Bernard   1936
Mehre, Harry   1919-20-21
Melady, Eugene   1887-88
Melinkovich, George   1931-32-34
Mello, Jim   1942-43-46
Menie, Tom   1970-71
Meno, Chuck   1956
Mense, Jim   1953-54-55
Mergenthal, Art   1944

Merkle, Bob   1964
Merlitti, Jim   1967-68-69
Mertes, Al   1906-07-08
Meschievitz, Vince   1950
Meter, Bernie (Bud)   1942-43-46
Metzger, Bert   1928-29-30
Metzger, Harry   1912
Meyer, John   1963-64
Michaels, Bill   1947
Michels, Andrew   1940
Michuta, John   1933-34-35
Mieszkowski, Ed   1943-45
Mikacich, Jim   1959-60-61
Milbauer, Frank   1922-23
Miles, Frank (Rangy)   1918
Miller, Creighton   1941-42-43
Miller, Don   1922-23-24
Miller, Earl   1918
Miller, Edgar (Rip)   1922-23-24
Miller, Fred   1926-27-28
Miller, Gerry   1922-23-24
Miller, Harry (Red)   1906-07-08-09
Miller, Howard   1921
Miller, John   1914-15-16
Miller, Ray   1911-12
Miller, Steve   1934-35-36
Miller, Tom   1940-41-42
Miller, Walter   1915-16-17-19
Miller, Ward   1916
Millheam, Curtis (Duke)   1931
Millner, Wayne   1933-34-35
Mills, Rupert (Rupe)   1913-14
Milota, Jim   1954-56
Minik, Frank   1960-61-62
Minnix, Bob   1969-70-71
Miskowitz, Lew   1973
Mittelhauser, Tom   1963
Mixon, Leo   1922
Modak, Dan   1949-50
Mohardt, Johnny   1918-19-20-21
Mohn, Bill   1918
Monahan, Bill   1897-98-99
Monahan, Tom   1960
Mondron, Bob   1955
Montroy, Jack   1928
Monty, Tim   1966-67-68
Mooney, Al   1937-38-39
Moore, Dan   1925-26
Moore, Elton   1973-74
Morales, Alfred   1916
Morgan, Larry (Red)   1917
Morgan, Steve   1910-11-12
Moriarity, Mike   1906-08-09
Moriarty, George   1933-34-35
Moriarty, Kerry   1974
Moritz   1896
Morrin, Dan   1971-72-73
Morrison, James   1894
Morrison, Paul   1938
Morrissey, Joe   1926-27-28
Morrissey, Rockne   1952-53
Morse, Jim   1954-55-56
Morse   1894
Mortell, John   1938
Mosca, Angelo   1956
Moynihan, Tim   1926-27-28-29
Mudron, Pat   1968-70
Muehlbauer, Mike   1957-58-59
Mueller, Art   1934
Muessel   1893
Mulcahey, Jim   1937
Mullen, Jack   1894-95-96-97-98-99
Muller, Nick   1962
Mullins, Larry (Moon)   1927-28-29-30

Mundee, Fred   1934-35-36
Munger, Harold   1911-12
Munro, Jim   1954-55-56
Munson, Frank   1905-06-07
Murphy, Dan   1904
Murphy, Denny   1960-61-62
Murphy, Emmett   1930-31-32
Murphy, Fred   1892
Murphy, Gene   1921-22
Murphy, George   1940-41-42
Murphy, Jerry   1916
Murphy, Johnny   1936-37
Murphy, John   1908
Murphy, John   1894-95-96
Murphy, Tim   1921-22-23
Murphy, Tom   1950-51-52
Murphy, Tom   1927-28-29
Murray, Joe   1897-98
Murray, John   1961-62
Murrin, George   1925-26-27
Musuraca, Jim   1970-71-72
Mutscheller, Jim   1949-50-51
Myers, Gary   1956-57-58

N

Naab, Dick   1959-60-61
Nadolney, Romanus (Peaches)   1918
Nagurski, Bronko   1956-57-58
Nash, Joe   1926-27-28-29
Nash, Tom   1968-69
Naughton, David   1897
Naughton, Mike   1971-72-73
Nebel, Ed   1958-59
Neece, Steve   1973-74
Neff, Bob   1940-41-42
Neidert, Bob   1968-69-70
Nelson, Patrick   1887
Nemeth, Steve   1943-44
Nickel, Russ   1936
Nicola, Norm   1962-63-64
Nicula, George   1953-54-55
Niehaus, Steve   1972-73-74
Niemiec, John   1926-27-28
Niezer, Charles   1897
Nightingale, Chuck   1970
Nissi, Paul   1960
Noon, Tom   1926
Noppenberger, John   1923
Norri, Eric   1966-67-68
Nosbusch, Kevin   1972-73-74
Novakov, Dan   1969-70-71
Novakov, Tony   1973-74
Nowack, Art   1953
Nowers, Paul (Curly)   1912-13
Noznesky, Pete   1954-55
Nusskern, John   1949
Nyere, George   1901-02-03

O

Oaas, Torgus (Turk)   1910-11
Oberst, Gene   1920-22-23
O'Boyle, Harry   1924-25-26
O'Brien, Coley   1966-67-68
O'Brien, Dick   1940-41
O'Brien, Johnny (One Play)   1928-29-30
O'Brien, Johnny   1938-39-40
O'Brien, Tom   1956
O'Connor, Bill (Bucky)   1942-46-47
O'Connor, Bill (Zeke)   1944-46
O'Connor, Dan   1968

O'Connor, Dan   1902
O'Connor, Paul (Bucky)   1928-29-30
O'Connor, Phil   1945
Odem, James   1914-15
O'Donnell, Hugh   1914-15
O'Donnell, John   1972-74
O'Donnell, Leo   1914
Odyniec, Norm   1956-57-58
O'Flynn, Ed   1906
O'Hara, Charlie   1960-61-62-63
O'Hara, Francis   1896
O'Hara, Joe   1916-19
O'Leary, James   1907
O'Leary, Tom   1965-66-67
Olosky, Marty   1961-62-63
O'Loughlin, Bill   1936-37-38
Olson, Bob   1967-68-69
O'Malley, Dom   1899-00-02
O'Malley, Hugh   1966
O'Malley, Jim   1970-71-72
O'Meara, Walt   1938-39-40
O'Neil, Bill   1911
O'Neil, Bob   1951-52
O'Neil, John   1904
O'Neill, Bob   1938-39
O'Neill, Hugh   1916
O'Neill, Joe   1934-35-36
Opela, Bruno   1945
O'Phelan, John   1903
Oracko, Steve   1945-47-48-49
O'Regan, Tom   1887
O'Reilly, Chuck   1936-37
O'Reilly, Martin   1940
Oriard, Mike   1968-69
Osterman, Bob   1939-40
Ostrowski, Chet   1949-50-51
O'Toole, Dan   1970-71-72
Owen, Tom   1918
Owens, Bill   1957

P

Page, Alan   1964-65-66
Paine, Bob   1907-08
Palladino, Bob   1943
Palmer, Ralph   1895-96
Palumbo, Sam   1951-52-53-54
Panelli, John   1945-46-47-48
Paolone, Ralph   1950
Papa, Bob   1964
Papa, Joe   1938-40
Parise, Tom   1973-74
Parisien, Art   1925-26
Parker, Larry   1970-71
Parker, Mike   1971-73
Parry, Tom   1944
Parseghian, Mike   1974
Pasquesi, Tony   1952-53-54
Paterra, Frank   1951-52
Patten, Paul   1940-41
Patton, Eric   1969-70-71
Patulski, Walt   1969-70-71
Payne, Randy   1974
Pearson, Dudley   1917-19
Peasenelli, John   1940-42
Penick, Eric   1972-73-74
Penman, Gene   1962
Penza, Don   1951-52-53
Pergine, John   1965-66-67
Perko, John   1943
Perkowski, Joe   1959-60-61
Perry, Art   1949-50
Peters, Marty   1933-34-35

Peterson, Elmer   1940
Petitbon, John   1949-50-51
Pfefferle, Dick   1932-34-35
Pfeiffer, Bill   1961-62-63
Phelan, Bob   1919-20-21
Phelan, Jim   1915-16-17
Philbin, Dave   1916-17
Philbrook, George   1908-09-10-11
Phillips, Denny   1961-62-63
Phillips, John   1918
Piccone, Cammille (Pic)   1942
Pick, John   1900-01
Piel, Ed   1901
Piepul, Milt   1938-39-40
Pierce, Bill   1930-31-32
Pietrosante, Nick   1956-57-58
Pietrzak, Bob   1958-59-60
Pilney, Andy   1933-34-35
Pinn, Frank   1954
Pivarnik, Joe   1931-32-33
Pivec, Dave   1962-63
Plain, George   1938
Pliska, Joe   1911-12-13-14
Ploszek, Mike   1974
Poehler, Fred   1951-52
Pohlen, Pat   1973-74
Pojman, Henry   1933-34-35
Polisky, John (Bull)   1925-26-27
Pomarico, Frank   1971-72-73
Pope, Al   1969
Porter, Paul   1945
Poskon, Dewey   1967-68-69
Postupack, Joe   1939
Potempa, Gary   1971-72-73
Potter, Tom   1945-46
Pottios, Myron   1958-59-60
Powers, John   1897
Powers, John   1917
Powers, John   1959-60-61
Prelli, Joe   1924-25-27
Prendergast, Dick   1955-56-57
Prokop, George   1918-19-20
Prokop, Joe   1940-41
Provissiero, John   1928
Prudhomme, Edward   1887-88-89
Pszeracki, Joe   1973-74
Puntillo, Chuck   1957-58
Puplis, Andy   1935-36-37

Q

Quehl, Steve   1972-73
Quinlan, Mike   1892
Quinn, Jim   1926
Quinn, Steve   1965-66-67
Quinn, Tom   1966-67-68

R

Raba, Elmer   1945
Racanelli, Vito   1967
Race, Joe   1935-36-37
Raich, Nick   1953-54
Rakers, Jim   1962-63
Rankin, George   1969-70
Ransavage, Jerry   1926-27-28
Rascher, Norb   1932
Rascher, Norb   1960-62
Rassas, George   1938-40
Rassas, Kevin   1966-67
Rassas, Nick   1963-64-65
Raterman, John   1969-70-71

Ratkowski, Ray   1958-59-60
Ratterman, George   1945-46
Rausch, Lorenzo   1914
Ray, John   1944
Ready, Bob   1951-52-53-54
Reagan, Bob   1921-22-23
Reedy, Joe   1925
Reese, Frank   1921-23-24
Reeve, Dave   1974
Regner, Tom   1964-65-66
Reid, Don   1967-68-69
Reilly, Clarence   1924
Reilly, Jack   1928
Reilly, Jim   1967-68-69
Rellas, Chris   1943
Renaud, Charles   1943
Reynolds, Frank   1956-57-58
Reynolds, Lawrence   1908
Reynolds, Paul   1951-52-54-55
Reynolds, Tom   1967
Rhoads, Bob   1965-66
Riffle, Chuck   1937-38-39
Rigali, Bob   1952-53
Rigali, Joe   1924-25
Riley, Charlie   1925-26-27
Rini, Tom   1958-59
Riordan, Will   1941
Rively, Clair   1939
Roach, John   1923-24-25-26
Roach, Tom   1932-33
Robertson, Bob   1935
Robinson, Jack   1932-34
Robinson, Tyrone   1972
Robst, Paul   1951-53
Roby, Charles   1892-93
Rockne, Knute   1910-11-12-13
Rogenski, Steve   1936-38
Rogers, John   1930-31
Rohan, Andy   1973-74
Rohrs, George   1931
Ronchetti, Pete   1916-17
Ronzone, Matt   1934
Roolf, Jim   1971-72
Rosenthal, Jacob (Rosy)   1894-95-96
Roth, Jesse   1908
Rovai, Frank   1944-45-46
Roy, Norb   1959-60-61
Royer, Dick   1956-57-58
Ruckelshaus, John   1925
Rudnick, Tim   1971-72-73
Ruell, Ulric   1908
Ruetz, Joe   1935-36-37
Rufo, John   1974
Ruggerio, Frank   1943-44-45
Russell, Bill   1945-46
Russell, Marv   1973-74
Rutkowski, Ed   1960-61-62
Rutkowski, Frank   1974
Ruzicka, Jim   1967-69
Ryan, Billy   1907-08-09-10
Ryan, Jim   1917
Ryan, Jim   1965-66
Rydzewski, Frank   1915-16-17
Rykovich, Julie   1943
Rymkus, Lou   1940-41-42

S

Sabal, Al   1957-58-59
Sack, Allen   1964-65-66
Sadowski, Ed   1936
Saggau, Bob   1938-39-40
Saggau, Tom   1948

Salmon, Louis (Red)   1900-01-02-03
Salmon, Joe   1911
Salvino, Bob   1954
Samuel, Al   1972-73-74
Sanders, Cy   1918-19
Sanford, Charles   1889
Sarb, Pat   1973
Sauget, Dick   1964
Savoldi, Joe   1928-29-30
Sawicz, Paul   1973
Sawkins, Edward   1887-88
Scales, Ed   1973
Scanlan, Ray   1906
Scannell, Bob   1954-55-56
Scarpitto, Bob   1958-59-60
Schaack, Ed   1892
Schaaf, Jim   1956-57-58
Schaefer, Don   1953-54-55
Scharer, Eddie   1924-25
Schilling, Joe   1936
Schillo, Fred   1892-93-94-96-97
Schiralli, Angelo   1966
Schiralli, Rocco   1932-33-34
Schivarelli, Pete   1969-70
Schlezes, Ken   1970-71-72
Schmid, Charles   1940
Schmidt, Oscar   1894
Schmitt, Bill   1906-07-08-09
Schneider, J. S.   1899
Schnurr, Fred   1966
Schoen, Tom   1965-66-67
Scholtz, Bob   1957-58-59
Schrader, Jim   1951-52-53
Schramm, Paul   1954-55-56
Schreiber, Tom   1944-45
Schrenker, Henry   1938-40
Schrenker, Paul   1933-34
Schultz, Herb   1927
Schulz, Clay   1959-60-61
Schumacher, Larry   1967-68-69
Schuster, Ken   1944
Schwartz, Charles   1929
Schwartz, Marchy   1929-30-31
Scibelli, Joe   1958
Scott, Vince   1944-45-46
Seaman, Neil   1957-58
Seaman, Tom   1950-51-52
Secret, Bob   1961
Sefcik, George   1959-60-61
Seiler, Leo   1960
Seiler, Paul   1964-65-66
Selcer, Dick   1956-57-58
Seyfrit, Frank (Si)   1920-21
Seymour, Jim   1966-67-68
Shakespeare, Bill   1933-34-35
Shamla, Dick   1934
Shanahan, George   1918
Shannon, Dan   1951-52-53-54
Sharkey, Ed   1974
Sharp, Art   1913-14
Shaughnessy, Frank (Shag)   1901-02-03-04
Shaughnessy, Rodney   1921
Shaughnessy, Tom   1914
Shaw, Lawrence (Buck)   1919-20-21
Shay, George (Dinny)   1927-28-29
Shea, Bill (Red)   1920-21
Sheahan, Jim   1968
Sheehan, Clarence   1903-04-05-06
Sheeketski, Joe   1930-31-32
Shellogg, Alec   1936-37
Shellogg, Fred   1936-37
Sheridan, Benny   1937-38-39
Sheridan, Phil   1938-39-40
Sheridan, Phil   1963-64-65

Sherlock, Jim   1960-61-62
Shields, Bob   1926
Shulsen, Dick   1955-56-57
Signaigo, Joe   1943-46-47
Silver, Nate   1902-03-04-05
Simmons, Floyd   1945-46-47
Simon, Jack   1961-62-63
Simon, Tim   1973
Simonich, Ed   1936-37-38
Sinnott, Roger   1896
Sipes, Sherrill   1954-55-56
Sitko, Emil   1946-47-48-49
Sitko, Steve   1937-38-39
Skall, Russell   1947
Skat, Al   1943
Skoglund, Bill   1966
Skoglund, Bob   1944-45-46
Skoglund, Len   1935-36-37
Slackford, Fred (Fritz)   1915-16-17
Slafkosky, John   1961-62
Slager, Rick   1974
Slovak, Emil   1945-46
Smith, Art   1911
Smith, Bill   1933-34
Smith, Dick (Red)   1925-26
Smith, Gene   1973
Smith, Gene   1948-49-50
Smith, Glen   1910-11
Smith, Howard   1927
Smith, John (Clipper)   1925-26-27
Smith, Lancaster (Lank)   1946-47-48
Smith, Maurice (Clipper)   1917-18-19-20
Smith, Pete (Red)   1921
Smith, Scott   1970-71
Smith, Sherman   1972-73-74
Smithberger, Jim   1965-66-67
Snell, Ed   1936
Snowden, Jim   1961-63-64
Snow, Jack   1962-63-64
Snow, Paul   1966-67-68
Snyder, Jim   1943
Solari, Fred   1933-34-35
Spalding, Tom   1917
Spaniel, Frank   1947-48-49
Springer, Frank   1887-88
Staab, Fred   1930
Stanczyak, Al   1945
Standring, Jay   1968-69
Stange, Gus   1922-23
Stanitzek, Frank   1954
Stanley, Basil   1917
Stansfield, John   1910
Statuto, Art   1943-44-46-47
Steenberge, Pat   1970-71
Steiner, Art   1902-03
Steinkemper, Bill   1934-35-36
Stelmazek, Ed   1945
Stenger, Brian   1966-67-68
Stepaniak, Ralph   1969-70-71
Stephan, Jack   1974
Stephan, Leo   1914-15
Stephens, Clay   1961-62-63
Stephens, Jack   1952
Stevenson, Harry   1937-38-39
Stevenson, Martin   1912
Stewart, Ralph   1944
Stickles, Monty   1957-58-59
Stilley, Ken   1933-34-35
Stine, Raleigh (Rollo)   1917-18
Stock, Jim   1972-73-74
Stoudt, Clement   1900
Strohmeyer, George   1946-47
Stroud, Clarke   1950
Studebaker, John   1893-94

Studer, Dean   1954-55-56
Stuhldreher, Harry   1922-23-24
Sullivan, Bob   1938
Sullivan, Danny   1936-37
Sullivan, Ed   1955-56-57
Sullivan, Eddie   1940
Sullivan, George   1943-44-46-47
Sullivan, Joe   1933-34
Sullivan, John   1937-38
Sullivan, Larry   1940-41-42
Sullivan, Tim   1971-72-73
Sullivan, Tom   1908
Sullivan, Tom   1963-64-65
Susko, Larry   1972-73
Swatland, Dick   1965-66-67
Swearingen, Tim   1967-68
Sweeney, Bob   1973-74
Sweeney, Chuck   1935-36-37
Swendsen, Fred   1969-70-71
Swistowicz, Mike   1946-47-48-49
Swonk, Frank   1897
Sylvester, Steve   1972-73-74
Szatko, Greg   1972-73
Szot, Denis   1962-63
Szymanski, Dick   1951-52-53-54
Szymanski, Frank   1943-44

T

Talaga, Tom   1963-64-65
Taylor, Bob   1951-52-53
Taylor, James   1896
Tereschuk, John   1970-71
Terlaak, Bob   1930
Terlep, George   1943-44
Tharp, Jim   1943
Theisen, Charles   1936-38
Theismann, Joe   1968-69-70
Thernes, Matt   1934-35
Thesing, Joe   1937-38-39
Thomann, Rick   1969-70-71
Thomas, Deane   1948
Thomas, Frank   1920-21-22
Thomas, Bob   1971-72-73
Thornton, Pete   1964-65
Tobin, George   1942-46
Tobin, John (Red)   1932-33
Toczylowski, Steve   1944
Todorovich, Mike   1943
Toneff, Bob   1949-50-51
Tonelli, Mario   1936-37-38
Torrado, Rene   1967
Toth, Ron   1956-57-58
Townsend, Mike   1971-72-73
Townsend, Willie   1970-71-72-73
Trafton, George   1919
Traney, Leon   1945
Trapp, Bill   1969-70-71
Traver, Les   1959-60-61
Tripucka, Frank   1945-46-47-48
Trombley, Cliff   1925
Trumper, Ed   1943
Tuck, Ed   1966-67-68
Tuck, Sweeney   1938
Twomey, Ted   1928-29

U

Urban, Gasper   1943-46-47

V

Vainisi, Jack   1945
Vairo, Dom   1932-33-34
Vangen, Willard   1946
Van Huffel, Al   1965-66
Van Rooy, Bill   1930
Van Summern, Bob   1945
Varrichione, Frank   1951-52-53-54
Vasys, Arunas   1963-64-65
Vaughan, Charles   1911
Vaughan, Pete   1908-09
Vejar, Laurie   1931-32
Vergara, George   1922-23
Vezie, Manny   1926-27-28-29
Viola, Gene   1959-60-61
Virok, Ernie   1945
Vlk, George   1928-29-30
Voedisch, John (Ike)   1925-26-27
Voelkers, John   1913-14-15

W

Wack, Steve   1968
Wadsworth, Mike   1963-64-65
Wagner, Earl   1899
Waldorf, Rufus   1904-05-06
Waldron, Ronayne   1943
Wallace, John   1923-24-25-26
Wallner, Fred   1948-49-50
Walls, Bob   1974
Walsh, Adam   1922-23-24
Walsh, Bill   1895
Walsh, Bill   1945-46-47-48
Walsh, Bob   1941
Walsh, Bob   1946
Walsh, Charles (Chile)   1925-26-27
Walsh, Earl   1919-20-21
Ward, Gilbert (Gillie)   1914-16
Ward, Bob   1955-56-57
Warner, Jack   1940-41
Washington, Bob   1971-72-73
Washington, Dick   1953
Wasilevich, Max   1973
Waters, Fred   1897
Waybright, Doug   1944-47-48-49
Webb, Bob   1940
Webb, Mike   1970-71-73
Weber, Robin   1973-74
Webster, Mike   1963-64
Weibel, John   1922-23-24
Weidner, Fred   1934
Weiler, Jim   1973-74
Weithman, Jim   1950-51-52
Welch, Bob   1944
Wendell, Marty   1944-46-47-48
Wengierski, Tim   1966
Westenkircher, Joe   1944
Weston, Jeff   1974
Wetoska, Bob   1956-57-58
Wheeler, Lucian   1895
Whelan, Ed   1950
Whelan, Jack   1951-52
Whelan, Jim   1925
Whipple, Ray   1915-16
White, Bob   1945
White, Carl   1911
White, Don   1957-58-59
White, Eddie   1925-27
White, Jim   1942-43
White, Richard   1918
Whiteside, Bill   1949-50

Wightkin, Bill   1946-47-48-49
Wilcox, Percy   1920
Wilke, Bob   1934-35-36
Wilke, Henry   1957-58-59
Wilke, Roger   1959-60-61
Wilkins, Dick   1955
Williams, Bo   1928
Williams, Bob   1956-57-58
Williams, Bob   1948-49-50
Williams, Cy   1910
Williams, George   1959-60-61
Williams, Scott   1969
Williams, Ted   1938
Wilson, George   1953-54-55
Winegardner, Jim   1966-67-68
Winsouer, Paul   1935-36
Winter, Frank   1898-99-00-01
Wisne, Gerald   1966-67-68
Witchger, Jim   1968-69-70
Witteried, George   1916
Wittliff, Phil   1968
Witucki, Jack   1954
Woebkenberg, Harry   1974
Wojcihovski, Vic   1934-35-36
Wolf, Louie   1915
Wolski, Bill   1963-64-65
Wood, Fay   1907-08
Wood, Greg   1962
Worden, Neil   1951-52-53
Wright, Harry   1940-41-42
Wright, Jim   1968-69-70
Wright, Tom   1970
Wujciak, Al   1973-74
Wunsch, Harry   1931-32-33
Wynne, Chet   1918-19-20-21
Wynne, Elmer   1925-26-27

Y

Yarr, Tommy   1919-30-31
Yeager, Leslie (Dutch)   1915-16
Yoder, Jim   1969-70
Yonakor, John   1942-43
Yonto, Joe   1945
Young, Jacob   1907
Young, John (Tex)   1933
Yund, Walter   1911-12

Z

Zajeski, Ben   1953-54
Zalejski, Ernie   1946-48-49
Zambroski, Tony   1949-50-51
Zancha, John   1949-50
Zanot, Bob   1972-73
Zappala, Tony   1973-74
Zehler, Bill   1945
Zeitler, Charles   1893-94-95
Zenner, Elmer   1935-36
Ziegler, Ed   1967-68-69
Zielony, Dick   1969-70
Ziemba, Wally   1940-41-42
Zikas, Mike   1969-70-71
Zilly, Jack   1943-46
Zimmerman, Jeff   1967-68
Ziznewski, Jay   1968
Zloch, Bill   1963-64-65
Zloch, Chuck   1968-69-70
Zloch, Jim   1972-73
Zmijewski, Al   1946-47-48-49
Zoia, Clyde   1917
Zontini, Lou   1937-38-39

Zubek, Bob   1966
Zuber, Tim   1970
Zuendel, Joe   1938
Zurowski, Dave   1964-66
Zwers, Joe   1935-36-37